MASTERING THE NEW TESTAMENT

THE COMMUNICATOR'S COMMENTARY SERIES

MASTERING THE NEW TESTAMENT

JAMES; 1,2 PETER; JUDE

PAUL A. CEDAR

LLOYD J. OGILVIE, GENERAL EDITOR

THE COMMUNICATOR'S COMMENTARY SERIES, Volume 11, *James, 1, 2 Peter, Jude.* Copyright © 1984 by Word, Inc. All rights reserved. No portion of this book may be reproduced in any form whatsoever, except for brief quotations in reviews, without written permission from the publisher.

The Bible text in this series is from The New King James Bible, New Testament, copyright © 1979 by Thomas Nelson, Inc., Publishers. All rights reserved. Used by permission. Brief Scripture quotations within the commentary text are also from The New King James Bible, unless otherwise identified, as follows: NEB, from The New English Bible, © 1961, 1970 by the Delegates of The Oxford University Press and The Syndics of The Cambridge University Press, used by permission; NIV, from the Holy Bible, New International Version, copyright © 1978 by the New York International Bible Society, used by permission.

Library of Congress Cataloging in Publication Data
Main entry under title:

The Communicator's commentary

  Includes bibliographical references.
  Contents: v. 11. James, 1, 2 Peter, Jude/Paul A. Cedar.
  1. Bible. N.T.—Commentaries—Collected works.
I. Ogilvie, Lloyd John. II. Cedar, Paul A.
BS2341.2.C65   225.7'7   81–71764
ISBN 0–8499–33277   AACR2

Printed in the United States of America

3 9 AGF 9 8 7 6 5 4 3

Contents

Editor's Preface

God has called all of His people to be communicators. Everyone who is in Christ is called into ministry. As ministers of "the manifold grace of God," all of us—clergy and laity—are commissioned with the challenge to communicate our faith to individuals and groups, classes and congregations.

The Bible, God's Word, is the objective basis of the truth of His love and power that we seek to communicate. In response to the urgent, expressed needs of pastors, teachers, Bible study leaders, church school teachers, small group enablers, and individual Christians, the Communicator's Commentary is offered as a penetrating search of the Scriptures of the New Testament to enable vital personal and practical communication of the abundant life.

Many current commentaries and Bible study guides provide only some aspects of a communicator's needs. Some offer in-depth scholarship but no application to daily life. Others are so popular in approach that biblical roots are left unexplained. Few offer impelling illustrations that open windows for the reader to see the exciting application for today's struggles. And most of all, seldom have the expositors given the valuable outlines of passages so needed to help the preacher or teacher in his or her busy life to prepare for communicating the Word to congregations or classes.

This Communicator's Commentary series brings all of these elements together. The authors are scholar-preachers and teachers outstanding in their ability to make the Scriptures come alive for individuals and groups. They are noted for bringing together excellence in biblical scholarship, knowledge of the original Greek and Hebrew, sensitivity to people's needs, vivid illustrative material from biblical, classical, and contemporary sources, and lucid communication by the use of clear outlines of thought. Each has been selected to contribute to this series because of his Spirit-empowered ability to help people live in the skins of biblical characters and provide a "you-are-there" intensity to the drama of events of the Bible which have so much to say about our relationships and responsibilities today.

The design for the Communicator's Commentary gives the reader an overall outline of each book of the New Testament. Following the introduction, which reveals the author's approach and salient background on the book, each chapter of the commentary provides the Scripture to be exposited. The New King James Bible has been chosen for the Communicator's Commentary because it combines with integrity the beauty of language, underlying Greek textual basis, and thought-flow of the 1611 King James Version, while replacing obsolete verb forms and other archaisms with their everyday contemporary counterparts for greater readability. Reverence for God is preserved in the capitalization of all pronouns referring to the Father, Son, or Holy Spirit. Readers who are more comfortable with another translation can readily find the parallel passage by means of the chapter and verse reference at the end of each passage being exposited. The paragraphs of exposition combine fresh insights to the Scripture, application, rich illustrative material, and innovative ways of utilizing the vibrant truth for his or her own life and for the challenge of communicating it with vigor and vitality.

It has been gratifying to me as Editor of this series to receive enthusiastic progress reports from each contributor. As they worked, all were gripped with new truths from the Scripture—God-given insights into passages, previously not written in the literature of biblical explanation. A prime objective of this series is for each user to find the same awareness: that God speaks with newness through the Scriptures when we approach them with a ready mind and a willingness to communicate what He has given; that God delights to give communicators of His Word "I-never-saw-that-in-that-verse-before" intellectual insights so that our listeners and readers can have "I-never-realized-all-that-was-in-that-verse" spiritual experiences.

The thrust of the commentary series unequivocally affirms that God speaks through the Scriptures today to engender faith, enable adventuresome living of the abundant life, and establish the basis of obedient discipleship. The Bible, the unique Word of God, is unlimited in its resource for Christians in communicating our hope to others. It is our weapon in the battle for truth, the guide for ministry, and the irresistible force for introducing others to God. In the New Testament we meet the divine Lord and Savior whom we seek to communicate to others. What He said and did as God with us has been faithfully recorded under the inspiration of the Spirit of God. The cosmic implications of the Gospels are lived out in Acts and spelled out in the Epistles. They have stood the test of time because the eternal Communicator, God Himself, communicates through them to those who would be communicators of grace. His essential nature is exposed, the plan of salvation is explained, and the Gospel for all of life, now and for eternity, is proclaimed.

A biblically rooted communication of the Gospel holds in unity and oneness what divergent movements have wrought asunder. This commentary series courageously presents personal faith, caring for individuals, and social responsibility as essential, inseparable dimensions of biblical Christianity. It seeks to present the quadrilateral Gospel in its fullness which calls us to unreserved commitment to Christ, unrestricted self-esteem in His grace, unqualified love for others in personal evangelism, and undying efforts to work for justice and righteousness in a sick and suffering world.

A growing renaissance in the church today is being led by clergy and laity who are biblically rooted, Christ-centered, and Holy Spirit-empowered. They have dared to listen to people's most urgent questions and deepest needs and then to God as He speaks through the Bible. Biblical preaching is the secret of growing churches. Bible study classes and small groups are equipping the laity for ministry in the world. Dynamic Christians are finding that daily study of God's Word allows the Spirit to do in them what He wishes to communicate through them to others. These days are the most exciting time since Pentecost. The Communicator's Commentary is offered to be a primary resource of new life for this renaissance.

In this volume on James, 1 and 2 Peter, and Jude by Dr. Paul Cedar we see exposition, illustration, and application blended together in a very helpful way. You will find the outline of these books particularly useful in the organization of your own exposition of the material. Each section gets to the core of the message in a way that encourages the reader to take the insight and develop it further, utilizing his or her own experience and study. Dr. Cedar gives us an example of sensitive, personal illustrations from his vast experience as a preacher, counselor, and pastor. His word pictures come alive in a way that enables us to feel we know the people whose experiences of the adventure in Christ he uses to illustrate the biblical message. The incisive application of these books from the life of the early church to our life today is challenging and thought-provoking. You will find that you better understand the minds of James, Peter, and Jude and will see the implications for your preaching and teaching today.

Dr. Cedar is the dynamic Senior Pastor of the large and growing Lake Avenue Congregational Church in Pasadena, California. His weekly expositions of the Scriptures draw large and enthusiastic crowds at three services each Sunday. In addition, his teaching of the Bible in classes is a vital part of his ministry. His strong biblical preaching has made him a sought-after speaker at conferences and retreats throughout the world. The congregation he serves is a model of contemporary church renewal. Dr. Cedar is a gifted leader in the equipping of the laity for its ministry. This is reflected in the energetic lay leadership of his church. Under his guidance, the church officers have developed a vital program of involving members in mission and evangelism. His church is distinguished for its giving and its support of local, national, and world missions.

I have had the pleasure of serving with Paul Cedar when he was the executive pastor of the First Presbyterian Church of Hollywood. Under his leadership, our church moved forward vigorously in its program of personal evangelism. His course, *Sharing the Good Life*, was first introduced while he served on our staff. Subsequently, this biblical course on how to communicate Christ's love has been distributed and used widely throughout the nation.

In this volume you will come to appreciate the author's ability to grasp the major themes of a biblical book, organize his exposition in a clear and vital way, and give specific helps for maximizing the preaching and teaching of the material. Here's how a creative preacher of a demanding, busy congregation does it. His commitment to Christ shines through on every page. And his winsome witness to what Christ has done in his own life through the passages he explains makes reading this commentary an experience of illuminating study and spiritual growth. I am delighted to have this straightforward, clearly ordered exposition of Jude, 1 and 2 Peter, and James as a part of the Communicator's Commentary.

LLOYD JOHN OGILVIE

Introduction to James

Recently, I visited a major bookstore in Southern California in search of a book on a specific "how to" subject. As I asked the salesperson about the book, I was escorted to a large "how to" section of the store. I was amazed to discover literally scores of books focusing on subjects which ranged from "how to build a house" to "how to pan for gold."

Our society is caught up in the excitement of learning how to do various things. The "do-it-yourself" craze has spread to most of us. For example, my wife and I have enjoyed "fixing up" houses which are in obvious need of repair.

James is also excited about "how to do it." His letter is a "how-to-do-it manual" for the Christian life. He writes in the most practical way for those of us who deeply desire to know how we can follow Jesus as Lord day by day. Many of us have that deep desire, but we simply don't know what to do or even where to begin.

James will help every serious reader who is concerned with the "how to" of Christian discipleship. In fact, I believe that James should be one of the first books read and mastered by the new Christian. Too often the Church has mastered the art of informing people regarding what they *should* be doing, but has failed to teach them *how* to do it!

James meets this problem head on. His subjects are as relevant for the contemporary reader as they were when he penned the epistle nearly two thousand years ago. "How to profit from trials," "how to obtain wisdom," "how to overcome temptation," and "how to communicate" are just a few of the vital subjects which James considers.

He is deeply concerned about active and vital Christian lifestyle.

It is not enough for us merely to believe; we must also do (James 1:22). If we lack wisdom, we shouldn't complain or despair; we need to simply ask God for it, and it will be given to us (James 1:5). If we are proud, James gives us the instruction we need to follow in order to become humble (James 4:1–10). Or, if we are ill, we should call for the elders of the church who will anoint us with oil and pray for us (James 5:14).

The list of "how to" subjects goes on and on. Indeed, James helps us to understand how to live the Christian life at its very best. His letter is a practical manual for vital Christian living. As we prayerfully study this book, we will learn how to live for Christ in our personal lives and how to encourage and assist others who desire to follow Christ day by day.

The Author

"James, a servant of God and of the Lord Jesus Christ," is the introduction which the author provides for us in the first verse of the first chapter of James. As one can readily see, we face an immediate problem in identifying just who this James was since he did not identify himself beyond this given name. And so Biblical scholars have debated for centuries the true identity of this author by the name of James.

Perhaps you would like to do some detective work on your own by taking your Biblical concordance and tracing the various persons in the New Testament who are identified with the name James. Among the most obvious are the two disciples of Jesus who bore the name James.

First, there was James the son of Zebedee, who was a brother of the Apostle John. He is mentioned several times in the Gospels as well as in the Acts of the Apostles including Mark 3:17, Luke 5:10, and Acts 1:13. Since he was the first apostle to be martyred for his faith in Christ in A.D. 44, most Biblical scholars believe that he could not have been the author of this letter which appears to have been written at a later date.

The second James among the twelve disciples of Jesus was known as James the son of Alphaeus. He is reputed to be a brother of Matthew and is mentioned in Matthew 10:3, Mark 3:18, Luke 6:15, and Acts 1:13. Very little is known of this James. However, Biblical scholars agree that it is unlikely that he is the author of this letter.

Another James who is identified in relationship to the twelve disciples is James the father of Judas, not Iscariot, who was one of the twelve. However, this James is merely a name used to identify his son. It is very unlikely that he could be the author.

In the account of the crucifixion of Jesus, one of His followers who stood at the foot of the cross, along with Mary Magdalene, was Mary the mother of James the Less (Mark 15:40). This Mary, the mother of James, is also identified in Matthew 27:56. Again, it is doubtful if this is the James who is our author unless the writers of the Gospels were referring to Mary the mother of Jesus, who was also the mother of a son named James.

This brings us to our fifth and final James who is identified in Scripture and who could be the author of this letter. This James is identified as a brother of Jesus in Mark 6:3 and in Matthew 13:55. William Barclay reminds us that brother James did not understand or sympathize with the ministry of Jesus and was actually hostile towards him (Mark 3:21, 31–35; Matt. 12:46–50; John 7:3–9). In fact, John states clearly that the brothers of Jesus, including James, did not believe in Jesus (John 7:5).[1]

However, in the Book of Acts we find a remarkable change in the life of James. He is identified as a prominent leader in the church at Jerusalem. For example, it is to James that Peter sent word of his escape from prison (Acts 12:17). This James presides over the Council of Jerusalem which agreed to allow Gentiles into the church. The vocabulary used in his speech to the Council is remarkably similar to that used in the epistle of James (Acts 15). And Paul came to James with his collection which he had received from the Gentile Christians to assist their brothers and sisters in the Jerusalem church who were in great need (Acts 21:18–25).[2]

Based upon this evidence, it is most likely that James, the brother of Christ, was the author of this epistle. In fact, in 1546, the Council of Trent acknowledged James, the brother of Jesus, as the author.

If this is true, his opening statement is all the more significant. James identifies himself not as the brother of Jesus, but as a servant of God and of the Lord Jesus Christ. How remarkable! The brother who had once opposed Jesus had become His faithful and humble servant who was committed to helping others live vitally for Jesus Christ as the Lord of their lives.

The Recipients

"To the twelve tribes which are scattered abroad" (James 1:1). The term "twelve tribes" is familiar to anyone who has studied the Old Testament. This speaks of the twelve tribes of Israel who were descendants of Abraham. Those twelve tribes were led by Moses in the Exodus to the promised land of Canaan where they occupied the land under the leadership of Joshua.

However, it is most likely that James is not referring to the twelve tribes of the old Israel but rather to the Jewish Christians who were part of the new Israel—the Church of Jesus Christ. Although James writes within the Jewish context and uses vocabulary and illustrations which could best be understood by Jewish Christians, it is probable that he is writing his letter to the entire Church at large—both Jewish and Gentile—who are recipients of the New Covenant through Jesus Christ.

A great deal of persecution had taken place in the church at Jerusalem, and so he is writing to brothers and sisters who have been scattered throughout the world. The technical name of this scatter of Christians is *Diaspora,* the same Jewish term used to identify those who had been exiled from Israel in the days before Christ, including the exile to Babylon of Daniel and thousands of his countrymen as recorded in 2 Kings 24.

The Occasion

The letter is written, then, to Christian believers who are scattered throughout the world because of the persecution they have endured for their faith in Jesus Christ. The letter was written probably in about A.D. 61 or 62. This suffering church was aware that life is very temporary. They were strangers in foreign lands and cultures. Many had lost everything they had in order to be faithful to Jesus.

As we can discern by the content of the letter of James, many of these believers were young in their faith. They needed practical instruction on how to live the Christian life. They also had to make some sense of their suffering and pain. They were in need of counsel and encouragement, and James responded with love and practical help.

A hypothetical question which has been posed to most of us is, "If you were stranded on an isolated island, what would be the one thing you would like most to have with you?" I believe I know how the scattered, tattered, faithful Christians who received this marvelous letter from James would have answered that question. Without a doubt, this letter was the lifeline used of God to rescue and encourage many of them. And it can be of that same kind of lifesaving and practical help to us as contemporary Christians who live in a society that is subtly hostile and in opposition to a vital Christian faith. We can learn "how to" live more effectively for Jesus Christ as our Lord.

Plan of Exposition

Our attempt to present an exposition of this remarkable book will be simply to expose the truth which was originally revealed to James by the Holy Spirit just as graphically and practically as possible. We need neither to add to nor subtract from the material.

Instead, we will approach the material inductively in an attempt to clearly understand what James was saying to the original readers and what God is attempting to say to us now in the contemporary sense of where we live. Then, in order to be true to the purpose of James and the God who inspired him, we will focus upon how we can practically apply these truths to our lives.

I am excited about what God has been doing in and through my own life as I have been prayerfully studying and expositing this practical letter. I believe that we will grow significantly in the grace and knowledge of Jesus Christ if we understand what God is teaching us through this book and as we allow the Holy Spirit to empower us to be not merely understanders but doers and obeyers of what He is saying to us. With this in mind, let us move on to the "how tos" of a vital Christian lifestyle.

NOTES

1. William Barclay, *The Letters of James and Peter* (Philadelphia: Westminster Press, 1960), p. 10.
2. Ibid., p. 4.

An Outline of James

I. How to Live with Faith and Trials: 1:1–27
  A. Greetings: 1:1
  B. How to Profit from Trials: 1:2–4
  C. How to Obtain Wisdom: 1:5–8
  D. How to Be Rich and Poor: 1:9–11
  E. How to Overcome Temptation: 1:12–15
  F. How to Receive Good Gifts: 1:16–18
  G. How to Communicate: 1:19–21
  H. How to Become a Doer: 1:22–25
  I. How to Be Authentically Religious: 1:26–27
II. How to Live with Faith and Works: 2:1–26
  A. How to Avoid Partiality: 2:1–7
  B. How to Fulfill the Law of Love: 2:8–13
  C. How to Make Faith Work: 2:14–26
III. How to Live with Faith and Wisdom: 3:1–18
  A. How to Live as a Teacher: 3:1
  B. How to Tame Your Tongue: 3:2–12
  C. How to Live with Wisdom: 3:13–18
IV. How to Live with Faith and Humility: 4:1–17
  A. How to Pray without Pride: 4:1–3
  B. How to Become Humble: 4:4–10
  C. How to Escape Judgment: 4:11–12
  D. How to Plan for the Future: 4:13–17
V. How to Live with Faith and Reality: 5:1–20
  A. How to Succeed in Spite of Riches: 5:1–6
  B. How to Be Patient: 5:7–11
  C. How Not to Swear: 5:12
  D. How to Pray for the Sick: 5:13–18
  E. How to Restore a Backslider: 5:19–20

CHAPTER ONE

How to Live with Faith and Trials

James 1:1–27

Christianity is much more than mere philosophy, theology, or religious teaching. It is a lifestyle based upon a vital relationship with God. He has invited us to love Him with all of our hearts, with all our souls, with all our minds, and with all our strength (Mark 12:30).

He desires for us to not only know about Him, but to know Him personally (1 John 4:7). We are to allow Jesus Christ to be the vine of our lives, and we are to be the branches (John 15:5). Christ asks that we not only receive Him but that we walk in Him and be rooted and built up in Him (Col. 2:6–7).

Our relationship with Him is one of great intimacy and utter dependence. We are asked to no longer live for ourselves but rather for Him. We are to be in Christ, and He is to be in us (2 Cor. 5:14–17). In fact, without Him we can do nothing (John 11:5). But through Him we can do anything He calls us to do (Phil. 4:13).

Love is at the very center of this relationship. It was God's love for us which caused Christ to live and die and rise from the dead. He was and is love personified (Rom. 5:8). Nothing in all of creation can separate us from Christ's love (Rom. 8:35–39). Where Christ is, there is love. His very character is love (1 John 4:8). Jesus said that it is by this love that His authentic disciples are to be recognized (John 13:35). This love must not only be expressed in word or in talk, but it must be expressed in action, in deed and in truth (1 John 3:18). Therefore, love is not an option for the Christian; love is at the very center of his or her lifestyle. And so are the other qualities of the "fruit of the Spirit" at the center of the Christian's life, including joy, peace, longsuffering, kindness, goodness, faithfulness, gentleness, and self-control (Gal. 5:22–23).

Love, and all of the other fruit of the Spirit, must be lived out in daily lifestyle. Possession is more than mere profession; authentic

Christianity is practical. That is what the Book of James is all about. James helps us understand "how to" live the Christian life.

He helps us to move from the place of merely possessing intellectual belief in Christ to the joy of knowing Him personally and following Him daily. Too often the church has merely told people that they "should" live for God or that they "must" do what is right. James moves beyond mere moralizing to teach us "how to" follow Jesus Christ as the Lord of our lives. His teaching is both practical and workable; his style is "show and tell." He tells us and shows us "how to" do it.

James is concerned with the matter of faith. For him, faith is not merely something which is believed; faith is something we do. It must be lived—in active obedience. The focus of his direct teaching regarding faith is found in the second chapter of his letter. However, the emphasis is found throughout the book beginning with the first chapter which focuses upon how to live with faith and trials.

GREETINGS

1 James, a servant of God and of the Lord Jesus Christ,

To the twelve tribes which are scattered abroad:

Greetings.

James 1:1

As we have seen in our introductory study, James identifies himself not as a brother of Jesus Christ, nor as a leader of the church, but rather as a servant of God and a servant of Jesus Christ. I believe that his identification is more than mere literary style. He is writing with a true Christian perspective of leadership.

James understands who he is and who the people of God are within the Christian family. His style is one of love and humility. Other leaders of the early church used a similar greeting in their epistles such as Paul (Phil. 1:1) and Peter (2 Peter 1:1).

James understood that his highest calling, and therefore his most accurate identification of his position, was that of a servant. Peter presents that teaching in a powerful manner as he addresses his "fellow elders" concerning the Christian style of leadership (1 Peter 5:1–

4). He is expounding the basic teaching of Jesus regarding the vital matter of servant leadership (Matt. 20:20–28).

Jesus taught clearly that the leaders of His Kingdom did not "lord over" or dominate others. Instead, the one who is the greatest in the Kingdom of God is the one who is the servant of all (Matt. 20:26). This is the understanding and conviction of James. He seeks to be the servant of God's people wherever they may be.

Our introductory study has shown us that James is writing to a scattered church often referred to as the *Diaspora*—those Christians who were dispersed throughout the Roman world as a result of severe persecution.

His reference to the twelve tribes appears to be a symbolic description of the scattered people of the New Covenant as opposed to the twelve tribes of Israel of the first covenant. These twelve tribes are the New Covenant people of the Church of Jesus Christ.

The simple word translated as "greetings" from James is the Greek word *chaírein,* which was used often in letters of that day. Although Paul and the other New Testament writers did not use it, the Jerusalem church used it in their letter to the Gentile believers in Antioch, Syria, and Cilicia (Acts 15:23).

In summary, James writes as a humble servant of Christ and His Church to fellow believers who are scattered throughout the Roman world by persecution for their faith. These are people who have a deep faith in Jesus Christ. James writes to give them practical counsel regarding how they can follow Christ as the Lord of their lives even more effectively.

How to Profit from Trials

> 2 My brethren, count it all joy when you fall into various trials,
> 3 knowing that the testing of your faith produces patience.
> 4 But let patience have its perfect work, that you may be perfect and complete, lacking nothing.
>
> *James 1:2–4*

Normal people do not enjoy trials. In fact, most of us do everything possible to avoid the trials of life. However, James is writing to people who were well acquainted with the pain and the challenge of trials.

Most of these Christians had faced severe trials even to the point of losing their homes, their jobs, and their security within a community. They had to flee literally for their lives to a strange place. Many of them faced not mere inconvenience, but the very survival of life itself. They were separated from family members and friends, not only geographically, but also spiritually. They were members of a new family—the Body of Christ. In the world they were aliens and foreigners and strangers, but they had become fellow citizens with the saints and members of the household of God (Eph. 2:19).

In these verses, James teaches us three practical principles regarding how to profit from trials. These principles are as relevant for us today as they were for the believers in the early church.

1. *Consider it pure joy whenever you face trials* (v. 2). Trials are seldom met with joy. However, James not only instructs us to face trials with joy, but with *pure* joy. In the Greek text, the word translated as pure is the word *pas* which is a primary word meaning all, every, and whole or thoroughly.

James is telling us not to "fake it." We should have a joy which is neither contrived or forced as some impossible religious obligation. To the contrary, we should have pure, unadulterated, all-encompassing, thorough joy! It should be the "real thing."

The second word we should explore should be the word for "trial," from the Greek *peirasmós*. The root of this word means "to assay, to examine, or to put to the proof. A good Biblical and theological definition might be "an external adversity which provides a testing towards an end."

For example, this is the word used to describe the exciting adventure of a young bird "testing" his wings. It is the word often translated as "temptation," as in the prayer Jesus taught His disciples (Matt. 6:13). The writer of Hebrews uses the word to describe the trials or temptations faced by the Children of Israel (Heb. 3:8).

One of the greatest promises regarding such trials or temptations is found in 1 Corinthians where Paul writes, "No temptation (trial) has overtaken you except such as is common to man; but God is faithful, who will not allow you to be tempted beyond what you are able, but with the temptation will also make the way of escape, that you may be able to bear it" (1 Cor. 10:13). It is with this kind of joy, hope, and optimism that we should face the trials of life.

A third word which we should explore in verse 2 is the word

translated as "various." It is a form of the Greek word *poikilós*, which means many or several kinds of trials. In my study of the Word of God and in my pastoral counseling, I have discovered at least three varieties of trials or temptations which are faced by sincere Christians.

The first is what I would call the cause-and-effect trial. It is the type of trial that adheres to a basic principle of Scripture which teaches us that we reap what we sow (Gal. 6:7). Many of the trials and temptations that come into our lives come through our own disobedience. In fact, James teaches us about this error in some detail later in this first chapter (vv. 13–16). Lust draws us away. We "play with fire" to see how close we can get to a given sin without being burned. We sow what we reap!

The second variety of trials which we can face as Christians is the spiritual trial. Peter tells us not to be surprised or "do not think it strange concerning the fiery trial which is to try you" (1 Pet. 4:12). He goes on to say that "If anyone suffers as a Christian, let him not be ashamed, but let him glorify God in this matter" (1 Pet. 4:16).

This confirms Jesus' teaching when he said, "In the world you will have tribulation, but in Me you will have peace" (John 16:33). Also, Jesus told His disciples to, "Remember the word that I said to you, 'A servant is not greater than his master.' If they have persecuted Me, they will also persecute you" (John 15:20).

There is that kind of trial which comes simply from living the godly life. As we have said, the one who follows Jesus as Lord and is a citizen of His Kingdom is out of step with his society. He or she is the bearer of light in the midst of darkness, and often those in darkness dislike the light and those who bear it (John 1:1–13).

Third, there is the kind of trial which I would call the spiritually mysterious trial. Without a doubt, this is the most difficult type of trial for us to accept and to express pure joy concerning its attack on our lives.

The problem is that there is simply no rational or logical reason for the trial—or at least not one that we can identify and understand. This is the kind of trial faced by Job.

His friends were convinced that Job was facing the trials because of hidden sin in his life, while his wife was certain that it was God's fault. Job asked many of the right questions, but he still didn't understand the "why" of his trials and suffering. Even at the conclusion of the Book of Job, he does not understand the reason or reasons for his suffering.

But God does give Job the solution that is proper for every form of trial. The solution was that he commit his utter trust and faith to God. He acknowledged the "mystery" of God's ways not being our ways and committed himself to his faithful God—who is always to be trusted.

Recently, my wife and I had a close friend who died from a painful disease. She suffered an incredible amount of physical pain during the last year of her life. She and her loved ones asked the logical question, "Why should she face such suffering and trial?"

It was certainly not a matter of cause-and-effect or a spiritual trial. As is true of many of the trials which we face in our lives, her suffering fell into the third and most difficult category of trials—the spiritually mysterious trial. Her solution was the same as Job's. She trusted herself to the Lord with all of her heart.

What blessing resulted from her trust and commitment to Christ. Her pure joy in the midst of her trials was unmistakable. And, as you might suspect, her joy and faith touched the lives of scores of people. She pointed them to Jesus as the One who gave her pure joy and who could make sense out of senselessness.

Yes, my friends, we should be those who consider it pure joy whenever we face the trials of life. And, whether the trials make sense or not, the solution is always the same. We need to turn to Jesus and trust Him for strength and wisdom and pure joy. He is to be trusted!

2. *The testing of your faith develops perseverance* (v. 3). God is not the author of evil, suffering, or trials, but He has a wonderful capacity to use them for our good. The Apostle Paul wrote, "And we know that all things work together for good to those who love God, to those who are the called according to His purpose" (Rom. 8:28).

Within this context, James contends that there is a very practical result of facing trials with pure joy and with deep faith in Jesus Christ. The result of such trials is the great virtue of patience or perseverance. Let us explore together how such testing can lead to patience or perseverance in our lives.

First, let us examine the word "testing." In the Greek text, we find the word *dokímion,* which literally means proving or trying. It is the word used by Peter when he writes about the "genuineness of your faith, being much more precious than gold that perishes, though it is tested by fire, may be found to praise, honor, and glory at the revelation of Jesus Christ" (1 Pet. 1:7).

This kind of testing can be compared to a refiner's fire which burns out all the alloys from the precious metal. As God allows this testing in our lives, He uses it for our good. As we turn to Him and commit ourselves to Him, He allows the impurities of motive and conduct to be removed from our lifestyles. And He leaves in their stead the wonderful gift of patience or perseverance.

Next, we must notice where this testing takes place. James refers to it as *"the testing of our faith"* (v. 3). This faith has its source in God. "So then faith comes by hearing, and hearing by the word of God" (Rom. 10:17). In fact, without faith it is impossible to please God (Heb. 11:6). (For a more complete study on the subject of faith— *pistis*—see p. 61.)

The testing which God allows to take place in our lives is at the place of greatest spiritual significance—our faith. It is by faith that we come to God; it is by faith that we follow Him, and it is by faith that we receive His wonderful promises, including life eternal. As we are tried, our faith grows. We trust God more fully and ourselves less fully. Indeed, "this is the victory that has overcome the world—our faith" (1 John 5:4).

I have a close friend who has been experiencing this kind of testing in his own life. Just a few years ago, he was a senior partner in a major law firm in Los Angeles. Then, he began to sense that God was calling him into a new phase of ministry. After a great deal of prayerful consideration, he resigned from his position and enrolled in a theological seminary to prepare for the pastoral ministry.

Of course, this required a great deal of personal sacrifice, including a substantial financial loss. But the primary commitment of his life was to Jesus Christ as Lord. He believed that he was doing the will of God.

He completed seminary with high honors and then received his first pastoral call to serve as an assistant pastor of a large church. During his first year of service in that church, he became ill. The medical examinations revealed that he was suffering from cancer. Since that time he has undergone a series of surgeries and a variety of cancer therapies.

The question could be asked, "Why would such a thing happen to a man who loved God so much and who sacrificed such a great deal in order to follow Jesus as Lord?" I am certain that my friend has wrestled personally with that kind of question.

However, there is a deeper question which has much more importance. How is his faith? Has it endured the testing or has it failed him? The good news is that God's grace has been sufficient. His faith has continued to grow. He has entrusted himself to the Lord not only in word but in action. His faith has been winning the victory. And he will readily admit that his painful experiences have wrought some very important results—including perseverance.

In fact, that is exactly what James is teaching. The testing of your faith results in perseverance or "patience," the quality of unswerving constancy or endurance. It is not "passive" patience which might be confused with laziness but, rather, "active" patience which denotes steadfastness and "staying power."

This is the attribute referred to the Apostle Paul when he wrote that "tribulation produces perseverance" (Rom. 5:3). And the writer of Hebrews counsels us to "lay aside every weight, and the sin which so easily ensnares us, and let us run with perseverance the race that is set before us, looking to Jesus . . ." (Heb. 12:1–2).

Probably the most helpful contemporary phrase we could use adequately to describe this Christian virtue would be, "Keep on keeping on!" God invites us to trust Him with all that we are and to realize that even the testing of our faith is for our good—it develops perseverance in our lives.

Later in his letter, James shares some additional insight and counsel regarding how we should respond to suffering and trials (James 5:7–11). Within that context, he refers to the examples of Job and the prophets. And he points us to Christ as the One full of compassion and mercy who finally brings about the solutions to our needs (James 5:11).

The suffering and trials of life are never wasted when we give them and our total selves to God. As a result of trials, there are some benefits which are extremely important for us to recognize and enjoy. James identifies three specific benefits that come to us as a result of experiencing trials in our lives.

3. *Perseverance—patience—helps us become mature, complete, and not lacking anything* (v. 4). James has told us that *"the testing of your faith produces patience"* (v. 3). He goes on to contend that *"patience* [*must finish*] *its perfect work that you may be perfect and complete, lacking nothing"* (v. 4).

What a profound statement! The facing of trials and the testing of our faith can be profitable to us if we will entrust ourselves to the Lord. He will use those negative experiences for very positive

results in our lives and personal characters by teaching us perseverance.

In the same way, experiencing perseverance is not an end in itself
even though perseverance is a very great Christian virtue. As we
continue to entrust ourselves to Jesus Christ as Lord, this quality
of perseverance will continue its work to ultimate completion so that
we may become mature, complete, and lacking in nothing. What
exciting potential! Let us examine these three characteristics individu-
ally in order to better understand what they can mean in our lives.

The first benefit we can enjoy in our lives as we allow perseverance
to finish its work is that of maturity. To be mature (*téleios*) means
to be perfect, complete, or full-grown.

This is the word which Jesus used in His Sermon on the Mount
when He said, "Therefore you shall be perfect, just as your Father
in heaven is perfect" (Matt. 5:48). Our human response to that command would be, "That's impossible; no one can be perfect but God!"

However, if that is true, why would Jesus give us such a commandment? Why would He tell us to be perfect? I believe that the answer
is quite simple. Although we can never reach the state of perfection
in this life, that should be our goal.

The Apostle Paul put this matter into proper perspective when
at the close of his ministry he wrote, "Not that I have already attained,
or am already perfected; but I press on, that I may lay hold of that
for which Christ Jesus has also laid hold of me. . . . I press toward
the goal for the prize . . ." (Phil. 3:12, 14).

In fact, to become mature or perfect is the goal or purpose of the
ministry of the church in our lives according to Paul as he wrote to
the Ephesian church. He said that within the church we should be
growing so that "all come to the unity of the faith and the knowledge
of the Son of God, to a perfect man, to the measure of the stature
of the fullness of Christ" (Eph. 4:13).

In other words, the church should be the place in which we are
growing and maturing to become more and more like Jesus Christ
Himself—measured by nothing less than His full stature, which is
perfection. This is our goal and our purpose.

In addition, James wants us to learn that God will use trials in
our lives to teach us perseverance and that this lifestyle of perseverance would continue to work in us to bring about spiritual maturity—
so that increasingly we would become perfect—like Jesus.

The second benefit is that we can be complete. James uses the word *"complete"* not merely to be redundant, but for emphasis and clarification. He means exactly what he is saying. Perseverance, when it finishes its perfect work, makes the believer complete. The Greek word used here is *holóklēros,* which means entire or perfect in every part.

This word is found in only one other place in all of the New Testament. In the closing blessing of his first letter to the Thessalonians, Paul states, ". . . may your whole (*holóklēros*) spirit, soul, and body be preserved blameless at the coming of our Lord Jesus Christ" (1 Thess. 5:23).

That is exactly what James is saying. As we allow patience to have its perfect work, we become increasingly complete, whole, entire, and perfect in every part. But if the first two statements are not clear enough, he proceeds to the third which places "the final nails in the box."

Verse 4 promises that we will be lacking nothing. The word for lacking, *leípō,* is the same word James uses in the next verse when he states, *"If any of you lacks wisdom . . ."* (v. 5). It cannot be translated any more graphically than "lacking nothing." It means just that. God desires for us to be deficient in nothing or to want for nothing.

What a powerful statement. When we allow patience to have its perfect work in our lives, we shall be growing to become more and more like Jesus—perfect, mature, full-grown, complete, entire, perfect in every part, lacking in nothing, deficient in nothing, wanting nothing!

In addition to the three results which James shares in verse 4 of chapter 1, there is a fourth benefit of perseverance in the face of trials that he exposes in verse 12. Within that context he states, "Blessed is the man who endures temptation; for when he has been proved, he will receive the *crown of life* which the Lord has promised to those who love Him."

There are immediate benefits from perseverance, but there is the ultimate benefit which supersedes all. It is life eternal, which no one can take from us. Life is not always fair nor are the victories for the Christian always obvious, but of one thing we can be sure: ultimate victory is ours in Jesus Christ. As we are faithful and as we persevere, the "crown of life" awaits us in the victory circle of the Kingdom of God!

How to Obtain Wisdom

> 5 If any of you lacks wisdom, let him ask of God, who gives to all liberally and without reproach, and it will be given to him.
> 6 But let him ask in faith, with no doubting, for he who doubts is like a wave of the sea driven and tossed by the wind.
> 7 For let not that man suppose that he will receive anything from the Lord;
> 8 he is a double-minded man, unstable in all his ways.
>
> *James 1:5–8*

Wisdom is one of the great and unusual qualities of life—even for the Christian. James teaches that the only source for godly wisdom, or that which comes from above, is God Himself. God is the source of wisdom.

There is a quality of the wisdom of men which comes primarily from the experiences of life. For example, a person shows wisdom when he or she does not touch a hot stove. Most of us have gained that little bit of wisdom through the painful experience of touching a hot stove at some time in our lives and gaining the desire never to do it again. That is the process of gaining early wisdom.

Of course, the longer we live, the more "hot stove" experiences we encounter; older people are usually wiser people. James is inviting us, however, to employ a quality of wisdom that far exceeds the early kind of wisdom.

The Apostle Paul contrasts the wisdom of God and the wisdom of men very graphically in the first two chapters of 1 Corinthians. The summary of his argument is simply this: "The foolishness of God is wiser than men, and the weakness of God is stronger than men" (1 Cor. 1:25). James and Paul agree that God desires for us to enjoy more than mere human wisdom, that He offers us the very wisdom of God! James teaches us three specific things about godly wisdom.

1. *We should ask God for wisdom* (v. 5). James states, *"If any of you lacks wisdom, let him ask of God. . . ."* The instruction is very clear: if we need wisdom, we should ask for it.

This asking is predicated upon recognizing the need for wisdom.

We simply will not ask if we do not realize that we have the need. One of the earmarks of sin is walking in darkness (1 John 1:6). Sin blinds us and prevents us from seeing the truth.

In contrast, God invites us to walk in the light as He is in the light (1 John 1:7). He desires for us to know the truth so that we might be free in Him (John 8:30–36). All of us need the wisdom of God! But there are those who do not recognize the need. They are wise in their own conceits—in the flesh.

Every day, we have repeated opportunities to trust in our own wisdom or to ask God for His; to live in the flesh or to walk in the Spirit; to be in the slavery of the darkness of sin or to be set free by the light of Jesus Christ. There is a godly wisdom that can be ours only when we come to God recognizing our need for Him and for His wisdom.

If we ask God for wisdom, we shall receive it. The promise is clear: if we lack wisdom and ask God for it, it will be given to us (v. 5). Of course, the focus is not upon us but rather upon the generous God who provides wisdom.

God is described as "liberal" (*haplōs*) and as "one who gives without reproach" (*oneidízō*). As we study the Word of God, it is obvious that God delights in giving. He is generous; His very character is to give. Love is His motive for giving. In fact, He loved enough to give His very best. "God so loved the world that He gave His only begotten son . . ." (John 3:16).

It is not only God's character to give generously; it is also His character to build us up. He does not wish to tear us down. Indeed, He neither refuses nor reproaches anyone; He never "puts anyone down." He is the Master Builder.

2. *We should ask in faith, with no doubting* (v. 6). As we have seen, faith is central to the teaching of James and is central to Christian lifestyle. James tells us that we must ask God for wisdom with faith. We must believe that God is capable of giving us wisdom as we need it and that He will give wisdom to us as we request it from Him.

Once again we see the practicality of our faith. It is active obedience. God has instructed us to ask Him for wisdom. As we do, we are actively obeying Him. We are asking in faith. To clarify what it means to ask in faith, James shares two graphic examples of what we should not do.

First, faith excludes doubting (v. 6). One cannot exist where the other is found. Where there is faith there is not doubt. As Elton Trueblood has said, "An empty, meaningless faith may be worse than none." The one who lives by faith has his or her life built upon the solid rock—Jesus Christ Himself (Matt. 7:24–25).

In contrast, James contends that the person who doubts is *"like a wave of the sea driven and tossed by the wind"* (v. 6). What a difference between faith and doubt. As usual, James uses a most practical example. He warns us against being up one day and down the next in our spiritual lives. We need to build our lives upon the rock and ask in faith.

Second, James tells us not to be double-minded. Such a person is unstable in all his ways (v. 8). In chapter 4, verse 8, James encourages the double-minded to *"purify your hearts."*

Jesus spoke directly to the problem of being double-minded in His Sermon on the Mount. He said, "No one can serve two masters; for either he will hate the one and love the other, or else he will hold to the one and despise the other. You cannot serve God and mammon" (Matt. 6:24).

Christian discipleship is based upon being single-minded. We must deny ourselves, take up our cross, and follow Jesus (Mark 8:34). We must cast off every sin which would weigh us down and run with resolution the race which lies ahead of us, looking only to Jesus who is both the author and finisher of our lives—our goal and purpose for living (Heb. 12:1, 2). We cannot be double-minded and be effective as Christians.

The conclusion is clear. If someone asks with doubts or is double-minded, *"let not that man suppose that he will receive anything from the Lord"* (v. 7). God is anxious to give to us, but we must ask Him in faith.

3. *If we ask God, we shall receive wisdom* (v. 5). The promise is so clear that none of us should miss it. If we ask, it will be given to us. It is always the desire of God to give what is good to His children.

Jesus taught this principle when He said, "Ask, and it will be given to you; seek, and you will find; knock and it will be opened to you" (Matt. 7:7). He continues that teaching by comparing our heavenly Father to our earthly father. As our earthly father loves us and wants to give us what is good, how much more our heavenly Father desires to do so (Matt. 7:9–11).

James also continues his teaching on this important subject in relationship to prayer (James 4:2–3). He states that we often do not have simply because we do not ask!

The Apostle John also reveals important insight on this subject when he writes, "Now this is the confidence that we have in Him, that if we ask anything according to His will, He hears us" (1 John 5:14). I believe that it is always the will of God to give His children wisdom.

The bottom line of this important teaching is clear—if we lack wisdom, we must recognize the need; we must ask God who alone can supply His quality of wisdom, and we shall receive it. That is His promise and guarantee.

In fact, it is an unlimited guarantee. We can come to our Father for wisdom as often as necessary. We never need to fall short of what He longs to give us. His wisdom is available all of the time in whatever quantity we need it.

In my own life, I find constantly the need to ask for the wisdom of God. For example, as I was invited to consider becoming the pastor of the church I am now serving, I found that I was greatly in need of the wisdom of God. In short, I wanted to do the will of God, but I desperately needed His wisdom in order to recognize His will. I joined with my wife and children in seeking God's wisdom.

The church that had invited me to be a pastoral candidate was within thirty minutes of the church I was then serving with a great deal of joy and fulfillment. For several weeks, I sensed the Lord leading me to drive over to the other church in my car and to drive around it while praying for His wisdom and His guidance. I wanted to be single-minded. I wanted to do His will alone.

As you may guess, God answered those prayers in a very marvelous manner. He clearly led us to the new church ministry while releasing us from the former. He supplied wonderfully for someone to replace me and then blessed marvelously in the beginning of our new ministry. In the most practical way, we sought the wisdom of God. And, in His love and generosity, He liberally gave His wisdom to us. And as a result, His blessings have flowed upon all who have been involved.

I am convinced that when we ask God for wisdom and commit our way to Him, we have the strength to do the right things. He will direct our paths. He will protect us from the wrong, and guide us to the right (Prov. 3:5–6). He is to be trusted!

How to Be Rich and Poor

9 Let the lowly brother glory in his exaltation,
10 but the rich in his humiliation, because as a
flower of the field he will pass away.
11 For no sooner has the sun risen with a burning
heat than it withers the grass; its flower falls, and its
beautiful appearance perishes. So the rich man will
also fade away in his pursuits.

James 1:9–11

One of the major areas in which we need the wisdom of God is
in relationship to riches. The love of God and the love of money
are mutually exclusive. Jesus said that we cannot serve God and
money (Matt. 6:24). He also said that it was "easier for a camel to
go through the eye of a needle than for a rich man to enter the
kingdom of God" (Matt. 19:24).

However, we must recognize that the inherent evil is not with
money, but rather with the "love of money." Paul wrote to Timothy,
"For the love of money is a root of all kinds of evil, for which some
have strayed from the faith in their greediness, and pierced themselves
through with many sorrows" (1 Tim. 6:10).

As we might suspect, James meets this potential problem head-
on by sharing practical advice both to those who are rich and those
who are poor. He recognizes that riches may be a snare not only to
the rich but also to the poor who might believe that their human
needs could be met if they only had more money. This philosophy
is in direct contradiction to the teaching of Jesus regarding riches
in Matthew 6:19–34.

The teaching of Jesus was simply that life's deepest needs can be
met only by Him—and that He desires to provide even the practical
needs of food, clothing, and shelter. He longs to care for us and to
provide for us if we will "seek first the kingdom of God and His
righteousness, and all these things will be added to you" (Matt. 6:33).

James is continuing this vital teaching. And we must remember
that he is writing to many believers who have lost everything they
had as a result of the persecution for their faith in Christ. They
had forsaken literally everything in order to be faithful in following
Jesus. Within this context, he begins by addressing the poor.

1. *The richness of humble circumstances* (v. 9). The words of James are

words of encouragement, *"Let the lowly brother glory in his exaltation"* (v. 9). In other words, those who find themselves in humble circumstances or a low position take pride in the fact that a high position awaits them in the Kingdom of God!

The word used for glory, *kaucháomai,* comes from the root word *auchéō* which means "to boast." That is what James is encouraging us to do in the best sense of the term. We should be boasting or rejoicing or glorying in the fact that our lowly estate is temporary.

God has invited us to the riches of His Kingdom. We are assured of an exalted and high position in the Kingdom of God. We are loyal subjects of the King of kings and Lord of lords! And, although the going may be difficult at times, there is a day that we will "cross over the Jordan" into the "Promised Land."

As I mentioned in my exposition of 1 Peter, it was this hope that inspired so many of the marvelous Negro spirituals which were sung and cherished by the Black slaves in the early history of the United States. For example, there is the marvelous spiritual:

> Swing low, sweet chariot,
> Coming for to carry me home.
> Swing low, sweet chariot,
> Coming for to carry me home.
>
> I looked over Jordan, and what did I see,
> Coming for to carry me home?
> A band of angels coming after me,
> Coming for to carry me home.
>
> If you get there before I do,
> Coming for to carry me home;
> Tell all my friends I'm coming too,
> Coming for to carry me home.
>
> I am sometimes up, I'm sometimes down,
> Coming for to carry me home,
> But still my soul feels heavenly bound,
> Coming for to carry me home.

The Scriptures are correct when they declare, "There is one who makes himself rich, yet has nothing; and one who makes himself poor, yet has great riches" (Prov. 13:7). Jesus stated the same truth in another way, "For where your treasure is, there your heart will be also." Within that context, He encourages us to "lay up for ourselves treasures in heaven" (Matt. 6:20, 21).

The encouragement of James is clear. Let those who are in humble or low circumstances be glad in the assurance that the best is ahead. We are assured of a high position in the Kingdom that matters not merely for the present, but for eternity.

2. *The potential poverty of riches* (v. 10). Next, James proceeds to discuss the appropriate way in which those Christians who are rich in this age should relate to those riches. In short, he says that we should not glory in our riches but rather in our humiliation. At first thought, this counsel seems very strange. In fact, it is contradictory to everything which our society would teach us about the power and glory of riches.

Of course, James is using "Kingdom talk" and is sharing his counsel in the perspective of the Kingdom of God. His analogy of the temporality of riches is again both graphic and practical.

He compares riches to the flowers of the field which are attractive when in full bloom. But, at best, their beauty is temporary. When the sun rises with a burning heat, it withers the grass and the flowers drop off their stems and their beauty comes to an end.

So it is with riches. They may be beautiful and attractive for the present, but they are temporary. They, too, will "fall" and be no more. And so James concludes, *"The rich man also will fade away in his pursuits"* (v. 11).

As we have seen, Jesus warned us clearly about the dangers of trusting riches. In His parable of the sower, He describes the seed that fell among the thorns, "And the cares of the world, the deceitfulness of riches, and the desires for other things entering in choke the word, and it becomes unfruitful" (Mark 4:19).

Riches can be very deceitful. Jesus not only spoke about the deceitfulness of riches, but He also warned us to "beware of covetousness, for one's life does not consist in the abundance of the things he possesses" (Luke 12:15). Within that context, He went on to share the Parable of the Rich Fool who planned to tear down his barns to build larger ones to contain all his wealth. Instead, the Lord required his soul that night.

Jesus concluded that story by saying, "So is he who lays up treasure for himself, and is not rich toward God" (Luke 12:21). That is the essence of the teaching of James. He instructs those who are rich not to be so foolish as to trust in their wealth. Instead, they should be rich toward God and should glory not in their riches, but in their humiliation.

The word in verse 10 translated as "humiliation" is *tapeinōsis,* which means "to be made low." It is from the root word *tapeinós* which is the exact word used in verse 9 to describe the brother who is lowly.

What a marvelous insight is ours! God has asked the brother who is lowly (*tapeinós*) to glory in his exalted estate in the Kingdom of God, while He asks the man who is rich to glory in his humble estate (*tapeinōsis*). In fact, this insight leads us to the basic truth which James desires to teach us.

3. *How to be rich and poor* (v. 11). In conclusion, James is contending for the rich and the poor to live in the same manner with the same priorities for living. Whether we are rich or poor, we are the Lord's— if we are serious about following Jesus as the Lord of our lives.

And, although James does not refer to it specifically, I believe that we are being fair to the text and to the basic conclusion of his teaching to suggest that James is encouraging his readers to enjoy the life of contentment.

Rather than pursuing the "things" which we do not have or trusting in riches, we are invited to "be without covetousness, and be content with such things as you have. For He Himself has said, 'I will never leave you nor forsake you' " (Heb. 13:5).

The Apostle Paul would teach us that the person who is truly rich is the person who has learned to be content. He wrote, "Not that I speak in regard to need, for I have learned in whatever state I am, to be content: I know how to be abased, and I know how to abound. Everywhere and in all things I have learned both to be full and to be hungry, both to abound and to suffer need" (Phil. 4:11–12).

He concluded by saying, "I can do all things through Christ who strengthens me" (Phil. 4:13). That is also the conclusion of James. The focus of godly living is in trusting the Lord for all things whether it be the perseverance to overcome trials, the need for wisdom, the need for the lowly to be encouraged by their promised exaltation in the Kingdom of God, or the need for the rich to be delivered from the snare of trusting in their riches to the joy of walking humbly with Christ.

Christ is the source for everything we need! He has promised to never leave us nor forsake us. He has promised to supply all of our needs (Phil. 4:19). He has invited us to seek first His Kingdom and His righteousness, and everything will be added unto us (Matt. 6:33).

Therefore, all of us should be both rich and poor, both exalted and humbled, both lowly and high. But whatever our earthly estate, the best is yet to come. The Lord is always to be trusted. His Kingdom shall come.

HOW TO OVERCOME TEMPTATION

12 Blessed is the man who endures temptation; for when he has been proved, he will receive the crown of life which the Lord has promised to those who love Him.

13 Let no one say when he is tempted, "I am tempted by God"; for God cannot be tempted by evil, nor does He Himself tempt anyone.

14 But each one is tempted when he is drawn away by his own desires and enticed.

15 Then, when desire has conceived, it gives birth to sin; and sin, when it is full-grown, brings forth death.

James 1:12–15

After dealing with the important subjects of wisdom and riches, James returns to his central theme of this chapter—facing trials. Within verses 2 to 4, he focused on ways that we could profit from the trials we face. Now he deals with the vital subject of "how to overcome trials or temptations."

The word for temptation in Greek is *peirasmós,* from the root word *peirázō* which literally means "to put to the test" or "to go through." To tempt means to entice, assay, examine, or try. Temptation, then, means "a putting to proof—for good" or "an evil solicitation—for bad."

In other words, temptation can be used for our good or for our harm. The outcome depends upon our response to the temptation. It is important to realize that temptation in itself is not sin. Jesus was tempted for forty days in the wilderness (Luke 4:1–13). But He did not submit to His temptation. He did not sin. Instead, He overcame the temptation which He faced.

How we respond to temptation is vitally important. James presents three vital truths concerning temptation that should help us to recognize temptation and then to overcome it.

First, in order to recognize and adequately deal with temptation, it is very helpful to realize what temptation is not. Verse 13 gives us the crucial information on this subject.

"Let no one say when he is tempted, 'I am tempted by God' " (v. 13). That statement presents a temptation within itself. From the beginning of the human race, we have faced the temptation of blaming others for our weaknesses or shortcomings.

Adam began this erroneous behavior by blaming Eve for the fact that he had eaten of the forbidden fruit in the Garden of Eden (Gen. 3:12). In turn, Eve blamed the serpent for her disobedience (Gen. 3:13).

And since that time, we have faced the temptation of blaming others for our actions. Flip Wilson, the American comedian, has made popular the phrase, "The devil made me do it!" However, the Scripture clearly teaches that we are responsible for our own actions and that each of us is to give an account of ourselves to God (Rom. 14:12).

Although it is difficult for us to understand because of our humanness and our tendency to sin, evil has no attraction to God. God is good, and He is the source of all good. Evil is contrary to the very nature of God. John writes that "all that is in the world—the lust of the flesh, the lust of the eyes, and the pride of life—is not of the Father but is of the world" (1 John 2:16).

Therefore, James makes his contention that God cannot be tempted with evil as a basic premise of truth (v. 13). He is God and He is good. He is not evil and He cannot be tempted by evil.

Neither does He tempt anyone with evil. God allows trials in the lives of His children but not with evil intent. He allows such temptations to be used for our good, if we will but trust Him to enable us to overcome the temptations.

As we have seen, the Biblical story of Job is a prime example of this truth. The Lord allowed Satan to tempt Job, but He stood available to enable Job to endure the temptations and to be the victor. That is exactly what ultimately happened. Job did trust in the Lord and did commit his way to God. As a result, he not only overcame the temptation, but "the Lord blessed the latter days of Job more than his beginning" (Job 42:12).

Temptation to do evil does not come from God, according to verse 13. The following verses, 14 and 15, reveal to us what the real source

36

of temptation is. In fact, James presents a four-step sequence of how temptation takes place in our lives.

First, we are tempted when we are drawn away by our own desires or lust. As John reminds us, because of our sinful nature, all of us are attracted by the lust of the flesh, the lust of the eyes, and the pride of life. As Jesus became man, He was tempted in every way which we are, yet without sin (Heb. 4:15). He faced the temptations of the lust of the flesh, lust of the eyes, and the pride of life (Luke 4:1–13).

Sower Krant summarized our dilemma well when he said, "If temptation struck no responsive chord, it would not be temptation." And so we sing in a marvelous hymn the descriptive phrase, "Take away my bent to sinning."

Temptation always begins with us and our tendency to sin. We face constantly the temptation to be drawn away by our own lusts and desires rather than to live and to walk in the Spirit. Indeed, walking in the Spirit with our eyes fixed intently on Jesus is a vital first step in overcoming temptation.

Second, we are enticed by the sin. The word "entice" is *deleázō*, which comes from the base "to entrap." It means to allure or beguile. In short, it is Satan who would tempt us with evil. He is the source of all evil just as God is the source of all good.

Satan knows our strengths and our weaknesses. He knows the "bait" which will most readily entice us. He wisely meets us at our tendency to lust or desire and then offers us that bait just as surely as he offered the forbidden fruit to Eve.

Recently, my son Mark and I were trout fishing in a small lake in the mountains of Southern California. We were using the usual bait of salmon eggs which are usually very attractive to trout. However, as we began to visit with other fishermen, we discovered that they were using another bait and were having great success in their fishing. Strangely enough, they were using marshmallows—and that unusual bait was enticing the trout!

Third, James contends that when this lust conceives, it gives birth to sin. Submitting to lust always leads to sin. The way of the flesh always results in evil just as certainly as the way of the Spirit always leads to good. Sin never adds quality to our lives. Although there are the momentary pleasures of sin and the lust of the flesh, sin ultimately subtracts from our lives. When we sin, we are always losers and never gainers in relationship to the eternal.

Finally, when sin is full-grown, it brings forth death. "The wages of sin is death" (Rom. 6:23). There is a way which seems right to man, but the end of that way is always death (Prov. 14:12).

Temptation that leads to evil begins with lust which leads to enticement which points to sin which results in death. That is the four-step model of the negative flow of temptation.

But God has invited us to overcome temptation. The key verse which addresses that subject within this passage is verse 12. The major instruction is in regard to enduring or overcoming temptation. Such a person will be blessed and "will receive the crown of life which the Lord has promised those who love Him" (v. 12).

The actual practical instruction regarding "how to endure or overcome temptation" is actually found in two other passages. The first is the earlier paragraph of James focusing on the subject of trials and temptation—James 1:2–4.

The second helpful passage is found in Paul's first letter to the church at Corinth. He writes, "No temptation has overtaken you except such as is common to man; but God is faithful, who will not allow you to be tempted beyond what you are able, but with the temptation will also make the way of escape, that you may be able to bear it" (1 Cor. 10:13).

The promises are clear. First, every temptation that we face is common to others. Second, God is faithful. He is to be trusted. He is to be the focus when we are being delivered from temptation.

Next, as we trust Him, He will not allow us to be tempted beyond what we are able to stand. In other words, His strength is greater than the enticement of Satan's bait. Finally, He will also make a way of escape so that we will be able to bear the temptation.

What a promise! We are brought back to the basic premise of discipleship and the Lordship of Jesus Christ. Our trust must be in Him. We must be walking in the Spirit rather than lusting in the flesh. We must keep our eyes and our minds upon Him.

Several years ago, I took our puppy to an obedience school. Although she learned a great deal during the eight weeks of classes, I believe that I learned even more. I learned one specific thing that will be helpful to me as long as I live. It is simply this: in order to prevent a dog from being distracted and enticed to go astray, the trainer must maintain eye contact with the dog. As long as the dog keeps his eyes upon the master and listens for his commands, the more certain he is to be oblivious to distraction and to be obedient to his master.

I believe that is the message which James is teaching us. We need to fix our eyes and minds upon Jesus. We need to tune in on His frequency. We need to trust Him fully and constantly. We need to depend upon His strength and wisdom and power. He will give us the victory.

How to Receive Good Gifts

16 Do not be deceived, my beloved brethren.

17 Every good gift and every perfect gift is from above, and comes down from the Father of lights, with whom there is no variation or shadow of turning.

18 Of His own will He brought us forth by the word of truth, that we might be a kind of firstfruits of His creatures.

James 1:16–18

As we have seen, James writes about very practical problems and needs of the Christian life. Although he writes in very practical "how to" kinds of principles, he does not always organize his material into specific paragraphs. For example, verse 16 is a transition verse between his teaching on the important subject of trials and temptations and his specific consideration of the goodness of God.

Therefore, the important teaching of verse 16 could have been considered with the past section on temptation or with this section. As you study and/or teach this passage, you will have the freedom to include it in either or both of the sections. I have decided to include it in this section. In any event, the interpretation of the important teaching of James on the subject of deception is appropriate.

1. *Do not be deceived* (v. 16). Sin is deceptive, and Satan is always seeking to deceive us. Eve was correct when she said, "The serpent deceived me" (Gen. 3:13). Peter was right when he warned us to "Be sober, be viligant; because your adversary the devil walks about like a roaring lion, seeking whom he may devour" (1 Pet. 5:8).

In contrast, God never deceives. He always deals with truth. Jesus came declaring, "I am the way, the truth, and the life" (John 14:6).

39

Jesus said if we would know Him we would know the truth, "and the truth shall make you free" (John 8:32). He proceeded to call the devil "a liar and the father of lies" (John 8:44).

And so the wise counsel of James is that we should not be deceived. And, since this verse is the transition between two important paragraphs of truth, it is appropriate for us to apply both truths to the teaching of this verse. First, we should not be deceived regarding the source of evil—that is Satan. He is the one who would tempt us to do evil and who would delight in leading us to sin and death.

Then, we should not be deceived concerning the One who is the source of all good—that is God. He is not only the source of good, but He is the One who is committed to making all things work together for good for His children, those who are called according to His purpose (Rom. 8:28).

2. *Every good gift and every perfect gift comes from God* (v. 17). James contrasts that which comes from Satan and that which comes from God. Within verses 17 and 18, he uses such descriptive words as good, gift, perfect, above, lights, and firstfruits. These are "life" words rather than the "death" vocabulary which he used in the preceding passage.

God loves us and desires what is best for us. As we have said, it is the character of God to give. Because He is good, He delights in giving good gifts to those who trust Him. The Bible contains story after story of how God has blessed those who obey Him. The Biblical promises of the blessing of God are literally innumerable.

Every good gift comes from God. And every perfect gift comes from Him. The word translated as "perfect" is *téleios,* the same word James uses in 1:4 when he speaks about letting patience *"have its perfect work, that you may be perfect . . ."*

God is perfect, and everything which He does is perfect. Therefore, His gifts are not only good, but they are also perfect. They come from above because that is James' concept of where God is. Literally, they come from God.

These gifts come down from "the Father of lights, with whom there is no variation or shadow of turning" (v. 17). The phrase "Father of lights" is found only in this passage of all the New Testament.

However, the reference to God as the God of light is frequent in the Scriptures beginning with the creation account (Gen. 1) and carrying through the Book of Revelation which describes the New Jerusalem as needing no lamp or light of the sun, "For the Lord God gives them light" (Rev. 22:5). Indeed, God is the Father of lights. There is little wonder that Jesus said, "I am the light of the world" (John 8:12).

The phrase which describes God as the One "with whom there is no variation or shadow of turning" (v. 17) is also very interesting. It is anchored in many promises of God including the one made to the Children of Israel as recorded in Deuteronomy 31:6 and promised anew in Hebrews 13:5. It is this marvelous promise, "I will never leave you nor forsake you." God is called a dependable friend who "sticks closer than a brother" (Prov. 18:24).

Jesus Christ is the same yesterday, today, and forever (Heb. 13:8). He is the rock upon which we should build our lives (Matt. 7:24–25). God is the One to be trusted; what He promises, He will do (1 Thess. 5:24). These and other promises concerning the steadfastness and faithfulness of God permeate both the Old Testament and the New Testament. As James says, He is not like the shifting shadows. You can depend upon Him.

3. *God offers us the very best of gifts.* One of the great mysteries of theology is the tender balance between the sovereignty of God and the free will of man (see commentary on 1 Peter 1:1–2, pp. 111). James reminds us in verse 18 of the fact that God initiated our salvation by His own will. Without a doubt, He is the aggressive lover; He is the initiator; He is the One who loved us while we were yet His enemies (Rom. 5:8).

"He brought us forth by the word of truth" (v. 18a). The phrase which is translated as "brought us forth" is the word *apokueō,* which literally means to beget or to produce, to breed.

In other words, when James refers to the fact that God "brought us forth," he is actually referring to our new birth. It has been His will to bring us forth to spiritual birth. As Jesus said, "who were born, not of blood, nor of the will of the flesh, nor of the will of man, but of God" (John 1:13).

God has brought us to this spiritual birth by using the vehicle of "the word of truth." Again, we must recognize Jesus as the personification of truth (John 14:6) and as the One who is the truth which "shall make you free" (John 8:32). Paul contends that he was called by God to share this word of truth which had been a mystery to all previous generations (Col. 1:24–27).

"That we might be a kind of firstfruits of His creatures" (v. 18b). Jehovah required the Children of Israel to give of their tithes and firstfruits as a part of the Levitical law (Lev. 27:30–33). This was a vital part

of God's covenant relationship with His people. He desired the best of the herds and flocks and of the crops of the land and the fruit of the trees. The first tenth of everything belonged to God.

As we have seen, James is writing to Jewish Christians who understood the requirements of the tithe and firstfruits. He is reminding us that as we trust in Christ by faith, we become a kind of firstfruits of His creatures.

God is a generous giver, and He has lavished us with many gifts including the new birth through Jesus Christ, the revelation of the mystery of the word of truth which had been hidden for generations, and the marvelous position in Christ which allows us to be a kind of firstfruit within the Kingdom of God. Through faith in Christ, we have become eternal creations which shall never pass away. The earth and heaven and the universe shall pass away; they are only temporary. But we shall never pass away. Death has no more dominion over us—we have life eternal!

How to Communicate

19 Therefore, my beloved brethren, let every man
be swift to hear, slow to speak, slow to wrath;
20 for the wrath of man does not produce the
righteousness of God.
21 Therefore lay aside all filthiness and overflow
of wickedness, and receive with meekness the
implanted word, which is able to save your souls.

James 1:19–21

Communication theory, as a discipline of the behavioral sciences, is primarily a phenomenon of the latter half of the Twentieth Century. However, the art of effective communication belongs to the ages. Without a doubt, God is the most perfect and effective communicator in all the universe. We should not be surprised that He shares some very helpful counsel for us in His Word regarding how we can communicate more effectively.

1. *Be swift to listen* (v. 19). One of the marvelous characteristics of God is that He listens to us. He is available at all times to hear our prayers, to listen to our concerns and even to be touched with the nonverbal communication of our feelings. God does not keep office

hours, nor does he require appointments. He hears us (Ps. 66:16–20).

In studying the earthly life of Jesus as reported in the Gospels, we are deeply touched with His marvelous ability to listen. While His disciples were arguing and talking, Jesus was listening to the deeper needs of them and of the people whom they encountered.

Jesus traveled the same roads and village streets as His contemporaries. Yet He heard and saw needs which no one else seemed to notice. His authentic love for people motivated Him to listen not only to words but to nonverbal communication. He was constantly meeting people at a point of need whether it was the Samaritan woman at the well or Zacchaeus who was up a tree. He listened.

And so our Lord invites us to the ministry of listening. Most of us would be amazed at how much more effective we would be in our witnessing if we stopped talking and began to listen. The most effective means of ministry, for example, is responding to need; not dumping our load.

Jesus gives us some wonderful insights concerning the importance of listening not only in our interpersonal relationships but also in our relationship to Him. In using the analogy of our being the sheep and of His being our Shepherd, He said, "He goes before them; and the sheep follow him, for they know his voice. Yet they will by no means follow a stranger, but will flee from him, for they do not know the voice of strangers" (John 10:4–5).

In the same way in which a sheep listens to his shepherd's voice, we should become acquainted increasingly with the voice of our Lord. And we should be following Him day by day.

Most of us do too much talking and not enough listening. Recently, I was invited to participate in a large Christian convocation which was to be held in the famed Rose Bowl. Thousands of Christians were invited to gather together to pray for revival and the spiritual renewal of our nation.

As I sat on the platform during the several hours of the service, I was deeply touched by the fact that we were doing far too much talking and far too little praying and listening to God. I face that problem frequently in my own life and ministry. I do not need to point to others. Like you, I need to make a commitment to my Lord that I will talk less and listen more.

2. *Be slow to speak* (v. 19). In fact, that is the next statement made by James. We should be slow to speak. The Bible has a great deal

of instruction on this subject. For example, Solomon suggests that "In the multitude of words sin is not lacking" (Prov. 10:19). He also contends that "even a fool is counted wise when he holds his peace" (Prov. 17:28).

James becomes involved in deeply practical teaching regarding the tongue and speech in the third chapter of his letter. In fact, he contends that if any one does not stumble in what he says, he is a perfect man (James 3:2). However, he goes on to contend that "no man can tame the tongue" (3:8). God is the authentic source of any person being able to control his or her tongue. We need God's help through the empowering of the Holy Spirit.

3. *Be slow to wrath* (vv. 19, 20). We should not only be slow to speak, we should also be slow to wrath or anger! The Greek word for wrath or anger is *orgē* which can be translated as anger, indignation, vengeance, or wrath. It is the same word used in Colossians 3:8 as one of the qualities which we should put off from our lives. The teaching of Paul concerning this quality of wrath or anger in 1 Thessalonians 5:9 is very interesting. He writes, "For God did not appoint us to wrath, but to obtain salvation through our Lord Jesus Christ."

Behavioral scientists tell us that this quality of wrath or anger usually comes as a result of frustration and that most frustration is caused simply by our not getting our own way. No wonder we should be slow to become angry!

In fact, James continues by asserting that "the wrath of man does not produce the righteousness of God" (v. 20). The righteousness of God comes to us as we seek to do His will as we follow Jesus as Lord. We are to "seek first the Kingdom of God and His righteousness." That kind of lifestyle is in sharp contrast to the person who becomes angry because he is not getting his own way.

The teaching is clear: be quick to listen, but slow to speak and slow to anger. In the following verse, James gives another one of his practical "how to" suggestions. We may be asking, "How can I do that?" And he answers by saying, "Lay aside all filthiness and overflow of wickedness, and receive with meekness the implanted word, which is able to save your souls" (v. 21).

James is saying to us, as you are slow to anger and to speak, carry that out in your daily living by laying aside all filthiness (*rhuparia:* dirtiness as contrasted to cleanliness) and the overflow of wickedness (*kakia:* evil or naughtiness). In short, our words and outbursts of anger reveal the true person within us. As we become more and more possessed by the Holy Spirit, we will increasingly enjoy not the overflow of filth, but rather the fruit of the Spirit of love, joy, peace, longsuffering, kindness, goodness, faithfulness, gentleness, and self-control (Gal. 5:22–23).

The key to that kind of lifestyle is the indwelling of the Holy Spirit. James also gives us practical advice concerning the influence of the Holy Spirit in our lives when he writes, "Receive with meekness the implanted word, which is able to save your souls" (v. 21).

That counsel is closely related to his teaching on being "quick to listen." In communication theory, we call the act of listening the "reception." The ears are often called our "receivers." If we are to receive the implanted Word of God, we must listen to His written Word, and we must have our receivers open to the revelation and guidance of the Holy Spirit. That Word becomes vital and powerful and alive as we allow the Holy Spirit to implant God's Word in us. We should receive that Word not with anger but with meekness.

How to Become a Doer

22 But be doers of the word, and not hearers only, deceiving yourselves.

23 For if anyone is a hearer of the word and not a doer, he is like a man observing his natural face in a mirror;

24 for he observes himself, goes away, and immediately forgets what kind of man he was.

25 But he who looks into the perfect law of liberty and continues in it, and is not a forgetful hearer but a doer of the work, this one will be blessed in what he does.

James 1:22–25

There is a progression in the teaching of James which goes something like this. First, be quick to listen; then be slow to speak; next, be slow to become angry; and, finally, do what God's Word tells us to do. "Doing" the Word of God is at the very center of the theology and practical teaching of James.

We must not merely give lip service or mental assent to the truth of God's Word. We must live it out in action. His teaching is simple but profound. He presents two major contentions. The first is as follows:

1. *Do not merely listen to the Word* (v. 22). As we have seen, listening

is terribly important. But it is not enough. Our lives can become spiritually stagnant like the Dead Sea when we only receive the Word of God and then do not translate it into appropriate action.

A lake can have the most beautiful spring water in the world flowing into its reservoir. But unless there are outlets, that beautiful water becomes stale and stagnant. The same phenomenon takes place in our lives if we are not living the life of active obedience and allowing the Holy Spirit to overflow into our lives. Nothing is more obnoxious to God than dead orthodoxy. To know the Word of God and not to live it is sin (James 4:17).

Frankly, this is the problem faced by many Christians within the contemporary church. They have become mere spectators who enjoy listening to the Word of God preached and taught Sunday after Sunday. Their heads are filled with Biblical knowledge and facts, but they ignore the translating of that knowledge into godly living.

Their spiritual heads grow fatter and fatter while their spiritual bodies are wasting away from lack of use. They are spiritual freaks who are of little value to themselves, the church or the world. In the words of James, they are deceived. They have deceived themselves by merely knowing without "doing."

To illustrate this point, James uses a very basic example of a person looking into a mirror. He simply glances into the mirror, compares himself with himself, and then goes away forgetting what he sees. That is the problem. When I look into a mirror or into a theology which is established by my standards, I always look all right. I am deceived into thinking that I am o.k.

Thousands of professing Christians are being deceived as they meet their own standards which they have established rather than God's standards. When I was a young boy, I was on vacation with my parents when we stopped to visit an old classmate of my father's. Before we arrived at the home, my parents shared with us children that we should not be disturbed when we met the little boy who lived at this house.

They explained that he was different from any other child we had met, but that we should not be frightened. His parents loved him deeply, God loved him deeply, and we should also love him.

After a friendly visit in the home, we were preparing to depart when the parents invited us into a nursery to meet their special little boy. I will never forget that precious little one. His body was that of a tiny baby but his head was nearly adult size.

I have often wept when I have thought of that dear little boy.

And, over the years, I have wept even more over the scores of Christians whom I have met who have the same distortion in their spiritual lives. Their spiritual heads are grossly enlarged with Biblical knowledge which has never been translated into lifestyle. They move from one Bible study to another or from one church service to another, but they never put the truths of God's Word into practice. They are deceived. They are hearers of the Word but not doers.

2. *Do what the Word says to do.* As usual, James speaks directly to the point. He not only instructs us to become doers of the Word, he gives us practical counsel in telling us "how to" do it.

Begin by looking intently into the perfect law (v. 25). The perfect law comes from God. As James has said, "Every good gift and every perfect gift is from above" (v. 17). Although James does not reveal the details of the perfect law, the New Testament speaks repeatedly about it. Jesus said, "Do not think that I came to destroy the Law or the Prophets. I did not come to destroy but to fulfill" (Matt. 5:17).

In reply to a question posed by one of the scribes, He answered him, "The first of all the commandments is: 'Hear, O Israel, the Lord our God is one Lord. And you shall love the Lord your God with all your heart, with all your soul, with all your mind, and with all your strength.' This is the first commandment. And the second, like it, is this: 'You shall love your neighbor as yourself.' There is no other commandment greater than these" (Mark 12:29–31).

This is the perfect law to which James is referring. Paul also presented this perfect law of Jesus which fulfilled all of the law and the prophets. For example, he wrote, "For all the law is fulfilled in one word, even in this: 'You shall love your neighbor as yourself' " (Gal. 5:14).

The perfect law has come from God and when we look intently into it, we see God. The object of looking into the law is not merely to catch a glance of ourselves. We need an in-depth look at God. The verb translated as "look" can be translated correctly as "peering into it." That is what we need to do with God's law.

As we do, James says that the law is not only perfect, but also that it is the law of liberty or freedom. Only in Christ can we actually be free. Only when we know the truth through Jesus Christ can we be free indeed (John 8:32). Being only hearers of the Word can lead us into the slavery of spiritual malnutrition. But being doers of the Word can lead us to freedom in Jesus Christ!

James again gets to the very heart of vital Christianity in verse 25. It is not enough to merely begin the race, we must continue in it. James pleads for us to be those who would look intently into the perfect law of liberty. That is essential. But it is not enough.

That action should become our lifestyle. We are to continue to look into the perfect law of liberty and to live the life of love which it reaches. We must never forget the truth we hear from God's Word. We should put it into action by doing.

The Christian life is always lived in the present tense. We do not have the luxury of clipping the coupons of the past. The verbs which describe vital Christian living are in the present tense such as the teaching of Jesus when He said, "Abide in Me, and I in you. As the branch cannot bear fruit of itself unless it abides in the vine, neither can you, unless you abide in Me" (John 15:4).

Glancing into the mirror is not enough. We should peer into the Lord and His Word day by day. We must listen closely to what He is saying to us. And then, by faith, we can be doers of His Word. We must follow Him in active obedience.

"This one will be blessed in what he does" (v. 25). The word "blessed" is a marvelous word in the Greek. It is *makários* which means happy, fortunate, or well off. This is the word which Jesus used in His beatitudes when He said, "Blessed are the poor in spirit . . . blessed are those who mourn . . . blessed are the meek . . ." (Matt. 5:3–11).

It is also the word that James uses when he writes, "Blessed is the man who endures temptation" (1:12). The person whose life is abiding in Christ is a blessed person. He or she is like a tree planted by streams of water, which yields its fruit in season and whose leaf does not wither. Whatever he or she does prospers (Ps. 1:3).

The life of the doer is the good life in Jesus Christ. There are some lifestyles which are far easier, but there is none better. The doer enjoys life at its very best. He or she is not deceived, but is set free in Jesus Christ to enjoy the life of liberty and blessing.

HOW TO BE AUTHENTICALLY RELIGIOUS

26 If anyone among you thinks he is religious, and does not bridle his tongue but deceives his own heart, this one's religion is useless.
27 Pure and undefiled religion before God and the Father is this: to visit orphans and widows in their trouble, and to keep oneself unspotted from the world.
James 1:26–27

James continues his theme of how to be a doer of the Word by focusing upon the subject of authentic religion. As we might suspect, he begins by telling us what pure and faultless religion is not and then proceeds to tell us what it is. Actually, his teaching is an expansion of that which he just presented.

1. *What pure and faultless religion is not* (v. 26). Religion (*thrēskeía*) has been defined as the outward expression of worship in ritual, liturgy, and ceremony. James believes that all of that religious expression is worthless if someone is not able to bridle his own tongue. This teaching must be taken within the balance of the previous teaching along with that which follows.

However, in short, James is saying that authentic religion is much more than outward expressions of worship. As Jesus said, all of that can take place but our hearts can still be far from Him (Matt. 15:8–9). We can simply be deceiving our own hearts if we think we are religious when we are not.

Again, James warns against the life of deception. Our own estimation of ourselves is usually wrong. We need more than a glance in the mirror of our lives; we need to peer into the perfect law of liberty. We need to see ourselves as God sees us. The goal of our lives needs to be to become more and more like Christ, measured by nothing less than His full stature (Eph. 4:13). Pure and faultless religion is not based upon deception, mere outward form, or a tongue which is out of control.

2. *What pure and faultless religion is* (v. 27). James presents a very concise definition of pure and faultless religion. This definition is not based upon human standards. He states clearly that this is pure and undefiled religion before God and the Father (v. 27).

First, it is a religion marked by a personal ministry. An excellent definition of ministry in the Biblical sense is as follows: Ministry is responding to the authentic needs of others with the love of Jesus Christ by the power of the Holy Spirit.

That definition describes the basic concern of James. He shares a specific ministry need of his society. The Church has been neglecting her widows and orphans. James is calling the Church to accountability. He is teaching us that pure and faultless religion must be carried out in action.

It is not enough to be "knowers." We must be "doers." The Apostle John teaches this same truth in his first letter, "By this we know love, because He laid down His life for us. And we ought to lay down our lives for the brethren. But whoever has this world's goods, and sees his brother in need, and shuts up his heart from him, how does the love of God abide in him? My little children, let us not love in word or in tongue, but in deed and in truth" (1 John 3:16–18).

Authentic religion shows itself in appropriate action. We need to minister to the specific needs of widows and orphans as well as other authentic human needs. We must love in action!

Then, we need to exhibit a personal purity. Again, the teaching of James is clear. In order to have a religion which is pure and faultless, we need to keep ourselves unspotted from the world (v. 27).

The word unspotted is *áspilos,* which literally means "without spot." The implication is clear, James is not suggesting that one be totally involved in the world or immersed by it. Rather he is calling us to the highest of godly lifestyles in which we would not have a single spot of the world visible to others.

This teaching is in concert with his concern stated earlier in the chapter when he warns us about being drawn away by our own lusts and enticed to sin (v. 14). Once again, we find John supporting the teaching of James when he writes, "Do not love the world or the things in the world. If anyone loves the world, the love of the Father is not in him" (1 John 2:15).

The Christian life is always a delicate balance between the positive and the negative. In this passage, James is instructing us to positively carry on personal ministry by responding to the authentic needs of widows and orphans. And, in the negative sense, we are to keep ourselves unspotted from the world.

As Jesus said in His prayer for His disciples and for us, "I do not pray that You should take them out of the world, but that You should keep them from the evil one" (John 17:15). We are to live in the world, but not be of the world. We are to love the world of people, but we are to hate the world system which has been devised by Satan himself. Again, it is characterized by the lust of the flesh, the lust of the eyes and the pride of life (1 John 2:16).

CHAPTER TWO

How to Live with Faith and Works

James 2:1–26

Now we come to the very heart of the message of James. Christians have always had great difficulty in understanding the relationship of faith and works. The early church struggled a great deal with this tension—especially those believers who had Jewish roots.

Of course, it was to these people—Jewish Christians—that James was writing. They understood the message declared by Paul to the church in Ephesus, "For by grace you have been saved through faith, and that not of yourselves; it is the gift of God, not of works, lest anyone should boast" (Eph. 2:8–9).

Like us, they faced the challenge of relating faith to works in their daily Christian living. The problem led them to one of two extremes. There were the Judaizers who taught that in order for one to be an authentic Christian, a person first had to become a Jewish convert and then be converted to Christ. Paul's letter to the Galatians meets that false teaching head-on. He writes in deeply theological terms regarding the fact that Jesus Christ came to set us free from the impossible demands of the law.

In fact, he calls the Judaizers "foolish" or "stupid" who would return to the slavery of living under the Jewish law (Gal. 3:1–5). Paul taught that, "The law was our tutor to bring us to Christ that we might be justified by faith. But after faith has come, we are no longer under a tutor" (Gal. 3:24–25).

That very teaching became central to the Protestant Reformation. Justification by faith alone, *sola fides,* was the focus of Martin Luther, John Calvin, and other leaders of the Reformation. For example, because of Luther's primary focus upon justification by faith, he had a major problem in understanding the message of James. He referred to the Book of James as an "epistle of straw."

However, since Luther's day, Lutheran scholars and other Reformation and Biblical scholars have come to understand that the teaching of James regarding the relationship of faith and works is not a refutation of Paul's teaching. Instead, James wrote to correct those who were distorting Paul's teaching.

The Christians of James' day faced a problem which many of us are facing in the contemporary day. In simple terms, many Christians were "coasting" in their commitment of following Jesus Christ as Lord. They were practicing what Dietrich Bonhoeffer referred to as "cheap grace." They believed incorrectly that Christian faith is merely a matter of "profession" and not "possession." In other words, they "talked" about Christian discipleship, but they didn't "live" it.

A number of years ago, a friend of mine was working with teenagers who were involved in gangs in one of the high-crime areas of New York City. Through his ministry, scores of those young people came to a personal faith in Jesus Christ and were set free from the slavery of crime and violence.

As this community of faith began to grow, those new Christians began to reach out with love to their former gang members. Whenever one of these tough gang members would profess to receive Jesus Christ as Savior and Lord, the more mature Christians would be concerned that they were really sincere about their commitment. They would share this message with the new converts. "Don't tell us that you are a Christian; we'll tell you!" In other words, don't merely say you are a Christian; prove it by the way in which you live.

These young people were saying to those new Christians what James is teaching in this chapter of his letter. Authentic Christianity is not merely a matter of talk; it must show itself in appropriate action! We will be known as Christians not simply because we *say* we have faith, but by how we *demonstrate* that faith in our lifestyles. Indeed, professed faith without appropriate deeds is worthless.

As James shares his practical teaching on this vital subject, he begins by discussing how we should "live out our faith" in the way we treat both the rich and the poor people who come into our lives, and specifically, who come into our churches. This is a graphic example of how we should put our faith to work.

HOW TO AVOID PARTIALITY

1 My brethren, do not hold the faith of our Lord
Jesus Christ, the Lord of glory, with partiality.

2 For if there should come into your assembly a
man with gold rings, in fine apparel, and there should
also come in a poor man in filthy clothes,

3 and you pay attention to the one wearing the
fine clothes and say to him, "You sit here in a good
place," and say to the poor man, "You stand there,"
or, "Sit here at my footstool,"

4 have you not shown partiality among yourselves,
and become judges with evil thoughts?

5 Listen, my beloved brethren: Has God not chosen
the poor of this world to be rich in faith and heirs
of the kingdom which He has promised to those who
love Him?

6 But you have dishonored the poor man. Do not
the rich oppress you and drag you into the courts?

7 Do they not blaspheme that noble name by
which you are called?

James 2:1–7

The sin of partiality is one of the most subtle of all sins. Partiality reveals a non-Christian sense of values. God shows no favoritism (Acts 10:34) and neither can His followers.

The members of the early church shared everything they had; they held everything in common (Acts 2:44–45). Those who believed were "of one heart and one soul; neither did anyone say that any of the things he possessed was his own, but they had all things in common" (Acts 4:32).

The simple result was that none of them lacked anything which he needed (Acts 4:34). As William Barclay said about those remarkable early believers, "None of them had too much and none of them had too little."

It was within the context of this kind of lifestyle that James writes to warn believers of the sin of partiality and to remind us of God's sense of values. In short, he instructs his readers to avoid partiality by observing three specific principles.

James begins his teaching with examples of how Christians would tend to treat two kinds of persons who might visit church. The illustration is hypothetical but extremely probable and practical.

First is the example of the rich man who would enter a church service. He would be wearing fine clothes and gold rings. The human tendency would be to welcome him warmly and to invite him to sit in the place of honor.

But why should you do such a thing? James asks, "Do not the rich oppress you and drag you into the courts?" (v. 6). "Do they not blaspheme that noble name by which you are called?" (v. 7).

We must be careful to realize that James is not asking us to discriminate against the rich. He has already addressed that important issue in chapter 1, verses 10–11. He is stating simply that rich people should not be treated with any special honor or favor. True value in the Kingdom of God has nothing to do with bank accounts, gold rings, or fine clothes.

In fact, Jesus said, "Assuredly, I say to you that it is hard for a rich man to enter the kingdom of heaven. And again I say to you, it is easier for a camel to go through the eye of a needle than for a rich man to enter the kingdom of God" (Matt. 19:23–24).

In His Sermon on the Mount, Jesus taught that we should not be worried about clothes or food or drink or riches. Instead, we should lay up for ourselves treasures in heaven, and we should seek first the Kingdom of God and His righteousness, and all these things will be added to you (Matt. 6:19–34).

The truly rich in the Kingdom of God are not those who have fine clothes, costly jewelry or great possessions. Only those who are rich spiritually are laying up treasures in heaven which shall last for eternity.

And so the teaching of James is clear; do not show favoritism to the rich. Do not give them special attention or bestow upon them special honor.

James presents a second hypothetical example to illustrate his warning against the sin of partiality. He suggests that a poor man might come into the Christian assembly dressed in filthy clothes. The tendency would be to treat him much differently than a rich person.

Rather than inviting him to sit in a good place, the Christians might ask him to stand in an inconspicuous place or to, "Sit here at my footstool" (v. 3).

Recently, I was reminded of James' example while I was worshiping in a fashionable Southern California church. During the worship service, a shabbily dressed man staggered into the beautiful sanctuary. He sat down next to me on a pew covered with a beautiful velvet pad.

An usher came running to him and asked him to leave the sanctuary. The man protested and refused to leave. Finally, the usher decided to allow him to remain where he was seated. However, the odor from his unbathed body began to offend some of the people seated near him. One by one, they began to depart. They did not understand the teaching of James. They were offended by the poor man and were not willing to reach out to him in love or even tolerate his presence.

James speaks to this kind of reaction. "Listen, my beloved brethren: Has God not chosen the poor of this world to be rich in faith and heirs of the kingdom which He has promised to those who love Him?" (v. 5). In summary, do not dishonor the poor (v. 6). Do not put down a person simply because he is poor. Many of the poor of this world are the rich of God's Kingdom!

The basic premise of the teaching of James regarding the sin of partiality is found in the first verse of chapter 2. "My brethren, do not hold the faith of our Lord Jesus Christ, the Lord of glory, with partiality." Those who follow Jesus Christ as Lord cannot be partial to either the rich or the poor.

The result of the sin of partiality is found in the ninth verse of chapter 2. "But if you show partiality, you commit sin, and are convicted by the law as transgressors." Indeed, partiality breaks the law of God and brings the judgment of the law. The result of sin is always spiritual death—and so the sin of partiality brings death to interpersonal relationships which could be meaningful and could serve as a bridge to introducing a visitor to eternal life through faith in Jesus Christ.

The solution to the problem of partiality is found in verse 8 of chapter 2. "If you really fulfill the royal law according to the Scripture, 'You shall love your neighbor as yourself,' you do well." Love is the key to overcoming partiality.

When you love another with Christ's love, you are always at eye level. You can neither look up at another nor down. Everyone who comes into our lives is on one level, whether rich or poor, bathed or unbathed, impressive or unimpressive.

God loves them all equally, and so must we. Indeed, the church should be the one social institution where all are treated equally. All are loved. Everything is shared. No person is violated. The lordship of Jesus Christ brings the indwelling presence of the Holy Spirit who generously shares the fruit of the Spirit and the unity of the Spirit.

All are one in Jesus Christ. "There is neither Jew nor Greek . . . slave nor free . . . male nor female; for you are all one in Christ

Jesus." (Gal. 3:28). That is the good news of the lifestyle of the Church of Jesus Christ. There is no partiality with God, and there can be no partiality in His Church!

HOW TO FULFILL THE LAW OF LOVE

8 If you really fulfill the royal law according to the Scripture, *"You shall love your neighbor as yourself,"* you do well;

9 but if you show partiality, you commit sin, and are convicted by the law as transgressors.

10 For whoever shall keep the whole law, and yet stumble in one point, he is guilty of all.

11 For He who said, *"Do not commit adultery,"* also said, *"Do not murder."* Now if you do not commit adultery, but you do murder, you have become a transgressor of the law.

12 So speak and so do as those who will be judged by the law of liberty.

13 For judgment is without mercy to the one who has shown no mercy. Mercy triumphs over judgment.

James 2:8–13

Love is the key to Christian lifestyle. In fact, love is the very essence of God. The most profound definition of love found in all of human literature is that revealed by John, the beloved apostle, "For God is love" (1 John 4:8). God's love (*agápē*) is unconditional love. There are no strings attached.

God has loved us from the beginning; even while we were yet sinners (Rom. 5:8). In fact, nothing can separate us from God's love (Rom. 8:35–39). It was this great quality of love that brought Jesus into the world to rescue us from our sins (1 John 3:16).

Jesus came teaching the importance of the life of love. He said, "A new commandment I give to you, that you love one another; as I have loved you, that you also love one another. By this all will know that you are my disciples, if you have love for one another" (John 13:34, 35).

James refers to this commandment of Jesus as "the royal law of love." As the reader might suspect, he not only relates to this law of love as essential; he teaches us how to fulfill this royal law.

1. *All of us have broken God's law* (v. 10). James begins by reminding us that all of us have broken God's moral law. He agrees with the Apostle Paul, "For all have sinned and fall short of the glory of God" (Rom. 3:23).

His argument is penetrating. He states simply that if we should keep the whole law, and yet stumble in one point, we are guilty of all (v. 10). Then he shares a vivid example of just what he means. If we should not commit adultery, but if we should murder someone, then we are guilty of breaking God's moral law. In other words, if you could live your whole life and just break God's moral law once, you would be guilty of breaking all.

I am reminded of a man with whom I counseled a number of years ago who had worked out of his own moral law. He envisioned God sitting at a great scale somewhere in the heavens. According to his theory, God placed every one of his actions on the scale.

All the good acts were placed on one side while the sinful acts were placed on the other. The man's goal was to keep the scale slightly balanced to the "good" side of his scale. And, if when he died the scale was tipped in the right direction, he would go to heaven.

Most of us have either consciously or unconsciously attempted to please God in that way. We have tried to live good lives. We have tried to "tip the scales" in the right direction! James refutes that argument as ridiculous. Only one sin in an entire lifetime would tip the scale the wrong way. We have all broken God's law. We have all sinned. We have all missed the mark.

2. *Only love can fulfill the law* (v. 8). In His Sermon on the Mount, Jesus stated, "Do not think that I came to destroy the Law or the Prophets. I did not come to destroy but to fulfill. For assuredly, I say to you, till heaven and earth pass away, one jot or one tittle will by no means pass from the law till all is fulfilled" (Matt. 5:17–18).

The Apostle Paul continues that teaching when he writes, "Owe no one anything but to love one another, for he who loves another has fulfilled the law" (Rom. 13:8). Then he continues by saying that the commandments of God's moral law such as "you shall not murder" and "you shall not steal" and any other commandment is "summed up in this saying, namely, 'You shall love your neighbor as yourself.' Love does no harm to a neighbor; therefore love is the fulfillment of the law" (Rom. 13:9–10).

This is what James calls the "royal law." Paul summarizes it well in Galatians 5:14, "For all the law is fulfilled in one word, even in this: 'You shall love your neighbor as yourself.'"

Of course, this "royal law" was first revealed by God to His covenant people as part of the Levitical law. (see Lev. 19:18). Jesus came to not only teach this law but to live it. Indeed, He is the personification of the royal law of love.

And so it is fitting that James should use "kingdom vocabulary" as he teaches about the life of love. Love is expected in the lives of those who follow Jesus Christ as Lord. In the fifth verse of chapter 2, James refers to Christ's Kingdom. In the seventh verse of the same chapter, he refers to "that noble name by which you are called." Of course, he is referring to the name of Jesus.

Then he refers to Christ's new commandment as the "royal law." He recognizes that this teaching was shared not merely by a great religious teacher, but by the King of kings! Indeed, Jesus Christ is the King of the Kingdom of God.

Jesus understands that we cannot keep God's moral law. However, the problem was not with His law. In fact, His law is good. The problem is with us because we are too sinful to obey it (Rom. 8:1–4).

And so God has sent to us a Savior to rescue us from our sins. Jesus Christ has come to not only save us from our sins, but to live in us and through us in the person of the Holy Spirit. To heal our rebellion and free us to obey. As Paul wrote, "The law was our tutor to bring us to Christ, that we might be justified by faith" (Gal. 3:24).

3. *Only Christ can supply that love* (vv. 12, 13). Jesus Christ is the source of *agápē* love. It can come only from Him. We cannot fabricate this quality of love. We cannot "fake it" or pretend that we have it. Only when we are in Christ and He is in us can we enjoy that love and express it to others.

John writes, "Beloved, let us love one another, for love is of God; and everyone who loves is born of God and knows God. He who does not love does not know God, for God is love" (1 John 4:7–8). Indeed, this love flows from God Himself. "If we love one another, God abides in us, and His love has been perfected in us. By this we know that we abide in Him and He in us, because He has given us of His Spirit" (1 John 4:12–13).

This dwelling in Christ and allowing Him to dwell in us in the person of the Holy Spirit is the key to the life of love and the fulfillment of the "royal law." As Paul declares, "I say then: Walk in the Spirit . . . if you are led by the Spirit, you are not under the law" (Gal. 5:16–18). Paul then goes on to compare the works of the flesh to the fruits of the Spirit.

Love is the first of the fruits of the Spirit. Where there is the Spirit of God, there is love! If we are to fulfill the "royal law" of love, then we must allow God to be in us and to live through us. Only then can love pour from our lives. Only then will we be recognized by our love. Indeed, "They will know that we are Christians by our love."

In this passage, James also refers to the law of love as the law of liberty. That, too, is the vocabulary of God's Kingdom. He has come to set us free from the yoke of bondage (Gal. 5:1). Jesus said, "And you shall know the truth, and the truth shall make you free" (John 8:32).

The life of walking with Jesus Christ in the Spirit will provide the fruit of love and the joy of liberty. Only in Christ can we be authentically free!

This liberty comes not from the law, but by Christ's mercy. And His mercy triumphs over judgment (v. 13). Therefore, writes James, because Christ has set us free to live and to love, we should "speak and so do as those who will be judged by the law of liberty" (v. 12). John teaches the same basic truth when he says, "Let us not love in word or in tongue, but in deed and in truth" (1 John 3:18).

We can fulfill the law of love only when we (1) acknowledge that we have broken God's law; (2) discover that only the life of love can fulfill that law; and (3) believe that only Christ can supply that love! Then we must receive the gift of the Holy Spirit day by day so that God's love can dwell within us and flow from us to touch the lives of others.

This lifestyle of living under the lordship of Jesus Christ sets us free to enjoy the life of mercy, the life of liberty and the life of love. "If you really fulfill the royal law . . . 'You shall love your neighbor as yourself,' you do well" (v. 8).

How to Make Faith Work

14 What does it profit, my brethren, if someone says he has faith but does not have works? That faith cannot save him, can it?

15 If a brother or sister is naked and destitute of daily food,

16 and one of you says to them, "Depart in peace, be warmed and filled," but you do not give them the things which are needed for the body, what does it profit?

17 Thus also faith by itself, if it does not have works, is dead.

18 But someone will say, "You have faith, and I have works." Show me your faith without your works, and I will show you my faith by my works.

19 You believe that there is one God. You do well. The demons also believe—and tremble!

20 But do you want to know, O foolish man, that faith without works is dead?

21 Was not Abraham our father justified by works when he offered Isaac his son on the altar?

22 Do you see that faith was working together with his works, and by works faith was made perfect?

23 And the Scripture was fulfilled which says, *"Abraham believed God, and it was imputed to him for righteousness."* And he was called the friend of God.

24 You see then that by works a man is justified, and not by faith only.

25 Likewise, was not Rahab the harlot also justified by works when she received the messengers and sent them out another way?

26 For as the body without the spirit is dead, so faith without works is dead also.

James 2:14-26

The central theme of James is practical Christianity. That is the thread woven throughout the pages of his letter. However, central to his teaching is that which this passage reveals—the relationship between faith and works. In the first chapter, he sets forth the proposition that we must not only be hearers of the Word, but also doers (James 1:22).

The result of being merely hearers and not doers is that we deceive ourselves into believing that we are something which we are not. And so it is with attempting to live a life of faith which does not demonstrate itself in appropriate works. Faith without works is worthless to James.

Let us define faith. Our English word "faith" as found in the New Testament is the translation for the Greek noun *pístis,* which is often defined as firm persuasion, conviction, or trust. The noun form *pístis* comes from the verb *peithó,* which is translated as believe, have confidence, persuade, trust, or obey.

This quality of faith is central to Christian living. In fact, the writer of Hebrews declares that without faith, it is impossible to please God (Heb. 11:6). This basic tenant of the Protestant Reformation and of Christian lifestyle is repeated four times in both the Old and New Testaments: "The just shall live by faith (Hab. 2:4, Rom. 1:17, Heb. 10:38, Gal. 3:11).

As we study the book of James, we should not be surprised to discover that he gives us some very practical definitions of faith. In this particular passage, he defines faith in four ways.

(1) *Saving faith must include deeds or works* (v. 14). In fact, any faith without works is "useless" (v. 20, NIV). (2) *Faith by itself, without works or action, is dead* (v. 17). As the body without the spirit is dead, so faith without works is dead (v. 26). (3) *Faith cannot be mere mental assent or intellectual belief.* The demons have that kind of belief (v. 19). (4) As we have seen, *Biblical faith is best defined as active obedience.* James uses two specific examples to reveal this vital truth: Abraham (vv. 23–24) and Rahab (v. 24). These examples coincide with all of the examples shared by the writer of Hebrews in chapter 11. The one common denominator of every person in Scripture who honored God by their faith is that they actively obeyed Him.

Now let us define works. The Scripture speaks about works in two categories. There are the works of persons which are done in the flesh, and there are the works which are done with the assistance of the Spirit which bring glory to God.

The works of the flesh are mentioned quite frequently in the New Testament. For example, Paul enumerates some of the works of the flesh in Galatians 5:19–21, which include adultery, fornication, uncleanness, licentiousness, idolatry, sorcery, hatred, contention, jealousy, outbursts of wrath, selfish ambition, dissensions, heresies, envy, murders, drunkenness, and revelry. He concludes by saying that those who practice such things will not inherit the Kingdom of God (Gal. 5:21). Paul also teaches that we are saved by grace through faith and not by our own works (Eph. 2:8–9).

The works of the Spirit do not originate with us. They do not come from our lust or flesh; they flow from the Holy Spirit. Paul teaches that we were created to live by such good works (Eph. 2:10).

In contrast to the works of the flesh, Paul enumerates the works or "fruit" of the Spirit in Galatians 5:22 and 23, which include love, joy, peace, longsuffering, kindness, goodness, faithfulness, gentleness, and self-control. What a contrast!

Of course, it is the works or fruit of the Spirit to which James refers when relating faith to works. He is not calling us back to live in the flesh nor to try to appease God or win the favor of God with our own works which are done in the flesh. He is instructing us to walk in the Spirit by faith and, as we do, our lives will manifest the works or fruit of the Spirit. Without these deeds of the Spirit, faith is dead.

Now that we have defined faith and works, let us examine the teaching of James regarding the relationship of the two. James proposes three major arguments concerning faith and works and shares at least one practical illustration to substantiate each of his arguments.

1. *Our faith must include appropriate works.* James' first argument is foundational. His statement is clear. Saving faith must manifest itself in appropriate works. He uses a very sensitive illustration. "If a brother or sister is naked and destitute of daily food, and one of you says to them, 'Depart in peace, be warmed and filled,' but you do not give them the things which are needed for the body, what does it profit?" (vv. 15–16).

It is inconceivable for a person who is walking in the Spirit to say that he has faith if that faith is not translated into appropriate works of the Spirit in reaching out and responding to the needs of a brother or sister. Saving faith responds with the appropriate works of the Spirit.

Recently, I heard a well-known Christian leader relate a story of a conference which he had conducted for lay leaders from a local church. Within the context of a discussion, he asked them how many friends they had in the church whom they could call for help if they encountered an emergency in the middle of the night.

Much to his surprise and dismay, not one single person in a group of some fifty church leaders could identify even one Christian friend whom they could count on in such a situation. How tragic! To those Christian friends, James would say, "You have missed the mark! Genuine faith must include appropriate works—even being available to be awakened in the middle of the night in order to respond to the needs of a brother or sister."

2. *Our faith must be accompanied by action.* The New English Bible

has an excellent translation of the seventeenth verse of chapter 2. "So with faith, if it does not lead to action, it is in itself a lifeless thing."

James has just shared the illustration of the brother and sister who are desperately in need of food. Now he shares two arguments which are a bit more theological in nature. He refutes those who would argue against him by sharing the ultimate spiritual futility of possessing a faith which is not accompanied by appropriate action.

First, he refutes those who say, "You have faith, and I have works." He responds by saying, "Show me your faith without works, and I will show you my faith by my works" (v. 18).

Then he shares his ultimate argument by stating, "You believe that there is one God. You do well. The demons also believe—and tremble" (v. 19). In other words, merely believing in the existence of God or even in His mighty power is not adequate for saving faith. Even the demons have that kind of faith. The faith which God requires must be accompanied by appropriate action. To believe in God and to not obey Him is the very essence of sin. It is missing the mark; it is falling short of the glory of God. Our faith must show itself in action.

3. *Faith without works is dead.* The "bottom line" of the arguments of James is this one which he repeats three times in verses 17, 20, and 26. It is that faith without works is dead. To substantiate his contention, James shares three vivid illustrations.

The first is that of Abraham. His faith was demonstrated when he offered his son, Isaac, on the altar (v. 21). What remarkable works were required of Abraham in order for him to put his faith into action. Indeed, this was "live" faith—not dead! For additional support of his contention, James quotes from Genesis 15:6, "Abraham believed God, and it was imputed to him for righteousness" (v. 21).

The second illustration is that of Rahab the harlot. James contends that she was "also justified by works when she received the messengers and sent them out another way" (v. 25). This impelling story is recorded in the second chapter of the book of Joshua. Rahab sheltered the two spies whom Joshua sent into Jericho.

She saved their lives, and, as a result, she and her family were spared when Jericho was defeated by Joshua and the Children of Israel. Even more remarkable is the fact that Rahab is mentioned in the genealogy of Jesus found in the first chapter of Matthew. Her faith was not dead; it was demonstrated by good deeds. And she, her family, and her descendents were blessed by her "live" faith—active obedience.

Third, there is an illustration which is not in the form of a Biblical story. Instead, James shares a very practical and vivid example. It is simply this, "As the body without the spirit is dead, so faith without works is dead also" (v. 26).

What an illustration! A reader may have some difficulty in identifying with Abraham or with Rahab. But everyone can easily understand the difference between a body which is dead in contrast to a person who is alive.

Life is an incredible mystery. Later in his letter, James declares that life is a vapor or mist "that appears for a little time and then vanishes away" (James 4:14). Those of us who have watched another person die have been deeply impressed with the validity of his statement.

How profoundly moving is the experience of seeing the spirit of a person depart leaving only a dead body to remain. The body is but the temporary dwelling place of the real person. When the spirit is absent, life departs and an empty, dead body is left.

That is what James is saying to us. Faith that is only intellectual or cerebral is not enough. It is dead. In the same way, works that are done in the flesh are inadequate. Also, they are dead!

But the Spirit brings life. And works done in the power of the Holy Spirit bring dead faith to life. Abraham and Rahab did not merely talk about faith—they acted it out. They did not only believe in God, they believed what He said and what He promised them. They responded to Him in active obedience. They practiced "live" faith.

Unfortunately, the stench of death hovers over many of our churches and over many of the lives of professing Christians. Often, we have mouthed the correct confessions and mastered the orthodox theology, but our faith has been dead.

Jesus described this dilemma well when He quoted the prophet Isaiah in saying, "These people draw near to Me with their mouth, and honor Me with their lips, but their heart is far from Me" (Isa. 29:13, Matt. 15:8).

There is a solution to this problem. We must move from deadness to life. We must forsake the life of the flesh in order to walk in the Spirit. We must not only believe in God; we must deny ourselves, take up our cross and follow Jesus (Mark 8:34). We must follow

Him with active obedience. That is what it means to live by faith.

Only when we have this "live" faith can we fulfill the Word of our Lord when He said, "Let your light so shine before men, that they may see your good works and glorify your Father in heaven" (Matt. 5:16).

CHAPTER THREE

How to Live with Faith and Wisdom

James 3:1–18

As faith is central to the teaching of James, so is God's gift of wisdom. In fact, some Biblical scholars compare the Book of James to the wisdom literature of the Old Testament both in relationship to content and to literary style.

In the truest sense, all of the Book of James deals with the practical application of God-given wisdom. In the first chapter, James refers to the need for God-given wisdom. He invites his readers to acknowledge the need for wisdom, ask God for it, and he says then it will be given (1:5).

In this chapter, he goes beyond those instructions to deal with the very issue of what God-given wisdom is and how we can recognize it. Of course, this teaching must be combined with that of the first chapter as well as with all of the related teaching in his letter regarding the "how to" of practical Christianity.

The third chapter of James deals with three specific matters which require God-given wisdom. The first is the awesome responsibility of serving as a teacher. The vital need to control one's tongue is the second, and then he teaches specifically about the unique quality of God-inspired wisdom.

HOW TO LIVE AS A TEACHER

1 My brethren, let not many of you become teachers, knowing that we shall receive a stricter judgment.

James 3:1

As James has been involved in his deep and passionate teaching regarding the relationship of faith and works, he now seems to change gears suddenly as he addresses a very important subject in just one sentence.

Although his words are few, his teaching regarding the awesome responsibility of serving as a teacher is very important. No other passage in all of the New Testament is as potent in its focus upon the great responsibility of being a teacher of Christian truth and lifestyle. It appears that James is teaching two major truths which are intertwined one with the other.

1. *Not many of you should become teachers* (v. 1). Within the New Testament church, the role of teaching was looked upon as the exercise of one of the leadership gifts given by the Holy Spirit. In Paul's letter to the church at Ephesus, he refers to the spiritual gift of teaching as one of five leadership gifts given by the Lord to His Church. The gift of teaching is clarified within that context along with the gifts of serving as apostle, prophet, evangelist, and pastor (Eph. 4:11).

Interestingly enough, this is the only reference of James in his entire letter to the gift or role of teaching. Although Biblical scholars speculate as to why he speaks concerning this matter within this context, the more important focus seems to be, "What is he saying to us?" Or, even more importantly, "What is God saying to us regarding the important role of teaching within the church?"

It appears that some of his readers may have been facing the temptation of becoming teachers when they were not actually called of God or given the spiritual gift of teaching. James is certainly not discouraging those who have received that calling and have that gift.

He is simply reminding his readers that few of us are called to be teachers. The leadership gifts are not given to all the members of the Body. And the gift of teaching is given but to a few. As true of any ministry, we should become involved in teaching only when we are called of God and gifted by the Holy Spirit to do so.

An appropriate paraphase of the teaching of James in this context might be, "Brothers and sisters, God has not seen fit to call many of us to be teachers. Don't be in a hurry to become teachers unless you are certain that God has called you and has entrusted to you the spiritual gift of teaching. Be content with whatever gifts and calling God gives to you. Don't try to be what you are not; joyfully be what God has called you to be. Use your gifts in ministry to others and to the glory of God. If you teach, do it to the glory of

God; if you do not teach, do it to the glory of God. Only then can you be truly fulfilled."

2. *Teachers shall receive a stricter judgment* (v. 1). As a part of the warning that James shares regarding the great responsibility of teaching others within the church, James presents the sobering information that those who teach will be judged more strictly than others. This statement raises at least two important questions. The first question is, "Why would a teacher be judged with greater strictness?" And the second question would be, "Who is going to do the strict judging?"

At least two principles of Scripture will help us to answer the first question adequately. The first is a principle taught by Jesus, "For everyone to whom much is given, from him much will be required; and to whom much has been committed, of him they will ask the more" (Luke 12:48).

In other words, both God and man require more from those who have been given more. When God calls a person to a place of leadership, much is required of that leader from God. And when one is given the great privilege and responsibility of teaching the truth of God's Word, there is little wonder that God would require a high standard of excellence and faithfulness.

Second, there is the principle of sowing and reaping which is very relevant to what James is teaching. The principle is as follows, "For whatever a man sows, that he will also reap" (Gal. 6:7).

Usually, teachers reproduce themselves in the lives of their students. A false teacher could do great harm by creating mediocrity in the lives of the people of God and by actually leading them astray. Much is written in the New Testament as a warning against false teachers, including the epistles of Jude (p. 252) and 2 Peter (p. 221).

A false teacher or an inept teacher would be "tearing down" the lives of the believers. A teacher who is called of God and gifted of God and who is properly equipped will have the joyous privilege of building the lives of God's people and of building the Body of Christ. The Biblical model for this style of teaching leadership is found in Ephesians 4:11–13. Such an act of teaching results in the Body of Christ being built up, becoming unified in faith, having the knowledge of Christ, and ultimately growing to become more and more like Jesus.

No wonder James shared his timely warning against those who would teach when they were not called to do so.

Concerning the second question, "Who is going to do the judging with greater strictness?" there seem to be two possible answers. Both of them have some probability. First, there is the obvious reality that God will judge those who teach His Word and His truth. This fact would be documented throughout Scripture including the statement of Paul, "So then each of us shall give account of himself to God" (Rom. 14:12).

Second, there is the strict judgment that shall come from our brothers and sisters in Christ; especially those whom we are teaching. There are many warnings in the New Testament concerning false teachers such as Peter's prophetic statement, "There will be false teachers among you, who will secretly bring in destructive heresies, even denying the Lord who bought them . . ." (2 Peter 2:1).

In summary, teachers should expect strict judgment from their brothers and sisters in Christ and from the Lord Christ Himself. To teach is a marvelous privilege and an awesome responsibility!

HOW TO TAME YOUR TONGUE

2 For we all stumble in many things. If anyone does not stumble in word, he is a perfect man, able also to bridle the whole body.

3 Indeed, we put bits in horses' mouths that they may obey us, and we turn their whole body.

4 Look also at ships: Although they are so large and are driven by fierce winds, they are turned by a very small rudder wherever the pilot desires.

5 Even so the tongue is a little member and boasts great things. See how great a forest a little fire kindles!

6 And the tongue is a fire, a world of iniquity. The tongue is so set among our members that it defiles the whole body, and sets on fire the course of nature; and it is set on fire by hell.

7 For every kind of beast and bird, of reptile and creature of the sea, is tamed and has been tamed by mankind.

8. But no man can tame the tongue. It is an unruly evil, full of deadly poison.

9 With it we bless our God and Father, and with it we curse men, who have been made in the similitude of God.

10 Out of the same mouth proceed blessing and cursing. My brethren, these things ought not to be so.

11 Does a spring send forth fresh water and bitter from the same opening?

12 Can a fig tree, my brethren, bear olives, or a grapevine bear figs? Thus no spring can yield both salt water and fresh.

James 3:2–12

The tongue is difficult to tame. In fact, James says it is humanly impossible to tame the human tongue. Yet, within that context, he shares some great insight as to how the tongue can be tamed by God.

James begins this section of teaching by exposing our human tendency to stumble in many things. He points to the ultimate solution which would enable us to overcome this stumbling. He contends that anyone who could stop stumbling in word would be a perfect person. If we could control our tongues, we could bring our whole body under control (v. 2).

James proceeds to share a long and seemingly disjointed discourse on the problem of taming or controlling the tongue. However, it is possible to organize his teaching into three specific contentions which will help us understand "how to tame our tongue."

1. *No one can tame the human tongue* (v. 2). James presents the problem or the need very clearly. In fact, his statement is so clear and is supported with so much evidence that the reader faces the possibility of misinterpreting what James is attempting to teach by concluding that he is fatalistic toward the probability of taming the tongue. To the contrary, he is simply attempting to establish the impossibility of the tongue being tamed by mere human endeavor. To establish that fact, he makes four specific contentions regarding the tongue.

(1) The tongue is a little member but boasts great things (vv. 2–5). To illustrate this point, he uses three practical examples which his readers would fully understand. First, he refers to the bit in the mouth of a horse. Although very small, it is very significant. By using the bit, the horse will obey us and will turn whatever direction we wish.

Then, there is the example of the rudder of a ship. It, too, is very small in comparison to the size of a large ship. But it also has great significance. By using the rudder, a ship can be turned and controlled.

Finally, there is the small fire. A very small fire or even a tiny spark can ignite a huge forest. What incredible power and significance belong to all three of these small things.

With a bit, one can control a horse; with a rudder, one can control a large ship; and with a spark, one can ignite a huge forest and destroy it by fire. So it is with the tongue; it is very small but very powerful and significant. If one can control it, one can control the whole body. Such a person would be perfect (v. 2).

(2) The tongue is a fire—set on fire by hell (v. 6). After establishing the significance and power of the tongue, James proceeds to address its great potential for destruction. His contention contains three specific statements regarding the destructiveness of the tongue.

First, as a fire, the tongue is *"a world of iniquity"* (v. 6). The word "iniquity" is *adikía* in Greek, a very strong word denoting moral unrighteousness. It is the same word used by Paul when he states, "Let everyone who names the name of Christ depart from iniquity" (2 Tim. 2:19).

Second, *"The tongue is so set among our members that it defiles the whole body"* (v. 6). As a world of iniquity, the tongue cannot be held in isolation. It corrupts the entire body. Just as a rudder affects a ship and a bit affects a horse, so the tongue affects the body and brings corruption. It defiles the whole body.

Third, the tongue not only corrupts the body, it sets on fire the entire course of one's life (v. 6). In other words, the tongue does not merely affect the physical body of a person, it brings corruption to our total life. It affects not only what we do but what we are. And the source of this fire is hell itself.

Once again James advances his basic contention that all evil comes from the devil. He is the source of the evil which plagues our tongues. No wonder we cannot control the tongue. In our own strength, we are incapable of overcoming evil. Such a person would have to be perfect.

(3) The tongue is an unruly evil, full of deadly poison (v. 8). James now levels his strongest attack of all on the evilness of the tongue. It is not only evil, it is an unruly or restless evil. It is the kind of evil which is not merely passive but is actively on the attack. And it is a deadly poison. It is poison, *iós*, like the poison of a deadly snake (Rom. 3:13).

(4) The basic conclusion: No one can tame the tongue (vv. 10–12). The tongue is an enigma; it is a defilement of the natural order created by God. A spring doesn't flow with both fresh and bitter water. Nor do fresh water and salt water flow from the same spring. Nor does a fig tree bear olives or a grapevine bear figs (vv. 11–12). Yet out of the same mouth can proceed both blessings and cursings (v. 10).

The conclusion of James is clear. The significance and influence of the tongue is great. It is a little member, but it has great power. It is a destructive fire which comes from hell. It corrupts one's entire life. It is an unruly evil, full of poison that is just as deadly as the venom of a snake! This can lead us to but one conclusion, according to James—**no one can control the tongue!**

In contrast, man can tame about everything else in all of creation including every kind of animal, bird, reptile, and creature of the sea. All of them have been tamed by mankind (v. 7).

James' conclusion in this matter is righteous before God. It should not be so; blessings should flow freely from our mouths—but not cursings. We have been created in God's image to bring glory to Him. Yet, because of sin, we are a strange mixture of good and evil. And our tongues betray us by expressing both blessings and cursings. No one can tame the tongue.

2. *If we could tame our tongue, we would be perfect* (v. 2). At the very beginning of this passage, James sets forth a hypothetical statement which can be very confusing to us. He states that if a person could tame his tongue, or bring it under control, such a person would be perfect.

This contention seems to stand in sharp contradiction to his later contention which states, "But no man can tame the tongue" (v. 8). In actuality, there is no conflict at all. James is drawing us back to God once again. His overwhelming evidence regarding the wickedness and destructiveness of our tongues establishes the fact that we are helpless in the human realm.

But we have great hope and potential in the spiritual realm. The problem with our tongues is a spiritual problem. They have been under the control of our sinful nature. All evil comes from Satan, and he has taken control of the tongues of human beings.

But, James teaches us, God is the source of all good and He is available to help us in every situation (1:16–18). If we need wisdom, we need only to ask for it (1:5). This brings us to the third and final contention of James concerning the tongue.

3. *God is perfect—He alone can control our tongues.* The first two contentions of James regarding the tongue are stated very clearly. This third contention comes by inference. It is related to all of the teaching which James has shared up to this point of his letter. Our reasoning is as follows:

Only God is perfect. Every good and perfect gift comes from Him alone (1:16–18). Only a perfect person could control his tongue (3:2). Such a person could not only control his tongue but also his total being. Since God is the only One who is perfect, He is the only One who can control the tongue. Our deep need is to be possessed by Him so that He can forgive all of our sin and enable us by the power of the Holy Spirit to control our tongues and our total being.

HOW TO LIVE WITH WISDOM

13 Who is wise and understanding among you? Let him show by good conduct that his works are done in the meekness of wisdom.

14 But if you have bitter envy and self-seeking in your hearts, do not boast and lie against the truth.

15 This wisdom does not descend from above, but is earthly, sensual, demonic.

16 For where envy and self-seeking exist, confusion and every evil thing will be there.

17 But the wisdom that is from above is first pure, then peaceable, gentle, willing to yield, full of mercy and good fruits, without partiality, and without hypocrisy.

18 And the fruit of righteousness is sown in peace by those who make peace.

James 3:13–18

"The greatest good is wisdom" according to St. Augustine. Those words would be a fitting summary for the teaching of James on the vital subject of the wisdom from above. James contends that this wisdom is not merely something which is intellectually understandable; it must be demonstrated practically in Christian lifestyle. This "wisdom" is *sophía,* which A. T. Robertson refers to as practical knowledge.

Earlier in his letter, James gives us guidance in how to ask for wisdom from God. He assures us that as we ask, we shall receive (1:5). Now he helps us to understand what wisdom from above is and how it should be used. First, we need to recognize the wisdom which is earthly as opposed to that which is godly. Good and evil are contrasted throughout Scripture. As we have seen, James is involved in this comparison repeatedly as he presents the practical examples of Christian lifestyle. Within the context of his consideration of wisdom, he shares a very vivid description of the wisdom which comes from below. The characteristics of such wisdom are as follows:

Bitter Envy (v. 14). The Greek word for "bitter," *pikrós,* is the same word James uses to describe the bitter water which comes from the spring (3:11). The word denotes a sharp, pungent characteristic. Envy is *zēlos,* which can also be translated as jealousy or zeal. In verse 16, James contends that such envy leads to confusion and every evil thing.

Self-Seeking (v. 14). This word in Greek is *eritheía,* which is better translated as "strife." The most graphic translation of the word would be "faction" or those involved in "party split." This is the expression of mankind's sinful nature which is preoccupied with the indulgence of wanting our own way—doing our own thing. It creates the "we-they" syndrome with which we are all so familiar. It is selfish ambition at its worst.

Boasting (v. 14). The word for "boast" is one with special meaning, *katakaucháomai,* which denotes not only boasting but boasting against or glorying against something. In this case, James says that it is a boasting against the truth. As we have seen, the Spirit always leads us to truth while the evil one leads us to oppose the truth—even in our boasting.

Lying (v. 14). "Lie" in Greek is the word *pseúdomai,* which means "to utter an untruth or to attempt to deceive by falsehood." From the same root we get such words as false, false teachers (2 Pet. 2:1), false prophets (Matt. 7:15), and false witness (Rom. 13:9). The prefix *pseudo* has become a part of our English vocabulary. We use it to denote something which is false or someone who is attempting to deceive us. James tells us that the wisdom from below attempts to lie against the truth.

As James concludes his graphic description of some of the characteristics of the wisdom from below, he focuses upon three sources of that wisdom. He lists three specific sources (v. 15). (1) Earthly: To be earthly, *epígeios,* is simply what the word implies. Such wisdom comes from the worldly system or from the earth. As James says, it does not come or descend from above (v. 15). (2) Sensual: Rather than originating in the spiritual realm, this wisdom from below originates in the natural, the animal, the flesh: *psuchikos.* As Jude teaches, the sensual is opposed to the spiritual (Jude 19). (See Commentary on p. 256). (3) Demonic: This term needs little definition. James states that the wisdom from below comes from the devil himself. Indeed, it comes from below and not from above.

Finally, after identifying the characteristics and the sources of this wisdom from below, James proceeds to identify two results which are manifested when this kind of wisdom is present (v. 16). First, where there is envy and self-seeking, confusion is present. The word translated as "confusion," *akatastasia,* means commotion or tumult. This is a condition that reflects instability and disorder. Godly wisdom brings peace, but earthly wisdom brings confusion. In addition to confusion, James contends that every evil thing will be present as a result of the wisdom from below. In other words, rather than giving a long, specific list of the various forms of evil that will be present, James simply summarizes and includes them all with his inclusive statement "every evil thing." Righteousness will be absent, and every evil thing will be there!

After describing the characteristics, sources, and results of the wisdom which comes from below, James is just as specific in detailing that wisdom which is from above (vv. 17, 18). He provides for us the most comprehensive and helpful definition of wisdom found in all of literature. Of course, this is the quality of wisdom from above; it is godly wisdom. The definition includes the following descriptions (v. 17):

Pure. In the first place, the wisdom from above is pure, which is *hagnós.* This quality of purity means "chaste, clean, innocent or perfect." It comes from the same root word as do the words holy, hallow, and sanctification.

Peaceable. Next, the wisdom from above is peaceable, which is *eirēnikós* coming from the root *eirēnē* which means "peace or quietness or rest." The words "pacify" and "pacific" come from the root. Godly wisdom is peaceable or "at one."

Gentle. To be "gentle," *epieikēs,* is to be patient or considerate. It is the very spirit of Jesus Christ (2 Cor. 10:1). Paul compares the quality of being gentle with not being a brawler (Titus 3:2).

Willing to yield. This Greek word, *eupeithēs,* is used but once in all the New Testament. It means literally "easy to be entreated." Various translators have attempted to find a contemporary word or phrase which would open its meaning to us. Some of those attempts are "open to reason," "conciliatory," "easily persuaded," and "ready to be convinced."

Full of mercy. The word for "mercy," *éleos,* is not used in the New Testament except in reference either to God Himself or to godly people. Mercy is a part of the very character of God. God is the source of mercy (2 Tim. 1:2), and God is rich in mercy (Eph. 2:4).

Full of good fruits. Karpós is the word translated simply as "fruit." The wisdom of God is full of good fruits according to James. Jesus said that only as we abide in Him can we bring forth much fruit (John 15:4–5). Paul describes the "fruit of the Spirit" for us in Galatians 5:22–23, and he refers to the same in Ephesians 5:9.

Without partiality. Adiákritos is derived from *diakrino* which is usually translated as "partial" or "to judge." James warns against the sin of partiality earlier in his letter (2:1–9). The wisdom from above shows no partiality or favoritism.

Without hypocrisy. Anupókritos is an assumed derivative of *hupokrínomai,* which means "to pretend" or "to act under a false part." It comes from the same root as our words "hypocrite" and "hypocrisy." As we know, Jesus spoke out loudly and clearly against hypocrisy— especially in the lives of the supposedly religious scribes and Pharisees (Matt. 6:2, 23:13, etc.). Godly wisdom is without pretense or hypocrisy. Since it flows from God, it manifests itself in truth and sincerity.

True justice (v. 18). The final verse of this chapter is most interesting. After listing specific characteristics of godly wisdom in verse 18, James makes a concluding statement which can be summarized under the heading "true or godly justice." The wisdom from above is concerned with justice and peace. As this wisdom is sown in peace by those who make peace, true justice is manifested.

As we have seen, James is always concerned that his teaching is practical and usable. He is concerned with our understanding the truth of God's Word and living it by faith. The same is true of his teaching concerning wisdom. Godly wisdom is not only to be recognized; it is to be lived.

In order to be able to understand how we should be living and enjoying this life of wisdom, let us pose the two questions that James answers for us.

The first question is, "How and where do we get this wisdom?" We have already found the answer to this important question in our study of the first chapter. James answers the question concisely and graphically. If any of us falls short of wisdom, we should ask God for it, and He will give it to us generously and without reproach (1:5).

"Who is actually wise and understanding?" is the second question. Once again, James answers the question directly. The one who shows "by good conduct that his works are done in the meekness of wisdom" (3:13). In other words, the one who actually possesses godly wisdom is the one who is manifesting good conduct and works in his or her daily lifestyle. Of course, this is done in humility.

Jesus said that we would know people by the fruit of their lives (Matt. 7:16). People who possess godly wisdom will not be able to hide it. Godly wisdom will manifest itself in the actions of their lives. The characteristics of such wisdom will stand in sharp contrast to the expression of the wisdom which comes from below.

I have known many godly men and women who have had little formal education but were wise beyond human comprehension. For example, we had such a woman come to faith in Christ in a parish which I served early in my ministry. She had very limited mental capacities and a very simple faith in Jesus Christ as her Savior and Lord. She became an effective prayer warrior who grew significantly to become more and more like her Lord.

As she grew in spiritual stature and wisdom, I found myself turning to her often for spiritual counsel and prayer. In fact, when I faced a major spiritual decision, I usually turned to her for her wise counsel rather than to my pastor or therapist friends.

She had genuine wisdom and understanding which comes only from God! And that same wisdom is available to us as we trust in Christ Jesus.

CHAPTER FOUR

How to Live with Faith and Humility

James 4:1–17

Humility is of great importance to James. It is the major focus of this fourth chapter. We are told that only as we humble ourselves in the sight of God will we be lifted up by the Lord (4:10).

Although James makes that direct statement about humility, he also makes many indirect statements which have great bearing upon Christian living. As usual, his teaching is both practical and workable. He is concerned that humility should be integrated into the lives of all of us who are sincere about following Jesus as Lord.

HOW TO PRAY WITHOUT PRIDE

1 Where do wars and fights come from among you? Do they not come from your desires for pleasure that war in your members?
2 You lust and do not have. You murder and covet and cannot obtain. You fight and war. Yet you do not have because you do not ask.
3 You ask and do not receive, because you ask amiss, that you may spend it on your pleasures.

James 4:1–3

James begins his teaching regarding the conflict of pride and prayer by posing an important question, "Where do wars and fights come from among you?" The basic assumption is that such conflicts are taking place within the interpersonal relationships of his readers.

The word James uses for "war" is *pólemos*, which means just that: war or battle. The word translated as "fights" is *máchē*, which can also be correctly translated as strife, struggles, or quarrelings. To be sure, both of these words denote interpersonal conflicts.

James not only poses the question; he gives a very graphic and appropriate answer. Simply stated, we are involved in conflicts because of our desires for pleasure or lusts that are in conflict within our very selves. We are at war inwardly so it is natural for us to be at war outwardly.

The word translated as "desires for pleasure" or "lusts" is the word *hēdonē* from which we get the English word "hedonism." In His parable of the sower, Jesus warned about the thorns of riches and the pleasures of this life which would come and choke the Word of God in our lives (Luke 8:14). Paul describes us who are now living in Christ as those who once served various lusts and pleasures (Titus 3:3).

In verse 2, James proceeds to describe the manifestations more specifically. He makes three specific statements concerning the dilemma of aggressively desiring but never getting what is desired. His is a description of the paradox of sin—always seeking but never finding, always desiring but never being fulfilled.

"You lust and do not have." The word that James uses for "lust" is different from that which he used in verse 1. Here the word is *epithumeō*. It means "to long for or to set one's heart's desire upon something or someone." It is sometimes translated as "covet."

The word can denote a negative form of lusting such as looking "at a woman to lust for her," as Jesus warned against (Matt. 5:28). Or it can be used positively to desire the right or godly thing, as in the statement made by Jesus at the Last Supper: "I have desire to eat this Passover with you before I suffer" (Luke 22:15).

The problem that Jesus describes is that we often desire something, but often we do not get it. In the most negative of terms, people who covet something or somebody do not receive the same without taking some kind of initiative. That brings James to his second statement.

"You murder and covet and cannot obtain." When a person covets, he or she often has to use evil means to get what they want such as stealing, scheming, or even killing. James gets directly to the point by describing killing or murder as the human solution to the sin of coveting. The word used for covet in this phrase is *zēlóō* from which we get our word zealous. The best translation is "to be moved with envy." Murder is the ultimate result of coveting and envying.

Yet, according to James, even with murder and envy we cannot obtain what we actually want. Again, we see the futility of sin. It promises us so much but gives us so little. Indeed, there are the pleasures of sin for the moment, but deep and lasting fulfillment can never come from sin—including lusting, coveting, and envying.

"You fight and war." James returns to his opening statement in verse 1. The result of lusting and murdering and coveting and not obtaining is more and more conflict—fighting and warring! And, although each of these words is a description of the life lived in the flesh without Jesus as Lord, James is acknowledging also that such wars and fightings also take place within the church. As Christians, we are plagued by a residual of our old nature which brings us to lusting, fighting, and conflicting.

A number of years ago, I had the privilege of working on the staff of the great evangelist Billy Graham. My first assignment was to work with Charlie Riggs, a veteran of many evangelistic crusades and a man who walked closely with God.

One day, as we were talking about conflicts within the church, Charlie shared an insight with me which I shall never forget. He quoted from Proverbs 13:10 which contends that "by pride comes only contention." I have found it to be so. Where there are conflicts and fightings and warrings within the church, the sin of pride is always present.

It is pride that makes us lust and covet and envy and murder and fight and war. Pride is to the life of the flesh what humility is to the life of the Spirit. It is at the very foundation of the lifestyle which displeases God. Pride always brings contention.

Have you ever noticed how the obvious in life can totally elude us? In our society, it seems that we have majored in making the simple complicated. To the contrary, Jesus had a great knack for making the complicated simple so that even I can understand it.

The teaching of James at this point is so simple, it is almost embarrassing to repeat it. In short, he is saying, "You can lust and covet and fight and war and murder and do anything else, but there is only one reason you do not have; it is because you do not ask" (v. 2). And, I might add, we should not merely "ask," we should "ask God!"

Is it not true that one of the great problems of your prayer lives is simply the fact that we don't pray? In the flesh, we do all the things which James enumerates such as lusting and fighting and warring. These things are natural for us to do. After all, haven't we been taught to "look out for number one—me?" And haven't we been told that "God only helps those who help themselves?" And so, even as Christians often we are tempted to try to get things through natural or fleshly means.

James is calling us back to the basics of Christian discipleship. He is reminding us that we no longer need to use tools of sin. They don't work well. Instead, God has entrusted to us spiritual tools—including prayer. We, ourselves, are no longer the source for our success. The Lord wants to be our Lord, not only in word but in deed. He simply desires to provide for us. He loves us and wants what is best for us.

Therefore, we do not need to be anxious or worry or fight or scheme or murder. We simply need to ask. We need to walk in the Spirit and commune with Him and ask for what we need. He has promised to supply all of our needs (Phil. 4:19). But so often our lives are empty and we go without what He longs to give us, simply because we do not ask!

In verse 3 James now leads us to the most challenging problem of all. This is the problem of asking God for something and not receiving it because we have asked for the wrong reason or with the wrong motive.

The problem with sin is the problem of missing the mark. That is the problem which James is identifying—to ask amiss. The phrase, "ask amiss," is translated from the Greek word *kakōs*, which is usually translated in the Scripture as "diseased" or "sick," as in Mark 1:32.

In other words, we can ask God for things with "sick" or "diseased" motives. In fact, James identifies what such motives are. He says that we ask amiss "that you may spend it on your pleasures." We are back to the word *hēdonē* which we found in verse 1. Our lusts or our desires for pleasure are not acceptable motives for prayer. They are characteristics of the flesh—not the Spirit. Like all sin, they will lead us to death rather than life.

In contrast, John shares with us the proper motive for prayer when he writes, "Now this is the confidence that we have in Him, that if we ask anything according to His will, He hears us" (1 John 5:14). The focus of Christian living and the motive of prayer are the same—God has called us to forsake doing our own thing and to seek to do the will of God. Only then can we be fulfilled and only then will God answer our prayers.

How to Become Humble

> 4 Adulterers and adulteresses! Do you not know that friendship with the world is enmity with God? Whoever therefore wants to be a friend of the world makes himself an enemy of God.
>
> 5 Or do you think that the Scripture says in vain, "The Spirit who dwells in us yearns jealously"?
>
> 6 But He gives more grace. Therefore He says:
> *"God resists the proud,*
> *But gives grace to the humble."*
>
> 7 Therefore submit to God. Resist the devil and he will flee from you.
>
> 8 Draw near to God and He will draw near to you. Cleanse your hands, you sinners; and purify your hearts, you double-minded.
>
> 9 Lament and mourn and weep! Let your laughter be turned to mourning and your joy to gloom.
>
> 10 Humble yourselves in the sight of the Lord, and He will lift you up.
>
> *James 4:4–10*

Humility is essential to Christian discipleship. Jesus spoke about the importance of humility on a number of occasions, including the time He called a child to Him and said, "Whoever humbles himself as his little child is the greatest in the kingdom of heaven" (Matt. 18:4). Jesus also said, "Whoever exalts himself will be abased, and he who humbles himself will be exalted" (Matt. 23:12). Following in the footsteps of his Master, Peter teaches us to "be clothed with humility" (1 Pet. 5:6).

James shares our Lord's deep concern that His followers walk humbly before Him. In the most practical and helpful way, James tells us not only that we should be humble, but also how to do it. James gives us three "how to" steps which will enable us to walk humbly with God.

First, resist the devil (vv. 7–9). We can never be truly humble if we are not willing to actively resist the devil. Not to do so is to be an adulterer or an adulteress (v. 4). To be involved in friendship with the world is to be at enmity with God (v. 4).

The Greek word for "enmity" is a very strong word, *échthra*, which is sometimes translated as "hatred." If that is so, James is saying that anyone who is in love with the world (a friend of the world, *philos*) hates God. In fact, that is the closing statement of verse 4, "Whoever therefore wants to be a friend of the world makes himself an enemy of God."

What a powerful and sobering statement. And, if that were not enough, James proceeds to substantiate that contention by presenting some very strong supporting evidence from the Scriptures. His first statement has caused much discussion among Biblical scholars since it is not a direct quotation from the Old Testament Scriptures but rather seems to be a paraphrase of Biblical truth.

Some scholars relate the phrase, "The Spirit who dwells in us yearns jealously" to Genesis 6:5 while others refer to Genesis 8:21 (v. 5). However, it seems more likely that James is referring to the concept of God being a jealous God (Exod. 20:5) who will not share his allegiance with another. In other words, we cannot serve two masters. We must serve God alone!

In the sixth verse, James quotes from Proverbs 3:34 which states, "Surely he scorneth the scorners: but he giveth grace unto the lowly." The statement of James is clear, "God opposes the proud." You cannot be living by pride and be accepted by God. But the promise is also clear. "God gives grace to the humble."

It was that promise which Christ made to the Apostle Paul, "My grace is sufficient for you, for My strength is made perfect in weakness" (2 Cor. 12:9). The grace of God is readily available to all who will trust in the Lord and follow Him. But He opposes the proud. We must resist the devil. We cannot be a friend of Christ and of the world. The two are in opposition to each other.

In addition, James gives some very specific suggestions regarding how we should resist the devil. In verses 8 and 9, he enumerates four specific steps we should follow in resisting the devil (vv. 8–9).

1. *"Cleanse your hands, you sinners."* This is an appeal to our outward lifestyle. Our conduct must be clean.

2. *"Purify your hearts, you double-minded."* This is another reference to our motives. Our spiritual hearts and motives must be pure before God. We must allow Jesus to be Lord of our lives and must forsake being double-minded (1:8).

3. *"Lament and mourn and weep."* This is an obvious reference to the act of repentance. We must not only acknowledge the existence of our sins, but we must feel sorry that we have sinned against God. We need to weep tears of repentance.

4. *"Let your laughter be turned to mourning and your joy to gloom."* This is a continuation of his call to godly repentance. He is not commanding us to forsake the joy of the Lord. Instead, he is asking us to depart from the shallow laughter and temporary joy that comes from the life of sin.

The summation of all this teaching is simply that we need to quit playing games with the devil and with sin and become serious about forsaking sin. We need to resist the devil in every area of our lives. We cannot play with the fire of sin without being burned. We cannot please God while we are playing games with Satan. We need to declare war on him. We need to resist him.

And, as we do, the promise is clear—he will flee from us. Through Jesus Christ, we are assured of victory over the devil. We cannot resist him in the flesh, but we can do so as we live in the Spirit! For example we should use the shield of faith with which we will be able to quench all the fiery darts of the wicked one (Eph. 6:16). Resist the devil—and he will flee from you!

As we have just discussed, the first step toward the life of humility is to resist the devil who is the source of all pride. The second step is to draw near to God (v. 8) who is the source of all authentic humility.

We begin our relationship with God by submitting to Him (v. 7). And that is the way we walk with Him day by day. He is the Lord—the Master, and we are the servants—the willing slaves. In order to follow Him, we must deny ourselves and take up our cross daily (Luke 9:23). There is no other way to be a Christian. Our wills need to be committed to know the will of God and to do it.

Submitting to God can sound cold and nonrelational. But it is not! God calls us to a relationship of love, trust, grace, forgiveness, openness, and all the other marks of a loving relationship. And yet, He will never force His love upon us. As someone has said, "God is not a divine rapist." He does not coerce or manipulate. He loves and invites and responds.

That is the context of, "Draw near to God and He will draw near to you" (v. 8). What a wonderful invitation and what an incredible promise. It takes risk to reach out to another or to attempt to draw near to someone else. God has promised not to "back off." He is always ready to respond appropriately to us with His love and grace.

As we draw near to Him and allow Him to draw near to us, a marvelous thing takes place. Jesus refers to this phenomenon as "abiding" in Him and He in us (John 15:4–5). As we are possessed more and more by Christ Himself, His character increasingly supplants ours. We become more and more like Him. As we die to self and are filled with the Holy Spirit, the "fruit" of the Spirit flow from our lives. We become more and more like Jesus—including becoming more and more humble. His humility becomes ours.

The third step we are to take is to humble ourselves in the sight of the Lord (v. 10). The steps are clear. If we are to be humble, we must begin by emptying ourselves of self and sin by resisting the devil. Next, that emptiness must be filled by the Holy Spirit as we draw near to God and we allow Him to draw near to us and to fill us to overflowing with Himself in the person of the Holy Spirit.

Only then can we accomplish the admonishment of James to humble ourselves. We cannot do so in our own strength. It is impossible for us to humble ourselves by our own cleverness or ingenuity. We need the power of God Himself.

A person who is truly humble is a person who has turned from sin and the devil and is walking with God. Authentic humility comes from God. A humble person is one who has seen himself as he really is in the sight of God, has repented of his sin, and is following Jesus as his Lord.

The promise to such a person is also clear. As we humble ourselves in the sight of the Lord, "He will lift you up" (v. 10). It is never God's desire to "put you down." It is sin that leads us down to death and destruction. The Lord delights in lifting you up. Indeed, he who humbles himself will be exalted.

How to Escape Judgment

> 11 Do not speak evil of one another, brethren. He who speaks evil of a brother and judges his brother, speaks evil of the law and judges the law. But if you judge the law, you are not a doer of the law but a judge.
> 12 There is one Lawgiver, who is able to save and to destroy. Who are you to judge another?
> *James 4:11–12*

James has warned us concerning the following sins: discrimination (2:1–11), cursing others with our tongues (3:9), envy and self-seeking (3:18), pride which leads to wars and fightings and conflicts of every kind (4:1–2). Now he comes to the specific instruction of warning us against the sin of speaking evil against others or judging others.

He begins by sharing one of his very direct statements. *"Do not speak evil of another"* (v. 11). Then, he proceeds with a series of very logical, connectional contentions. Do not speak evil of another because that is judging another, and that is judging of the law and that means that you are not a doer of the law but a judge, and there can be only one judge—God Himself!

The term "speak evil," or *katalaléo,* can be translated as malign or disparage. This is in contrast to Paul's encouragement to speak "the truth in love." (Eph. 4:15). Once again, it is the sinful activity of putting others down rather than the conduct of the Spirit of building others up with love.

One of the most common expressions of our sinful natures is to attempt to build ourselves up by tearing someone else down. As many of us have discovered, that approach simply does not work. The ones involved in such behavior find that they are simply torn down as they malign others. In this regard, John Calvin wrote, "Hypocrisy is always presumptuous and we are by nature hypocrites, fondly exalting ourselves by calumniating others."

In the same way, the sin of judging others or criticism causes destruction rather than construction. I have met Christians who have told me that they have the gift of criticism. And, unfortunately, as I have listened to them, they have proved their contention. However, the gift of criticism is not a gift of the Spirit but comes from the devil himself.

Jesus warns us about seeking a speck in a brother's eye when we have a plank in our own. He states very clearly, "Judge not, that you be not judged" (Matt. 7:1–5). That is a strong warning against this subtle sin. We are to be judged in the same manner as we judge others.

It is very freeing to discover that God has not commissioned us to go and to judge others. Instead, He has sent us to go and to share the Good News (Mark 16:15) and to share love (Mark 12:28–34). In fact, there is only one who is qualified to be a judge and lawgiver (v. 12). The term "Lawgiver," which is used some six times in the Old Testament, occurs just once in the New Testament. In each situation in which the term is used, "Lawgiver" refers to God and God alone. He is the only Lawgiver. And it is the reasoning of James that only the one who gives the law is qualified to judge the law. It is the pride of sin that motivates a person to think that he is capable of judging another. And so James poses the direct question, "Who are you to judge another?" (v. 12).

James refers not only to the Lawgiver, but also to the law. He writes about the royal law, "You shall love your neighbor as yourself" (2:8). He goes on to state that we should speak and act as those who will be judged by the "law of liberty" (2:12). And, as he speaks about being a doer of the Word and not just a hearer, he refers to "the perfect law of liberty" (1:25).

In addition to there being just one Lawgiver, James contends that He alone is able to save and to destroy. This is a direct quotation from Deuteronomy 32:39 where the Lord declares, "I kill and I make alive!"

In this context, we can clearly understand why judging others is sin. When we judge others, we are taking upon ourselves a role which belongs only to God. He alone is qualified to pass judgment on others. And it is by His mercy that we are not judged (2:13).

Verses 12 and 13 are closely related to the earlier teaching of James concerning judgment and mercy. In contrast to the sin of judging others, James clearly teaches that as Christians, we are called of God to love and to show mercy. In referring to the royal law, James quotes that commandment which fulfills all the others, "You shall love your neighbor as yourself" (James 2:8). How different that is from judging!

Then, James reminds us that if we are following Jesus Christ as Lord, we will be judged by the law of liberty. Since this is so, we should live by that law and remember that mercy triumphs over judgment. This is the good news of the Gospel and of the good life in Jesus Christ. If Christ has shown mercy to us, surely we should show it to others.

How to Plan for the Future

13 Come now, you who say, "Today or tomorrow
we will go to such and such a city, spend a year there,
buy and sell, and make a profit";
14 whereas you do not know what will happen

tomorrow. For what is your life? It is even a vapor that appears for a little time and then vanishes away.

15 Instead you ought to say, "If the Lord wills, we shall live and do this or that."

16 But now you boast in your arrogance. All such boasting is evil.

17 Therefore, to him who knows to do good and does not do it, to him it is sin.

James 4:13–17

James gives us very practical advice regarding how to plan for the future. However, before sharing that counsel, he considers three specific sins which would prevent us from planning for the future according to God's will.

The sin of presumption (vv. 13–15). The sin of presumption is an arrogant display of pride. James warns about this sin within a context very familiar to his readers. He uses the analogy of a Jewish merchant who makes his plans to go to another city, spends a year there by buying and selling, and then returns home with a profit.

This merchant presumes that his plans are his to make, and that God has nothing to say about it. He plans, and it is done. Solomon warned about such presumption as he shared the proverb, "Do not boast about tomorrow, for you do not know what a day may bring forth" (Prov. 27:1).

We tend to forget that we are mere human beings who are finite. We do not know what tomorrow will bring. Only God has that ability. He alone is infinite and all-knowing.

James tells us not to be presumptuous about our plans, but we should also not be presumptuous about life itself. Life is like a vapor or mist which appears for awhile and then vanishes away (v. 14). Our lives are not in our hands. They are in God's hands.

Jesus reminded us of this important truth as he presented a graphic parable of a rich man who was so wealthy that his barns were filled to overflowing. He said to himself, "I will pull down my barns and build greater, and there I will store all my crops and my goods." But the Lord said, "You fool! This night your soul will be required of you" (Luke 12:15–21).

It is presumptuous to think that we can live and plan without God. Presumption denies who we are, who God is, and how much we need God day by day. Indeed, life is a gift of God which comes by His love and mercy.

The sin of boasting (v. 16). The second sin about which James warns us is the sin of boasting. The Greek word for boasting is *alazoneia* which finds its roots in the characteristic of a wandering quack which was not unlike the medicine man of the frontier days in America. This quack offered cures which were not cures; he boasted of things which he was unable to do.

That provides a graphic description for the sin of boasting. This sin is based upon the invalid assumption that we are able to control our own destiny; that we have the power to determine the course of our own lives.

Interestingly enough, the word "boasting" appears just two times in the New Testament—in this James passage and in 1 John 2:16 where it is translated "pride of life." James says that this boasting is evil. This is the same word for evil, *poneros,* which is used in the prayer which the Lord taught his disciples in saying, "deliver us from evil" (Matt. 6:13). And it is the same word that James uses in warning us about becoming "judges with evil thoughts" (2:4).

The sin of omission (v. 17). Finally, James warns against the sin of omission when he writes, "To him who knows to do good and does not do it, to him it is sin" (v. 17). Without a doubt, this is a most difficult form of sin with which to deal.

Sin is missing the mark by not only doing wrong, but by failing to do what is right. Again, James is urging us to be "doers." To know what is right and then not to do it is a form of disobedience. The Lord gives us a commandment, and we either ignore it or simply fail to do it.

Jesus shared a prime example of such a person in His parable of the talents. Two of the men who received talents from their master invested them wisely and received great reward from their master who was well-pleased. However, one of the men buried his talent and simply returned to the master what he had received. With him, the master was exceedingly displeased and punished him harshly (Matt. 25:14–30).

The man had sinned against his master and against himself. In fact, this is one of the great sins of contemporary Christians within our society. God has given us so much, and we often do so little with it. We miss the mark repeatedly because we fail to do what the Lord is calling us to do.

After identifying the three specific sins, in verse 15 James shares with us a practical formula which we should use in making our plans for the future. This simple and important formula contains one basic contention, "If the Lord wills, we shall live and do this or that."

Instead of presuming or boasting or missing the mark by failing to do God's will, we should commit ourselves to the Lord and to doing His will. Our planning is based upon the conviction that our lives and our future are not in our own hands but in the Lord's! We need a dual sensitivity to the world around us and to the guidance of the Holy Spirit.

The phrase the Apostle Paul shared, "If the Lord will permit" (1 Cor. 16:7) was more than literary style—it was the conviction of his life. And so it should be the conviction of our lives. The great Latin phrase, *Deo volente* (God willing), should become the motto of our lives. We should live with utter dependence upon the sovereign will of God. Our lives are His, and the future is His.

Several years ago, a Presbyterian pastor friend of mine died very suddenly in the prime of his life. As I phoned his wife long distance to express our sympathy and love for her, she shared a wonderful story. At that time of deep grief, she was finding her greatest source of comfort to be coming from the words of a poem which her husband had written shortly before his unexpected death. The title of that poem, which was its major theme, is a wonderful commentary on this passage of James and upon authentic godly planning for the future. "Whate'er my God ordains is right! I trust Him utterly!"

CHAPTER FIVE

How to Live with Faith and Reality

James 5:1–20

God invites us to live a life based upon truth and reality. James understands that basic truth and delights in presenting its "how tos" in most practical terms. He completes his letter by sharing counsel regarding a number of areas of vital Christian faith and lifestyle including facing the challenge of riches, perseverance, swearing, praying for the sick, and restoring the backslider.

HOW TO SUCCEED IN SPITE OF RICHES

1 Come now, you rich, weep and howl for your miseries that are coming upon you!

2 Your riches are corrupted, and your garments are moth-eaten.

3 Your gold and silver are corroded, and their corrosion will be a witness against you and will eat your flesh like fire. You have heaped up treasure in the last days.

4 Indeed, the wages of the laborers who have mowed your fields, which you kept back by fraud, cry out; and the cries of the reapers have reached the ears of the Lord of Sabaoth.

5 You have lived on the earth in pleasure and luxury; you have fattened your hearts as in a day of slaughter.

6 You have condemned, you have murdered the just; he does not resist you.

James 5:1–6

Once again, James addresses the special problems of the rich. He builds upon his argument set forth in chapter 1, verses 9–11. Like the teaching of Jesus concerning the dangers of money and wealth shared in His Sermon on the Mount (Matt. 5–7), James warns against the misuse of riches.

He begins by calling the rich to repentance because they are in serious trouble (v. 1). His language is most graphic. His warning is clear, "Weep and howl for your miseries that are coming upon you!"

The word used for "weep" is *klaiō*, which is the same word used to describe the weeping of Peter as he repented of his sin following the denial of Christ (Luke 22:62). Indeed, the rich who have misused their wealth for their own sordid gain should weep such tears, for judgment is coming upon them.

Not only should they weep, but they should literally howl (*ololúzō*) for the miseries which are to come upon them. The word means literally to "howl" or "shriek." Misery (*talaipōría*) is the strong word used by Paul in conjunction with destruction in Romans 3:16, a direct quotation of the prophet Isaiah's warning (Isa. 59:7–8).

In verses 2 and 3 James makes four prophetic statements concerning the conditions that will indicate that trouble is coming.

"Your riches are corrupted" (v. 2). Once again, James sounds a great deal like Jesus in His Sermon on the Mount as He warns us, "Do not lay up for yourselves treasures on earth, where moth and rust destroy . . ." (Matt. 6:19). In short, your riches and your clothes will be destroyed.

"Your gold and silver are corroded" (v. 3). To be corroded (*katíōtai*), means literally to "rust down" or to be "cankered." Again, we have the vocabulary used by Jesus when He warns about rust destroying riches and counsels us to, "Lay up for yourselves treasures in heaven where neither moth or rust destroy . . ." (Matt. 6:19–20).

"Their corrosion will be a witness against you" (v. 3). Now James becomes much more personal in his warning. He no longer talks about the inanimate objects of money and clothing. Instead, he talks about persons who are rich and who have misused their wealth. The corrosion of their riches will be a witness against them. This witness (*martúrion*), or testimony, is the very kind of testimony given in a court of law. In this case, it will be very incriminating.

"And will eat your flesh like fire" (v. 3). Most of us have had the experience of some form of corrosion "eating" or "burning" our flesh. Probably the most common experience we encounter is having the acid

from our car battery "eat" our flesh. And it certainly does burn like fire.

The final sign that the rich are in trouble will not merely be the destruction of their wealth and clothing, nor merely the witness of corroded gold and silver. Instead, the very flesh of the rich who have been wicked will be destroyed.

The warning of James does not take place within a void. To the contrary, he presents specific reasons which lead to the proposed trouble (vv. 4–6). He uses practical cause-and-effect logic. After identifying the effects, he now enumerates the specific causes which are leading to the coming judgment.

First, *"You have heaped up treasure in the last days"* (v. 3). To heap up treasure merely for the sake of having treasure is at the very root of sin. Such an activity leads to trusting in the treasure for security and power. It is the motivation of making that treasure a person's god.

This was the problem of the rich farmer whom Jesus described in His parable. He trusted in his wealth. "But God said to him 'You fool! This night your soul will be required of you; then whose will those things be which you have provided?' " Then Jesus made the personal application by concluding, "So is he who lays up treasure for himself" (Luke 12:20–21).

That is one of the problems with wealth. At best, it is temporary. People who trust in it will ultimately lose it. Only treasures stored in heaven are eternal (Matt. 6:19–20).

Second, the unpaid wages of your laborers cry out (v. 4). The second problem with the unrighteous rich is that they have cheated those who have labored for them by withholding their wages. The rich have been deceived into thinking that they have gotten away with this disastrous deed, but the cries of those who have been cheated have reached the ears of the Lord of the Sabaoth.

The term *Sabaōth* is derived from a Hebrew military term which is used here to denote the sovereignty of God. Many people believe that they have succeeded in cheating others and God, but James warns the rich that such a belief is pure deception. Ultimately, the Lord rewards the righteous and punishes the wicked.

Third, *"you have lived . . . in pleasure and luxury"* (v. 5). Having wealth is not a sin in itself. Indeed, some of the Lord's most faithful servants were persons of great wealth including Abraham, David, and Solomon.

However, there is a misuse of wealth that is contrary to the very essence of spiritual living. The true meaning of this passage is that these rich people lived for the very purpose of their extravagance instead of for God. They had become ungodly hedonists who lived for the pleasures that could be derived from wealth. They trusted their money instead of God. They lived for money instead of for God.

Fourth, *"you have condemned . . . and murdered the just"* (v. 6). The ultimate manifestation of the rich who trust in their wealth rather than in God is that they are never satisfied with what they have. They must always have more.

And to gain more, they condemn the just and even murder them to get what belongs to them. The greed of Ahab and Jezebel led to the murder of Naboth and Jezreelite in order to steal his vineyard (1 Kings 21). That same greed is the motivation for the rich to condemn and kill the just who do not even resist (v. 6).

No wonder James warns against the sin of the misuse of wealth. It is a deadly sin that leads to destruction.

HOW TO BE PATIENT

7 Therefore be patient, brethren, until the coming of the Lord. See how the farmer waits for the precious fruit of the earth, waiting patiently for it until it receives the early and latter rain.

8 You also be patient. Establish your hearts, for the coming of the Lord is at hand.

9 Do not grumble against one another, brethren, lest you be condemned. Behold, the Judge is standing at the door!

10 My brethren, take the prophets, who have spoken in the name of the Lord, as an example of suffering and patience.

11 Indeed, we count them blessed who endure. You have heard of the perseverance of Job and seen the purpose of the Lord, that the Lord is very compassionate and merciful.

James 5:7–11

After sharing his warning regarding the misuse of wealth, James seems to reach the conclusion that the rich to whom he has been

referring are the non-Christians who have been oppressing the believers. In the midst of this oppression, James counsels the Christians
to be patient until the coming of the Lord which he believes is at
hand (vv. 7–8). He makes three specific contentions concerning the
believer and patience.

1. *Be patient until the Lord's coming* (vv. 7–9). In counseling us to be
patient until the coming of the Lord, James uses the example of the
farmer who waits for the precious fruit of the earth until it is ready
to harvest. He waits for the early rains and the latter rains.

James was writing within the context of the climate of Israel which
receives its early rain in late October and early November, and then
receives its late rain in April or May. That is a long time to wait
for the harvest. And yet the farmer patiently waits realizing that
he cannot hurry the process.

In the same way, James assures us that God is always on time
and that we cannot hurry the process. Instead, we should establish
(*stērizō*) our hearts which means to fix or strengthen. The prophet
Isaiah shared the same counsel when he wrote, "You will keep him
in perfect peace, whose mind is stayed on You; because he trusts
in You" (Isa. 26:3).

And, as we wait, we should not grumble or complain against one
another. Such judging of others can lead to our own condemnation,
warns James. The Judge is standing at the door (v. 9).

The Lord's coming is near! In fact, Peter contends that the only
reason that the Lord has not returned is that He is patient (in the
same way in which He desires for us to be patient) and is not willing
that any should perish but that all should come to repentence
(2 Pet. 3:3–9).

2. *Be patient in the face of suffering* (vv. 10–11). James is writing to a
suffering church. He writes not merely to instruct but to comfort
and encourage. As he encourages his readers to be patient in the
midst of their suffering, he gives two vivid examples from the Old
Testament Scriptures which should serve as great encouragement to
all of us.

He begins by inviting us to look at the prophets who have spoken
in the name of the Lord as examples of suffering and patience (v.
10). The writer of Hebrews describes some of the things these men
suffered. They were stoned, sawn in two, slain with the sword; they
wandered in sheepskins, being destitute, afflicted, and tormented
(Heb. 11:37).

A vivid example of such a prophet would be Jeremiah who was known as the "weeping prophet." He was beaten, placed in stocks, imprisoned, and thrown in a cistern. Yet he trusted in the Lord.

Job is example number two. He was blessed because he endured, and because of his patience and perseverance, he is an example to show us the purpose of the Lord through suffering.

Job suffered for no legitimate reason. And yet he committed his way to the Lord and trusted in Him. God was compassionate and merciful to Job and returned to him much more than he possessed prior to the time of suffering (Job 42:12).

In the same way, encourages James, the Lord will be compassionate and merciful to us as we trust Him and follow Him as Lord (v. 11). Indeed, we will also be blessed if we endure.

3. *Be patient and you will be blessed* (v. 11). This is the third contention of James. He believes that the result of being patient and enduring suffering will be the blessing of God. He states, "We count them blessed that endure."

James may be referring to the teaching of Jesus on this important subject. Jesus said, "Blessed are you when they revile and persecute you, and say all kinds of evil against you falsely for My sake. Rejoice and be exceedingly glad, for great is your reward in heaven, for so they persecuted the prophets who were before you" (Matt. 5:11–12).

To be "blessed" is to be "happy." Our Lord offers us a quality of happiness which we can enjoy even in the midst of suffering and persecution. It is no wonder that we consider those "blessed" or "happy" that endure. The promise to us is that our Lord's coming is near. He is compassionate and merciful, and He will reward those who are "overcomers" (Rev. 21:3–4).

HOW NOT TO SWEAR

12 But above all, my brethren, do not swear, neither by heaven nor by earth nor with any other oath. But let your "Yes" be "Yes," and your "No," "No," lest you fall into judgment.

James 5:12

Once again, James surprises us by a seemingly abrupt change of direction. As he comforts those who are suffering and counsels us to endure suffering which comes into our lives with patience and perseverance, he now sounds another note of warning. He begins chapter 5 by warning against the misuse of riches, and now he warns against the misuse of speech by swearing.

Again, he emphasizes a teaching of Jesus. James states that we should not swear (*omnúō*) either by heaven or by earth or with any other oath. Jesus taught, "Do not swear at all; neither by heaven, for it is God's throne; nor by the earth, for it is His footstool; nor by Jerusalem, for it is the city of the great King. Nor shall you swear by your head, because you cannot make one hair white or black" (Matt. 5:34–36).

As we can see, James is proclaiming the teaching of Jesus in most practical terms. In fact, his teaching is almost word for word what Jesus had declared.

James concludes his teaching concerning swearing by stating, *'Let your 'Yes' be 'Yes,' and your 'No,' 'No,' lest you fall into judgment."* Again, he is quoting directly from Jesus in His Sermon on the Mount (Matt. 5:37). Jesus went on to state that whatever we say which is more than merely "yes" or "no" is from the evil one (Matt. 5:37).

The warning is clear! We should not swear in any form nor for any reason. Swearing is an affront against God, and it brings His judgment upon us (v. 12).

How to Pray for the Sick

13 Is anyone among you suffering? Let him pray. Is anyone cheerful? Let him sing psalms.

14 Is anyone among you sick? Let him call for the elders of the church, and let them pray over him, anointing him with oil in the name of the Lord.

15 And the prayer of faith will save the sick, and the Lord will raise him up. And if he has committed sins, he will be forgiven.

16 Confess your trespasses to one another, and pray for one another, that you may be healed. The effective, fervent prayer of a righteous man avails much.

97

17 Elijah was a man with a nature like ours, and
he prayed earnestly that it would not rain; and it did
not rain on the land for three years and six months.
18 And he prayed again, and the heaven gave rain,
and the earth produced its fruit.

James 5:13-18

James makes another practical suggestion concerning how the believer should relate to suffering. His counsel is simple and clear, "Is
anyone among you suffering? Let him pray." The word translated
as suffering, *kakopathēo*, is used only five times in the New Testament.
It is sometimes translated as "afflicted."

Prayer is appropriate for every situation of life and it is certainly
appropriate for times of suffering and affliction. Our human tendency
is to pray in terms of "why?" Job, his wife, and his friends fell into
that trap.

A much deeper and more appropriate prayer in times of suffering
is that of "what?" "Lord, what are you saying to me through these
difficulties?" "Father, what do you want me to learn, or what do
you wish for me to do?"

Sometimes, the most appropriate prayer is, "Help!" That prayer
is predicated upon our understanding of who we are and who God
is. It is an acknowledgement of our need for His help.

Or sometimes the appropriate prayer is that of praise and thanksgiving as Paul and Silas demonstrated in the Philippian jail as they
prayed and sang hymns of praise to God after being beaten with
rods, placed in stocks, and locked in the inner prison (Acts 16:23–
34).

There is the second word of counsel in these verses. James continues,
"Is anyone cheerful? Let him sing psalms" (v. 13). The word for
being cheerful is *euthumēo*, which is often translated as "to be merry."
It is a wonderful word in the Greek which is a blend of the two
words meaning "well" and "soul." Thus it means being in "good
spirits" or in a "happy mood."

Next, comes the counsel which is the major focus of this passage.
The question of James is, "Is anyone among you sick?" He answers
that important question by sharing a three-part solution to the problem of sickness in the life of a believer.

1. *"Call for the elders of the church"* (v. 14). Just as James gives a direct
and practical answer to his first two questions, so he responds just

as directly and practically to this question. When a believer is sick, he or she should call for the elders of the church.

This is the only passage in the New Testament which gives such direct advice concerning the ministry of healing within the church. However, additional passages do address this vital subject. Of course, Jesus was involved in a very effective ministry of healing. A vivid example of His healing ministry is that of His healing of the paralytic. The crowd who witnessed the healing was filled with awe and praised God (Matt. 9:1–8).

The Gospel of Mark relates the account of Jesus sending His disciples out with a ministry of healing (Mark 6:13). And the Book of Acts relates numerous reports of the healing ministry of the apostles such as the account of Paul's healing ministry on Malta (Acts 28:1–10).

In addition, the ministry of healing is enumerated as one of the "grace" gifts or spiritual gifts by Paul in his letter to the Corinthian church. In his major treatise on the functioning of the Body of Christ and the use of spiritual gifts for the common good of the body, Paul refers specifically to the spiritual gift of healing in the twelfth chapter of 1 Corinthians, verse 9, and again in verse 30.

With all of that knowledge plus the many references to the ministry of healing in the Old Testament (i.e., Gen. 20:17, Num. 12:13, 2 Kings 5:14, and 2 Kings 20:1–5), James now calls for believers to call for the elders of the church. The inference of his statement is clear. He believes that God has entrusted the ministry of healing and, therefore, the spiritual gift of healing, to the elders of the church.

2. *Let them anoint him with oil* (v. 14). In turn, the elders should anoint the sick person with oil in the name of the Lord. The term "anointing with oil" has at least two significant meanings within the context of the Scriptures. First, there is the example of the anointing with oil as medicine. In Jesus' parable of the Good Samaritan, the Samaritan bathed the wounds of the injured traveler with oil (Luke 10:34).

Second, in the Old Testament, anointing with oil was often symbolic or sacramental; the prophet Samuel anointed Saul with oil when he was declared the King of Israel. That custom was followed within the kingdom of Israel. Jesus referred to this fact when the woman bathed the feet of Jesus with an alabaster flask of fragrant oil (Luke 7:37–38). Jesus used the occasion to teach those present, and us who read the account, a basic spiritual lesson by saying, "You did not anoint My head with oil, but this woman has anointed My feet with fragrant oil" (Luke 7:46).

The logical question now arises, should we anoint sick people with oil for medicinal purposes or for sacramental purposes? Some within the church would contend for the former and others for the latter. I would personally contend for both. I believe that God has given medical science every insight that has been gained. We should blend medicine and prayer together as we care for the sick.

When our oldest son, Daniel, was a little boy, he contracted a very serious illness. He was rushed to the Denver Children's Hospital where he was under the care of an outstanding pediatrician who was a committed Christian. As my wife, Jean, and I stood with the doctor next to Dan's bed which was covered by an oxygen tent, the doctor shared some counsel with us which I shall never forget.

He said, "I have done everything I can do. Dan has the best that medicine can offer. Now we must entrust him to God." He then continued, "I have found the best combination for healing is a healthy blend of penicillin and prayer."

That is the very message of James! Let the anointing of oil represent both the spiritual and medicinal. God is the source of both.

3. *"Let them pray over him"* (v. 14). Prayer is the key word in this entire passage. Over and over again James encourages us to pray. Pray when in trouble—verse 13. Pray when you are sick—verse 14. Pray for one another—verse 16. The prayer of a righteous man is powerful and effective—verse 16. Elijah is a vivid example of a man of prayer—verses 17–18.

Notice how clearly this teaching corresponds to that of chapter 4, verses 1–3. We often do not have because we do not ask or because we ask amiss (4:2–3). Now the promise is clear; if we ask according to the will of God (1 John 5:14), "The prayer of faith will save the sick, and the Lord will raise him up" (v. 15).

I believe that it may not always be the choice of God to heal physically, but I believe that it is always proper to call for the elders of the church, to be anointed with oil, and to pray for healing. Then we can leave the results with God. He is to be trusted with our lives and our bodies and all that we have and are. He is our Lord.

There is one more phrase which we must expose if we are to be faithful to the text. It is the closing sentence of verse 15, "And if he has committed sin, he will be forgiven." There are those in the church who believe that all illness is the result of sin. James does not concur with that teaching. He uses the word "if."

"If" he has sinned, he will be forgiven. This corresponds with the teaching of Jesus as He responded to a question posed by His disciples concerning the man who was blind from birth. They asked Jesus whether this man was blind because of his sin or his parents' sin. Jesus answered, "Neither this man nor his parents sinned, but that the works of God should be revealed in him" (John 9:3). The conclusion of James is clear; if a person has sinned and prays the prayer of repentance and faith which is necessary for healing, those sins will be forgiven (v. 15).

How to Restore a Backslider

> 19 Brethren, if anyone among you should wander from the truth, and someone turns him back,
> 20 let him know that he who turns a sinner from the error of his way will save a soul from death and cover a multitude of sins.
>
> *James 5:19–20*

As James has discussed the ministry of physical healing, he now closes his letter with some practical teaching on the important subject of spiritual healing. Without a doubt, this is the most difficult passage within the Book of James to exposit and to understand.

As a result, the church has not always agreed upon the interpretation of this passage. However, we will attempt to reveal the basic tenets of truth that will be applicable and practical for all who follow Jesus Christ as Lord.

1. *"If anyone among you wanders from the truth . . ."* (v. 19). In James 1:16, we are warned against erring. Now James shares counsel for those who have "erred" or "wandered" from the truth. The Greek word for this activity is *planáō* which can also be translated as "deceived" or "gone astray."

The "wandering" or "straying" has taken the person away from the truth. Jesus Christ is the personification of truth. He came declaring that "I am the way, the truth, and the life . . ." (John 14:6). He stated that if we would know Him, we would know the truth, and the truth would make us free" (John 8:31–32).

To err from the truth is a great tragedy. James calls upon his fellow Christians to respond to such a problem with directness.

2. *"And someone turns him [the sinner] back . . ."* (v. 19). Theologians and Biblical scholars have debated the meaning of this passage for centuries. The usual question which is posed is, "Does this passage teach that a Christian who errs from the truth is saved or lost?" This leads to the theological argument between the Calvinists and the Arminians.

Frankly, I don't believe that the question which separates Calvinists and Arminians is the most vital question of this passage. I find that all Christians agree that an erring brother or sister is in deep trouble, and that he or she needs to repent and return to Christ.

The more vital question is, "How do we become involved in the ministry of restoring such a backslider?" James focuses much more on the need to be involved in such a ministry than he does in explaining to us how to do it. How do we turn (convert) a sinner from the error of his way and save a soul from death therefore covering a multitude of sins?

All of us realize that we cannot "convert" another person. God does not allow us to violate anyone nor does He violate anyone. He does not force His will upon us. He invites us and longs for us to know and to do His will—but the decision to do so is ours.

Therefore, based upon other teachings of the Word of God, I believe there are at least three steps we can take to be involved in the vital ministry of "restoring" backsliders. First, we must take the initiative. I believe that the strong implication of the teaching of James is that we should not be passive about a brother or sister who is erring from the truth. We should take the initiative to do something about it.

Second, we should pray. In the preceding verses, James repeatedly instructs us to pray when we are in need. It is always appropriate to pray for those in spiritual need.

Third, we can love. The ministry of love is the primary calling of every Christian. Jesus said that the life of love was the distinguishable mark of the Christian (John 13:35). God has called us to prayerfully activate the ministry of the Holy Spirit to love and invite, to woo and draw sinners to repentance.

3. *"Will save a soul from death . . ."* (v. 20). Some Biblical scholars believe that this reference is to physical death. They cite the reference of Paul in 1 Corinthians 11:29–30 when he speaks of those believers who are sick or dying because of their spiritual sickness.

However, because James specifically refers to the phrase, *"will save a soul from death,"* it is more likely that he is referring to spiritual death. The word for soul is *psuchē* which refers to the spiritual part of man rather than the physical. This, of course, is in keeping with the clear teaching of Scripture that "the wages of sin is death" (Rom. 6:23).

4. *"[This will] cover a multitude of sins"* (v. 20). The teaching of James ends with the focus on grace and forgiveness. Peter teaches that love covers a multitude of sins (1 Pet. 4:8). And John teaches that God is the source of love; God is love! (1 John 4:8).

With God's love comes grace as opposed to judgment and forgiveness in contrast to condemnation (John 3:16–18). When a sinner turns from his or her wandering from the truth and returns to God, all the resources of God's love are unleashed. The psalmist declares that as far as the east is from the west, so far does our Lord remove our sins from us when they are confessed to Him. He forgives and forgets (Ps. 103:12).

Jesus, the One who came to save us from our sins, shared great truth of great joy when He said, "Likewise, I say to you, there is joy in the presence of the angels of God over one sinner who repents" (Luke 15:10). No wonder there is such great joy in the church when an erring brother or sister repents and returns to the living Christ!

Introduction to 1 Peter

A few days ago, I read a very remarkable book written by a contemporary missionary, Peter Brashler, who has just completed a total of thirty-five years of missionary service in Africa.[1] He relates a fascinating and moving story of the remarkable spread of Christianity in central and eastern Africa in the midst of great difficulty and persecution.

African Christian brothers and sisters have suffered greatly during the past two decades simply because of their faith in Jesus Christ. In spite of the persecution and hardship, the church has grown phenomenally within an unusual atmosphere of spiritual revival.

As I read Peter Brashler's sensitive portrayal of his loving ministry to the African church, I thought of another Peter who ministered under very similar circumstances nearly two thousand years ago. The Apostle Peter wrote to a suffering church. The believers had been scattered through Asia Minor. Peter writes to them with the love of a pastor who is caring for his flock as a shepherd cares for his sheep or as a mother cares for her children.

Peter identifies with their pain without being evasive or fatalistic. He speaks very directly about their suffering. He refers to their suffering some sixteen times as he brings them comfort and practical counsel. His teaching can be summarized in the words of the Apostle Paul, "For I consider that the sufferings of this present time are not worthy to be compared with the glory which will be revealed in us" (Rom. 8:18).

And within this context, Peter speaks about hope. In fact, hope is a central theme in this epistle. When we live our lives as strangers upon the earth, and when we live in constant communion with God, we can enjoy the life of hope regardless of the external circumstances and the present sufferings.

However, Peter is not only writing to comfort Christians who have known suffering, but he is preparing them for increased suffering which is about to come under the deranged hand of Nero, the infamous emperor of Rome.

As many of our Christian brothers and sisters are suffering for their faith in Christ in other parts of the world, it is possible that we, too, will face increased suffering in the days ahead. Therefore, his words of instruction are also appropriate for us today.

We will do well to study the book inductively. Our concern should not be only for what our Lord was saying to Peter's contemporaries through this epistle, but what He is saying to us personally. We need to be strengthened and encouraged in the faith in the same way as the early Christians were.

The Author

Peter, an apostle of Jesus Christ (1 Pet. 1:1). This is the introduction of the author of this letter. The internal evidence is clear. The Apostle Peter is identified as the writer.

In addition, the author identifies himself as a fellow elder and a witness of the sufferings of Christ in the first verse of chapter 5. Peter is writing as a loving elder of the Church of Jesus Christ.

The Recipients

To the pilgrims scattered throughout Pontus, Galatia, Cappadocia, Asia, and Bithynia (1 Pet. 1:1). These pilgrims, or "strangers," have been scattered throughout Asia Minor because of their faith in Christ.

As James writes his epistle primarily to the Jewish Christians of the Diaspora, Peter writes his letter primarily to the Gentile or non-Jewish believers. This is documented in several ways within the content of the letter.

For example, Peter refers to his readers as those "who once were not a people but are now the people of God" (2:10). He, of course, is referring to the fact that Gentiles were not a part of the first covenant which God made with the Jewish people. But now we are the people of God as a part of the new covenant through the blood of Jesus Christ.

Again, in chapter 4, verse 3, Peter refers to the fact that his readers once lived as the Gentiles live, but now they should live by the will of God. Of course, Jewish readers would not have lived the lifestyle of the Gentiles.

However, the messages in 1 Peter and James are appropriate for both Jewish and Gentile believers. We are now the people of God. We are a new nation of people who belong to the Kingdom of God. In Jesus Christ there is neither Jew nor Greek nor Gentile nor Swede nor American—we are **one** in Christ Jesus. "Christ is all and in all" (Col. 3:11).

The Occasion

As we have seen, Peter is writing to a suffering church. The date of the writing of this epistle is probably about A.D. 64. This was the time in which the persecution of the church under Nero was just beginning. Peter is writing not only to encourage and comfort, but also to prepare the believers for the persecution that lies ahead.

Tradition tells us that Peter faced this persecution in his own life and was actually crucified upside down on a cross sometime about A.D. 67. When he was sentenced to be crucified, he requested that he be hung upside down because he was not worthy to die in the same manner as his Master.

It is likely that Peter wrote this epistle from Rome. The only internal evidence we have for this contention is Peter's use of the phrase "greets you" within his salutation from "Babylon" (5:13). Within Peter's lifetime, there were three possible geographical locations which could have been identified as Babylon.

The first was a military outpost in Egypt where the city of Cairo is now located. The second was a small village located on the Euphrates River. Although there was a small colony of Christians there, we are told that they had fled under violent persecution in about A.D. 41. It is unlikely that Peter wrote from either of those two locations.

It is more probable that he was writing from Rome which has traditionally been referred to as "Babylon" within the Christian church. Tradition contends that Peter spent the latter years of his life and ministry in Rome. And it is upon this tradition that the Roman Catholic church bases its papacy in Rome.

Plan of Exposition

Once again, we will study this epistle by using the inductive approach. First, we shall attempt to understand what the Holy Spirit was saying to the original recipients in Asia Minor. Then, we shall examine our own lives so that we will be open to the guidance and revelation of the Holy Spirit for truth which we should apply to ourselves.

Like James, Peter shares very practical advice for us to follow so that we can grow in the grace and knowledge of Jesus Christ. We will notice that there are several teachings which are common to both epistles, such as the instruction of 1 Peter 1:6–7 concerning rejoicing as we face various temptations and the testing of our faith. James shares that same counsel in James 1:2–3.

The message of 1 Peter might be best summarized in practical terms by Peter himself when he writes, "But sanctify the Lord God in your hearts, and always be ready to give a defense to everyone who asks you a reason for the hope that is in you, with meekness and fear" (1 Pet. 3:15).

NOTE

1. Peter J. Brashler, *Change* (Wheaton: Tyndale House Publishers, 1979).

An Outline of 1 Peter

I. What Salvation Is All About: 1:1–25
   A. Why Has God Chosen You?: 1:1–2
   B. The Fringe Benefits of the New Birth: 1:3–5
   C. How Trials Can Bring Joy: 1:6–9
   D. The Priority of Salvation: 1:10–12
   E. Called to Be Holy: 1:13–16
   F. Living like Strangers Here on Earth: 1:17–21
   G. Loving from the Heart: 1:22–25
II. What Christian Living Is All About: 2:1–25
   A. Growing Goes Better with Milk: 2:1–3
   B. Building with Living Stones: 2:4–8
   C. The Truth about Self-Image: 2:9–10
   D. Goodness, Freedom, and Servanthood: 2:11–17
   E. Called to Be Servants: 2:18–25
III. What Being Good Is All About: 3:1–22
   A. How to Be a Good Christian Wife: 3:1–6
   B. How to Be a Good Christian Husband: 3:7
   C. Repaying Evil with Good: 3:8–12
   D. Sharing the Hope: 3:13–16
   E. Suffering for Doing Good: 3:17–22
IV. What Suffering Is All About: 4:1–19
   A. Living for the Will of God: 4:1–6
   B. The End Is at Hand: 4:7–9
   C. You Are Called to Ministry: 4:10–11
   D. Suffering as a Christian: 4:12–19
V. What Christian Leadership Is All About: 5:1–14
   A. Priorities for Christian Leadership: 5:1–4
   B. Clothing Yourselves with Humility: 5:5–7
   C. Standing Firm in the Faith: 5:8–11
   D. Final Greetings: 5:12–14

CHAPTER ONE

What Salvation Is All About

1 Peter 1:1–25

Salvation is at the very core of Christianity. It was for our salvation that Jesus Christ came to us as a man and lived among us as a servant. Indeed, Jesus Christ came to seek and to save that which was lost! He is the Lamb of God who came to take away the sins of the world.

The very name, Jesus, means "savior." The message proclaimed by the angel to the shepherds on the night of Christ's birth was, "For there is born to you this day in the city of David a Savior, who is Christ the Lord" (Luke 2:11). And long before this majestic event, the prophets had declared the coming of the Savior.

In fact, the entire Bible is an account of salvation history. The coming of Jesus was not a mistake or an incident of chance. His role as a Savior had been determined before the creation of the world (1 Pet. 1:20).

And so Peter begins his letter to a suffering, scattered church by reaffirming the basics of salvation. He uses marvelously expressive words such as "elect," "living hope," "abundant mercy," an "incorruptible and undefiled inheritance," and "salvation." Salvation is assured for all of those who trust in Jesus Christ, and this wonderful knowledge results in genuine hope.

WHY HAS GOD CHOSEN YOU?

1 Peter, an apostle of Jesus Christ,

To the pilgrims scattered throughout Pontus,
Galatia, Cappadocia, Asia, and Bithynia,
2 elect according to the foreknowledge of God the

Father, in sanctification of the Spirit, for obedience
and sprinkling of the blood of Jesus Christ:

Grace to you and peace be multiplied.

1 Peter 1:1–2

Peter writes as an apostle of Jesus Christ. It was Peter who was
among the inner circle of Christ's disciples. It was he that Jesus addressed when He stated, "You are Peter, and on this rock I will build
My Church, and the gates of Hades shall not prevail against it" (Matt.
16:18).

And, although Peter denied the Lord at a time of fear and weakness,
his fellowship with Christ was wonderfully restored (John 21). After
being filled with the Holy Spirit on the Day of Pentecost, it was
Peter who stood on the street in Jerusalem and courageously proclaimed the Gospel of Christ. And, as he was empowered by the
Holy Spirit, some three thousand responded to his message and received Christ as their Savior.

That was just the beginning of Peter's ministry. He continued to
see scores of people come to salvation through faith in Jesus Christ.
No wonder he believed in salvation!

He addressed the letter to the *"elect according to the foreknowledge of
God the Father"* (v. 1). This concept of a special people or the *"elect"*
comes from the first covenant which God had made with the Jewish
people. Jehovah had said, "You are a holy people to the Lord your
God; the Lord your God has chosen you to be a people for Himself,
a special treasure above all the peoples on the face of the earth"
(Deut. 7:6).

Now this special choosing or election has been extended through
the New Covenant to all who would experience salvation through
faith in Jesus Christ. Peter reminds the Gentile Christians, "You once
were not a people but are now the people of God" (1 Pet. 2:10).

Peter begins by reminding these elect and chosen ones that they
are strangers in the world in which they live (v. 1). He specifically
addresses the Christians who are scattered in five provinces of Asia
Minor. Three of these provinces were represented when Peter
preached at Pentecost—Pontus, Cappadocia, and Asia (Acts 2:7–12).

Galatia is mentioned in Acts 16:6 as being visited by Paul and
his companions. Of course, we know that Paul established churches
there and later wrote them the letter which became one of our books

in the New Testament—Galatians. Paul and his companions also ministered in Bithynia, according to Acts 16:7.

The word translated in verse 1 as *"scattered"* is the Greek word *diasporá*, the same term that James uses in describing the Christians to whom he is writing (James 1:1). As mentioned in the introduction (p. 14), this was a term commonly used to describe the Jewish people who had been exiled over the years of the existence of the kingdom of Israel. In the New Testament context, it came to refer to the Christians who had been dispersed or scattered all over the world because of their faith in Christ.

But the true meaning of Peter's phrase "sojourners in the world" (1 Pet. 2:11) goes much deeper than just a social or geographical identification. Peter speaks about the deepest meaning of being a Christian. Our King is God and our Kingdom is heaven. We are strangers and pilgrims (Heb. 11:13), aliens in the world. Our citizenship is in heaven (Phil. 3:20).

There is a traditional statement attributed to Jesus which contends, "The world is a bridge. The wise man will pass over it, but he will not build his house upon it." That is what Peter is teaching. Our life on earth is only temporary. But the salvation of the Lord is eternal. That is why he encourages these suffering brothers and sisters to focus upon the hope that is theirs and ours as we trust in Christ Jesus.

Peter next points out that election requires obedience to Jesus Christ (v. 2). There is a great and marvelous mystery in our understanding of the Scripture regarding the relationship between the sovereignty of God and the freedom of the will of man. The Bible teaches that both exist. As mere fallible human beings, we have difficulty in understanding how they can coexist. And so, historically, systematic theologians have tended to emphasize one more than the other.

In verse 2 Peter makes three specific statements about the election of God. These statements are not contradictory in any sense of the term. Instead, they are complementary.

First, we are elected by God *to obey Him*. Obedience is at the very heart of vital Christianity. (See our study on the subject of obedience in the commentary on James 2:14–26, p. .) To obey Him is better than sacrifice (1 Sam. 15:22). And to love God, I must obey Him. Anything less than obedience is hypocrisy (John 14:21).

We are also elected *according to the foreknowledge of God*. All of us realize that God knows everything—past, present, and future. And yet it is difficult for us to grasp the practical implications of His fore-knowledge. Peter uses that same term in his sermon at Pentecost when he refers to the crucifixion of Christ (Acts 2:23).

Third, we are elected *according to the sanctification of the Spirit.* *"Sanctification"* (*hagiasmós*) comes from the same root as does our word "holy" (*hágios*). It means to separate or to set apart. That is what Peter is attempting to teach us: that we are to be strangers in this world; that we are to be separated from the evil worldly system which is in total opposition to the things of the Spirit. We cannot be a friend of the worldly system and of God (1 John 2:15–17).

The term *"sprinkling of the blood of Jesus Christ"* (v. 2) is most interesting. It would mean a great deal to Jewish Christians who were familiar with the traditions of the Old Covenant, but for the Gentile Christians to whom Peter is writing it would be rather difficult to understand. Within Old Testament Law, there were three occasions in which there was the "sprinkling of blood." (1) *Cleansing:* When a leper was healed, he or she was sprinkled with blood of a bird (Lev. 14:1–7). (2) *Setting apart for service to God:* Aaron and the priests of the tabernacle were sprinkled with the blood of the sacrificial lamb when they were "sanctified" for their priestly service (Exod. 29:20–22, Lev. 8:30). (3) *Obedience to God's covenant:* When the people of Israel responded to God's invitation to establish a covenant with Him, Moses sprinkled half the blood of the oxen on the people and half on the altar. The people stated, "All that the Lord has said we will do . . ." (Exod. 24:1–8). Again, the key word in the covenant was "obey."

THE FRINGE BENEFITS OF THE NEW BIRTH

3 Blessed be the God and Father of our Lord Jesus
Christ, who according to His abundant mercy has
begotten us again to a living hope by the resurrection
of Jesus Christ from the dead,
4 to an inheritance incorruptible and undefiled and
that does not fade away, reserved in heaven for you,
5 who are kept by the power of God through faith
for salvation ready to be revealed in the last time.
1 Peter 1:3–5

One evening not long ago, we were invited to the home of some new Christian friends for a wonderful evening of dinner and fellowship. As the evening drew to a close, our host asked me to pray, and then he led us in singing the doxology. All of us were moved to tears as we joined together in simply offering praise and thanksgiving to God.

In the same way, Peter begins his letter with a note of praise and doxology. "Blessed be the God and Father of our Lord Jesus Christ, who according to His abundant mercy has begotten us again to a living hope by the resurrection of Jesus Christ from the dead!"

"Mercy" is a key word which we must understand in order to grasp the fullest meaning of Peter's teaching on the subject of salvation. Within the context of verse 3, Peter reminds us that new birth has come to us through the mercy of God (v. 3). The phrase ". . . *begotten us again"* is better translated as the "new birth."

As Paul said, "According to His mercy He saved us" (Tit. 3:5), and the writer of Lamentations contended that it is by God's mercies that we are not consumed. Peter later declares that without God we were without mercy, "but now have obtained mercy" (1 Pet. 2:10).

The Bible teaches us that the "new birth" is the beginning of new life in Jesus Christ. Whenever I hear that simple truth, I remember the first little sermon I ever preached. I was seventeen years old, and I shared a message entitled "The New Birth Is Only the First Step!" with my church youth group.

That's what Peter is declaring. Being born anew of the Spirit is not the end of Christian experience; it is the beginning. The most obvious benefit of the new birth is eternal life, but Peter teaches us that there are also some very profitable and enjoyable "fringe benefits" including the following:

1. *A living hope* (v. 3). Peter wastes no time in identifying with suffering and hurting people. In Jesus Christ, God has given us a *"living hope"* which is not dependent upon our environment or outward circumstances. The word "living" denotes that which is dynamic, vital, alive. This hope is like living waters flowing from a perennial spring which never runs dry. Such hope comes from the very source of God Himself.

The word "hope" is a uniquely Christian word. It makes no sense without the resurrection of Jesus Christ. This quality of hope is more than wishful thinking. It is more than the little train who said, "I think I can; I think I can!" As Peter declares, this hope has come to us by the resurrection of Jesus Christ from the dead (v. 3).

Peter goes on to contend that because God raised Christ from the dead and gave Him glory, our faith and hope are in God (1:21). And Peter believes so deeply that we should live the life of hope, that he instructs us to be ready to give an answer to the person who asks us the reason for that hope. That reason is the resurrection of Jesus Christ experienced in our own lives as we are born again of the Spirit.

Such hope finds expression in many ways including the singing of a marvelous hymn about hope.

> My hope is in the Lord
> Who gave Himself for me,
> And paid the price of all my sin at Calvary.
> For me He died
> For me He lives,
> And everlasting life and light He freely gives.[1]

2. *A heavenly inheritance* (v. 4). The new birth not only offers us eternal hope, but it also guarantees us a heavenly inheritance. This inheritance has several outstanding characteristics: It is (1) *"incorruptible."* It will never perish; it is indestructible. It is the same word used in Romans 1:23 in describing the glory of the incorruptible God. It is (2) *"undefiled"*—unpolluted and fresh. It will never spoil or decay. It is (3) *unfading.* It remains bright and vital. This description reminds me of an experience I had recently in visiting Milan, Italy to view *The Last Supper,* the great masterpiece of Leonardo da Vinci. Thousands of dollars are being spent in an attempt to restore some of the fading colors. Even the greatest of masterpieces ultimately fade. But the heavenly inheritance that our Lord provides for us will never fade.

Peter declares that this heavenly inheritance is reserved in heaven for us (v. 4). The word translated as "reserved" is *tēréō,* which is better translated as "to guard" or "to keep." In military terms it means "to guard." That is the promise of our Lord. He will guard, keep, and reserve our heavenly inheritance for us.

3. *A powerful shield* (v. 5). The phrase "kept by the power of God" is translated in the New International Version of the Bible as "shielded by God's power." That is the promise of God to us. Until the day we claim our heavenly inheritance, God has promised to provide for us a living hope, and He has promised to shield us with His power.

This powerful shield is ours if we live by faith in the living Christ. Faith is absolutely essential for Christian discipleship. It is by faith that we come to Christ, and it is by faith that we live for Him day by day (Gal. 3:11). Paul instructs us to use the shield of faith to quench all the fiery darts of the wicked one (Eph. 6:16).

The key to using this shield is to do so in God's power (*dúnamis*) and not our own. The promise of Jesus to us is that when we receive the Holy Spirit, we also receive the power of God (Acts 1:8). The Acts of the Apostles is a wonderful commentary of those brothers and sisters in the early church who lived by the power of God. Paul encourages us to realize that God does not give us a spirit of weakness, but of power (2 Tim. 1:7).

This shield of faith will keep us by God's power until our salvation is ready to be revealed in the last time (v. 5). Peter is speaking about the apocalypse—the ultimate revelation of Jesus Christ when He returns to reign as King of kings and Lord of lords. There will be a new heaven and a new earth (Rev. 21:1). God "will dwell with men . . . and they shall be His people, and God Himself will be with them and be their God. And God will wipe away every tear from their eyes; there shall be no more death, nor sorrow, nor crying; and there shall be no more pain, for the former things have passed away (Rev. 21:4).

What a day that will be! Until that day, our Lord has promised to be with us. He has promised us life eternal which no one can take from us. And He has offered us some wonderful fringe benefits including a living hope, a heavenly inheritance, and a powerful shield.

How Trials Can Bring Joy

6 In this you greatly rejoice, though now for a little while, if need be, you have been grieved by manifold temptations,

7 that the genuineness of your faith, being much more precious than gold that perishes, though it is tested with fire, may be found to praise, honor, and glory at the revelation of Jesus Christ,

8 whom having not seen you love. Though now you do not see Him, yet believing, you rejoice with joy unspeakable and full of glory,

9 receiving the end of your faith—the salvation
of your souls.

1 Peter 1:6–9

After beginning his letter with words of affirmation and encouragement, Peter proceeds with loving counsel for those who are facing
trials and suffering. Although he discusses the matter of suffering
more thoroughly later in his letter, he does not hesitate to face the
subject immediately with love and sensitivity.

Peter knows what it means to face temptations and trials. He remembers well the pain of falling to temptation when he denied his
Lord on the night of Christ's betrayal. Undoubtedly, Peter continued
to face trials in the succeeding days, and he discovered that in addition
to the grief that trials bring, there are also benefits which God brings
to pass. And so he shares with the suffering church three specific
results of the trials which God allows to come into our lives.

1. *The grief of trials* (v. 6). Peter begins by acknowledging the legitimate grief that comes from manifold trials. Grieving (*lupéō*) is an important human emotion. God created us with the capacity to grieve.
Jesus demonstrated the depths of human grief when he stood before
the tomb of his dear friend Lazarus who had been dead for three
days. Jesus wept (John 11:35).

It is right for us to grieve when pain and death and suffering come
into our lives. Our Lord has promised to be our comforter and encour-
ager. The period of grieving is a time for the healing of our inner
being. Trials, temptations, and suffering bring grief to our lives. Our
Lord identifies with the feelings of our infirmities. He has been
tempted in every way in which we are tempted (Heb. 4:14–16).

The word translated as "temptation" in verse 6, is the Greek word
peirasmós, which is better translated as "trials" within this context.
Peter is speaking about that undeserved, unexplainable trial which
comes from without as opposed to the temptation to do evil which
comes from within our spiritual being.

This is the same form of trial that James writes about when he
states that the testing of our faith produces patience. (See the commentary on James 1:2–4, "How to Profit from Trials," on p. 20).

These trials are manifold or various. They come in a variety of
forms. The word for "manifold" is *poikilos*, which also means "many-
colored." We, too, face the trials of life in many forms and many

117

colors. With these trials comes a very legitimate expression of grief. To deny that grief is only to exaggerate the pain of the trials.

2. *The purpose of trials* (v. 7). But in the midst of that grief, God is graciously assuring us that there is a positive purpose in our suffering. God is not the cause of suffering and pain, but He does not allow it to be wasted. He uses every trial for our good if we commit ourselves to Him (Rom. 8:28).

Peter exposes at least two specific benefits we can experience from every trial. Of course, these benefits are only for those who are enjoying the fringe benefits of the new birth by walking in a personal relationship with Jesus Christ as Lord.

First, we suffer trials so that our faith may be proved genuine (v. 7). The key word here is "faith." Trials can and often do destroy the lives of those who have no faith in Christ. But for those who are trusting in Christ with vital faith, the trials of life will actually strengthen us.

Peter uses the analogy of gold which is tested or refined with fire. That process removes all of the impurities and makes the gold more pure and precious. That is how God uses trials in our lives. He allows the trials to come so that the impurities of sin may be removed from us and so that our faith may become more precious. We grow to be more and more dependent upon our Lord, and less dependent upon ourselves. We become more and more like Jesus Christ, our Lord.

Peter tells us a second benefit of trials is that we may be found to praise, honor, and glory at the revelation of Jesus Christ (v. 7). Peter always puts our lives into perspective. The suffering of life is only temporary. It is an inconvenience that we must endure for the present. And God, in His grace, will use even that for our good.

But our focus should not be upon our suffering, trials, and temptations. We should be looking forward to the ultimate revelation of Jesus Christ. The genuineness of our faith will bring praise, honor, and glory to Christ when He comes again to reign as King of kings and Lord of lords.

Whenever I hear that kind of talk, I think about the slaves who suffered so much in the early history of the United States. Many of the Negro spirituals which we have come to admire and enjoy came out of the hearts and lives of those who were suffering. But those Christian slaves lived with great hope for the future. They looked forward to "crossing the Jordan." They were suffering in the present, but they looked forward to the joy of the future when they would be with Christ.

3. *The joy of trials* (v. 8). Peter now focuses upon the marvelous subject of joy. In the midst of trials, we can experience authentic joy. The joy of the Lord does not come from the externals of life. It can be experienced only as we walk in the Spirit and receive joy as one of the fruit of the Spirit (Gal. 5:22–23).

The possession of joy is always dependent upon living in a vital relationship to Christ. Where the Lord is, there is authentic joy. Peter speaks of Jesus when he states that "although we have not seen Him, we love Him; and although we do not see Him now, we believe in Him; and as we believe we do rejoice with joy unspeakable and full of glory" (v. 8).

This joy is more than transitory; it is unspeakable and full of glory. It is an inexpressible and glorious joy. If you have experienced that quality of joy in your own life, you know how it can come in the midst of trial and pain. The joy of the Lord can shine through the tears that come into our lives.

I have a pastor friend who has just returned from Uganda. He spent significant time with Christian brothers and sisters who have suffered so much in the past few years. Most of them have lost several loved ones who have been murdered or killed in various uprisings. Many Christians have been martyred for their faith. Most of the believers have lost everything they owned. They are struggling for food and survival.

In the midst of all of these trials and hardships, they are joyful people. In fact, my friend shared that he had never been among such genuinely joyful people in all of his life. He serves a church which is comprised of members who are very affluent and who possess nearly everything that money can buy. Yet his people do not display the joy which he observed in the lives of the suffering Christians of Uganda.

What a lesson for us to learn! Joy does not come from the abundance of things we have. Joy comes from the indwelling of the Holy Spirit in our hearts and lives. The joy of the Lord can be ours only when Jesus is Lord and we are possessed by the Holy Spirit. Authentic joy cannot be contrived or fabricated. It must come from the heart.

The end of it all is the end of our faith—the salvation of our souls (v. 9). Once again Peter brings us back to the basics of salvation. He presents the perspective of the "eternal" rather than the temporary.

The gold in which so many people trust is temporary; it will perish (v. 7). But the salvation of the Lord is eternal. No wonder we can have joy unspeakable and full of glory even in the midst of temporary trials and pain. We are assured of victory through our Lord Jesus Christ! We are able to bring praise, honor, and glory at the revelation of Jesus Christ!

This end or goal of our faith is not the conclusion. The *"end"* (*télos*) is the actual consummation of our faith. Its final end will be the salvation of our souls.

THE PRIORITY OF SALVATION

10 Of this salvation the prophets have inquired and searched diligently, who prophesied of the grace that would come to you,

11 searching what, or what manner of time, the Spirit of Christ who was in them was indicating when He testified beforehand the sufferings of Christ and the glories that would follow.

12 To them it was revealed that not to themselves, but to us, they were ministering the things which now have been reported to you through those who have preached the gospel to you by the Holy Spirit sent down from heaven—things which angels desire to look into.

1 Peter 1:10–12

Salvation is the major theme of this letter. Peter never allows us to lose sight of the priority of salvation through faith in Jesus Christ. It was this basic message that Peter proclaimed to the Sanhedrin when he and John were arrested for preaching the resurrection of Jesus Christ.

Peter declared, "Nor is there salvation in any other, for there is no other name under heaven given among men by which we must be saved" (Acts 4:12). It is of this salvation that Peter now writes. He shares two important truths concerning this salvation.

1. *This salvation was spoken by the prophets* (vv. 10–12a). Long before the birth of Jesus, the prophets were inquiring about this salvation and were searching for it (vv. 10–11). The Holy Spirit had revealed

to them the coming of this salvation. They longed for it to take place in their lifetimes.

And yet, it was revealed to them that they were not serving themselves but rather us who were to be born in later generations (v. 12). They testified long before Christ's birth and His sufferings concerning the glories that were to follow His death and resurrection (v. 12).

For example, Isaiah prophesied concerning the suffering of Jesus when he wrote, "He is despised and rejected by men, a man of sorrows and acquainted with grief. And we hid, as it were, our faces from Him; He was despised, and we did not esteem Him. Surely He has borne our griefs and carried our sorrows; yet we did esteem Him stricken, smitten by God, and afflicted. But He was wounded for our transgressions, He was bruised for our iniquities; the chastisement for our peace was upon Him, and by His stripes we are healed" (Isa. 53:3–5).

In contrast, the psalmist writes about the glory that was to be revealed in Jesus Christ. "Therefore my heart is glad, and my glory rejoices; my flesh also will rest in hope. For You will not leave my soul in Sheol, nor will You allow Your Holy One to see corruption. You will show me the path of life; in Your presence is fullness of joy; at Your right hand are pleasures forevermore" (Ps. 16:9–11).

The prophets were called not only to minister to their contemporaries, but they came to understand that they were sharing prophecies which would be a source of instruction and blessing to those of future generations. This salvation has come not merely from the mind of man, but from the Lord Himself.

2. *This salvation is a heavenly message* (v. 12). This message has come by the Holy Spirit sent from heaven. It is a message which is eternal. It has been good news to every past generation which has received it, and it shall continue to be good news to every future generation which shall receive it until the coming again of our Lord Jesus Christ.

It is difficult for our minds to conceive just how unusual it is for a message to have eternal qualities—for it to be good news for every generation. Let me attempt to illustrate this fact by asking you to review the front page of your morning newspaper. Your first challenge will be to find any good news.

However, the major challenge will be to recognize the temporariness of the relevancy and urgency of this morning's headlines. By tomorrow, new developments will replace those things which seem so urgent today. Within a week, most of the news will be out of date. And if you save that newspaper for several years, it will have historical value and your grandchildren will enjoy reading about the good old days, but it will have little contemporary news value.

But the message of salvation is always relevant and urgent. It is appropriate for every generation, every culture, every person. It is a heavenly message brought by the Holy Spirit and will never become outdated.

In fact, it is such a marvelous message that even the angels of heaven desire to look into it. Can you imagine that? The angels in heaven are in the presence of the glory and majesty of God. Yet they long to look into this message of salvation. The verbal form translated as "look into" is a marvelous word in the Greek. It is *parakúpto,* and it means to "stoop down to take a peek." Isn't that wonderful? The angels of heaven want to take a peek at this wonderful salvation which has been declared by the prophets, revealed by the Holy Spirit, and is available for all who will receive it by faith in Jesus Christ as Savior and Lord!

The writer of Hebrews summarizes the situation well when he poses the question, "How shall we escape if we neglect so great a salvation?" (Heb. 2:3). For all who receive this great salvation it is blessed; it brings joy unspeakable and full of glory; and it promises life eternal.

CALLED TO BE HOLY

13 Therefore gird up the loins of your mind, be sober, and hope to the end for the grace that is to be brought to you at the revelation of Jesus Christ;

14 as obedient children, not conforming yourselves to the former lusts, as in your ignorance;

15 but as He who has called you is holy, you also be holy in all your conduct,

16 because it is written, *"Be holy, for I am holy."*

1 Peter 1:13–16

Holiness is a subject often avoided by even Christian people. For some reason, it is very uncomfortable for us to talk about being holy. We seem to have little trouble in ascribing holiness to God as we sing, "Holy, Holy, Holy, Lord God Almighty" as one of our hymns of worship.

And yet when we make the transition to speak about the holiness of our lives, we often visualize the caricature of what none of us wants to be—a person who is "holier-than-thou!" Jesus refuted that kind of lifestyle as it was demonstrated by the scribes and the Pharisees.

Instead, God calls us to the life of authentic holiness. Charles Haddon Spurgeon said that "holiness is the architectural plan upon which God buildeth up His living temple." That is a graphic summation of the teaching of Peter on this important subject of holiness.

There is a great need within our society for men and women, young people and children to live holy lives. Peter reveals three steps which we should follow if we are to live the life of holiness.

1. *Be prepared* (v. 13). Holiness begins with proper preparation of our minds. Peter uses the Middle Eastern phrase, "Gird up the loins of your mind." This refers to the custom of men who were wearing long, flowing robes. When they were preparing to run or to do physical work, they usually lifted their robes and secured them with a belt or girdle around their waist. This allowed them freedom of movement.

In the same way, we are to "gird up the loins of our minds" or to use a contemporary expression, we are to "roll up the sleeves" of our minds. In other words, we are to take the initiative in preparing our minds for the life of holiness.

Behavioral scientists have discovered that human behavior is determined to a great extent by the subconscious mind. The computer vocabulary graphically describes the potential of human behavior, "Garbage in; garbage out." In the same way, holy living begins with our minds. Our minds must be holy if our behavior is to be holy.

"For as he thinks in his heart, so is he" is the proposition of Proverbs 23:7. The Apostle Paul warns us not to be conformed to this world, "but be transformed by the renewing of your mind, that you may prove what is that good and acceptable and perfect will of God" (Rom. 12:2). And he instructs us to think on the things which are true and noble, just and pure, lovely and of good report (Phil. 4:8).

Authentic holiness begins with the proper preparation of our minds. In addition, we should be sober (v. 13). The word translated as "sober" is often rendered as "self-controlled" or "steady." It is the word *nēphō* which denotes abstinence from wine or strong drink. Our minds need to be under the control of the Holy Spirit and not under intoxication of any kind. We are truly self-controlled only when we are God-controlled.

Peter then talks about hope. A part of the preparation for holy living is to live the life of hope. So many Christians fail at this point. Many of us tend to be negative and pessimistic and judgmental and even fatalistic.

It should not be so! We should be enjoying the life of hope. The word *hope* is a uniquely Christian word. It had little meaning except for wishful thinking until the resurrection of Jesus Christ. Through faith in Him, we have a living hope. Victory is assured!

That is the focus of the teaching of Peter in this passage. He tells us to base our hope on the grace "that is to be brought to you at the revelation of Jesus Christ" (v. 13). What a promise! There is a day that Jesus Christ shall be revealed in His fullness and power, and He shall reign as King of kings and Lord of lords! We should live every day with that marvelous hope.

Remember that Peter is writing to suffering people. He is asking them to be filled with hope in spite of their external circumstances. Joseph Addison summed it up well when he wrote, "A religious hope does not only bear up the mind under her sufferings, but makes her rejoice in them." And a fellow Christian adds the following words of hope, "Life with Christ is an endless hope, without Him a hopeless end."

2. *Be obedient* (v. 14). The life of holiness is predicated on a lifestyle of active obedience. Peter instructs us to be as obedient children. This concurs with the warning of Paul that we should not be children of disobedience (Eph. 2:2).

Obedience is at the very foundation of Christian lifestyle. If we are to be disciples of Jesus, we must deny ourselves, take up our cross and follow Him (Mark 8:34). Jesus said that the person who authentically loves Him is the one who obeys Him (John 14:21).

Peter warns us not to conform to our former desires as we once did when we lived in ignorance of sin. The word "conform" (*suschēmatizomai*) denotes a fashioning that is superficial and transient. It is to be compared to the fashions in both men and women's clothing that are constantly changing from one season to another.

Jesus Christ is the rock of our salvation who is the same yesterday, today, and forever (Heb. 13:8). When we obey Him, we will not be conforming to our former lusts. These "natural appetites" are always before us. They promise us fulfillment and purpose but ultimately bring us only disillusionment and death.

These lusts are of the flesh and are opposed to the life of the Spirit (Gal. 5:17). They are of the worldly system which is diametrically opposed to God's design for us and for all of creation (1 John 2:15–17). To disobey the Lord and to follow our former lusts is to return to our place of spiritual ignorance or spiritual blindness.

3. *Be holy* (vv. 15–16). There is only One who is fully holy. "Holy, holy, holy is the Lord of hosts; the whole earth is full of His glory" (Isa. 6:3). God is holy. He, says Peter, is the One who has called us. He is the true source of holiness. If we are to be holy, we must recognize the source of holiness. We must know Him, love Him, and obey Him. We must walk in fellowship with Him. As Samuel Lucas wrote, "The essence of true holiness consists in conformity to the nature and will of God."

But what does it mean to be holy? How could we recognize holiness in a life if we saw it? How can we understand holiness in the character of God so that we can appropriate His holiness in our own lives?

In the Old Testament, God declares, "For I the Lord your God am holy." In verse 16 of this first chapter of 1 Peter, we find this direct quotation from Leviticus 19:2 in which the Lord not only declares that He is holy, but He instructs the Children of Israel to be holy as He is holy. Peter emphasizes that same instruction for the Christian believer. We are to be holy.

The Hebrew word used in the Leviticus 19:2 passage is *gadosh,* which denotes apartness, holiness, sacredness, or hallowedness. To be holy is to be separated from sin, pure, or hallowed. The Greek word which Peter uses, *hágios,* also means to be without sin, blameless, or separated from uncleanness.

No wonder we are intimidated by the command of our Lord to be holy. There is only one who is truly holy—God Himself. If we were to be holy, we would have to be like God.

That is exactly what Peter is teaching. We are to be holy in all that we do. We are to become more and more like our Lord, and we are to live as He lives. His holiness should increasingly replace our natural character of lust and evil appetites. A spiritual transformation needs to take place which displaces our character of sin by His character of holiness. He longs to donate a new heart to us just as certainly as a physical heart may be donated in transplant surgery.

And when our lives communicate the holiness of God, we will

not need to declare it to anyone. D. L. Moody spoke well to the point when he said, "It is a great deal better to live a holy life than to talk about it. Lighthouses do not ring bells and fire cannons to call attention to their shining—they just shine."

Blaise Pascal wrote, "The serene, silent beauty of a holy life is the most powerful influence in the world, next to the might of the Spirit of God." Holiness is not meant to be merely a matter of our theology nor simply words on the page of our hymnals. The holiness of God is meant to be lived out in our daily lives.

As we are controlled increasingly by the Holy Spirit, the holiness of His presence and power will shine from our lives. If we try to live holy lives, we shall always fail. If we follow Jesus Christ as the Lord of our lives and allow the Holy Spirit to live in and through us, we shall be channels for the holiness of God. "Let your light so shine before men, that they may see your good works and glorify your Father in heaven" (Matt. 5:16).

LIVING LIKE STRANGERS HERE ON EARTH

> 17 And if you call on the Father, who without partiality judges according to each one's work, conduct yourselves throughout the time of your sojourning here in fear;
> 18 inasmuch as you know that you were not redeemed with corruptible things, like silver or gold, from your futile conduct received by tradition from your fathers,
> 19 but with the precious blood of Christ, as of a lamb without blemish and without spot.
> 20 He indeed was foreordained before the foundation of the world, but was manifest in these last times for you
> 21 who through Him believe in God, who raised Him from the dead and gave Him glory, so that your faith and hope are in God.
>
> *1 Peter 1:17–21*

The Apostle Paul instructs us to "work out your own salvation with fear and trembling" (Phil. 2:12). He then goes on to encourage us regarding the power and strength which the Lord provides, "for it is God who works in you both to will and to do for His good pleasure" (Phil. 2:13).

There is a great deal of difference between attempting to live for God, and allowing Him to live in and through us. Both Peter and Paul acknowledge the impossibility of the former and the absolute necessity of the latter. Peter not only calls us to the living out of our salvation, he offers us practical help in how we can do it.

1. *Live as strangers on the earth* (v. 17). Peter reminds us that we should live as those sojourning here or as strangers. The word for sojourning is *paroikía* which is translated as "stranger" in Acts 13:17. As Christians, our major citizenship is not of the United States of America nor any other nation of the world.

Our highest calling is to give our primary allegiance to the King of kings and to His kingdom. As Peter declares in chapter 1, verse 1, (see commentary on p. 111) we are merely pilgrims or strangers here on earth. This is our temporary dwelling place. But we have a citizenship in the Kingdom of God which is eternal.

As Peter speaks about this exciting concept, he reminds us of who God is and who we are. We should remember who it is that we call upon as Father. He is the One who judges, without partiality, each one's work. Three times in this epistle, Peter reminds us of God's role as judge. Within this context, he informs us that God judges without partiality (v. 17).

In discussing the trial and crucifixion of Jesus, Peter declares that Jesus "committed Himself to Him who judges righteously" (1 Pet. 2:23). Then, as a warning to those who would live for their natural desires, Peter teaches, "They will give an account to Him who is ready to judge the living and the dead" (1 Pet. 4:5).

With this in mind, we should conduct ourselves in reverent fear (v. 17). The word for fear is *phóbos* from which we get our English word "phobia." However, the kind of fear which Peter suggests is not caused by emotional illness. It is a healthy kind of fear.

This is the kind of fear described by Luke in Acts 2:43. "Then fear came upon every soul, and many wonders and signs were done through the apostles." Perhaps a better English translation for this word would be "awe." We should be in awe or reverent fear in the way we live in the presence of God. We need to live in constant recognition of who God is and who we are.

2. *Live as redeemed* (vv. 18–20). We need to live not only as strangers, but as those who have been redeemed by Jesus Christ. Peter makes

three significant statements about living this life as those who have been redeemed.

First, he says that we have not been redeemed by the futile conduct received by the tradition from our fathers (v. 18). The word translated as *"futile"* is the Greek word *mátaios,* which means "vain" or "empty." It is the word which Paul uses to describe the wisdom of this world as opposed to godly wisdom (1 Cor. 3:20).

One generation can only pass down the temporary things of life from one generation to another. We come into this world with nothing, and we leave this world with nothing. Peter suggests that even gold and silver are ultimately perishable. At best, these things are ultimately vain. They provide a false sense of security. These things motivated Solomon, one of the richest men who ever lived, to write, "Vanity of vanities . . . All is vanity" (Eccles. 12:8).

I have conducted funerals for both the rich and the poor, and they are basically the same. Whether a casket is made of wood or gold makes little difference to the one who is dead. All we have gained in life is lost except for eternal salvation for those who have trusted in the living Christ. We have been redeemed from the futile conduct which focuses merely on this life.

Second, Peter points out that we have not been redeemed with corruptible things, like silver or gold (v. 18). Peter uses an example of what is corruptible and what is imperishable, in an exaggerated sense. We think of gold and silver as being examples of the more permanent things of our world. For example, gold and silver coins can be passed down for generations.

In comparison to eternity, Peter correctly states that they are corruptible; they are temporary at best. Our salvation has not been bought with the corruptible or the temporary which ultimately perishes. Our salvation has been bought with the eternal and with that which is so precious that all of the gold and silver in the world could not purchase it—the death and resurrection of Jesus Christ.

But we have been redeemed with the precious blood of Christ (v. 19)! This blood was given by the Lamb of God who was without blemish and without spot. He is the fulfillment of the Passover lamb which was to be without spot or blemish, the very best of the flock. The Passover lamb was sacrificed and its blood was placed over the doorposts of the people of Israel to protect the life of the firstborn son and all who dwelled within the house (Exod. 12).

John the Baptist came introducing Jesus in the following manner,

"Behold! The Lamb of God who takes away the sin of the world" (John 1:29). Indeed, we have been redeemed by the very blood of the Lamb of God—Jesus Christ our Savior and Lord.

Peter continues by stating that Jesus was foreordained to be our redeemer before the foundation of the world (v. 20). In other words, Jesus did not shed his blood on the cross by accident nor by a terrible mistake wrought by hateful, sinful persons. His death and the shedding of His blood was the plan of God from the beginning of the world.

"God so loved the world that He gave His only begotten Son, that whoever believes in Him should not perish but have everlasting life" (John 3:16). Paul confirms this marvelous truth concerning our redemption by declaring that "He chose us in Him before the foundation of the world, that we should be holy and without blame before Him in love" (Eph. 1:4).

Although Jesus was chosen before the foundations of the world to be our redeemer, He has been revealed, or manifested, as the Savior only in these last times (v. 20). The prophets searched for this Redeemer, but within God's perfect plan, He was revealed centuries later in Jesus Christ (see commentary on 1 Pet. 1:10–12, p. 120).

He was not manifested or revealed within a vacuum. Peter contends that He was manifested for us who would believe in God through Him. This Redeemer is the source of our salvation.

3. *Live with faith and hope* (v. 21). Because we have been redeemed by the precious blood of Jesus Christ, we are to live with our faith and hope in God. Through Him we have come to believe in God. The Gospel message of John 3:16 has been fulfilled in our lives as we have believed in Jesus.

This God is the One who raised Jesus Christ from the dead. The teaching of the resurrection of Christ is central in the proclamation of Peter. It was preeminent in his first sermon at Pentecost after being filled with the Holy Spirit (Acts 2:31). It is the focus of his first teaching in this letter (1 Peter 1:3).

Peter understood the significance of the resurrection of Jesus Christ not only in theological concepts but through his personal experience. He knew the agony, the sorrow, and the disillusionment that he experienced after he had denied his Lord. What darkness and despair!

Peter also knew the joy of the resurrection. It was he who ran with John to the tomb where Jesus had been laid—it was empty! (John 20). He saw the resurrected Christ and he visited with Him.

His broken relationship was healed, and once again he walked with Jesus (John 20–21).

But he knew even more about the resurrection of Christ than that. The deepest understanding took place on the Day of Pentecost when he was filled with the Holy Spirit even as Jesus had promised. The resurrection power of Jesus Christ flooded into his life. He was able to minister in the power of the resurrected Christ. Indeed, Jesus Christ had been resurrected in his life, and he was now ministering in Christ's power. Jesus had told him that this would happen—and now it had (John 14:15–18; 16:5–15).

The God who raised Jesus Christ from the dead is the same God in whom we believe. His power is available to us day by day as we trust in Christ Jesus and as we allow the Holy Spirit to live in us and through us.

And God has given glory to Christ. The word *"glory"* in the Greek is *dóxa,* which can also be translated as "honor," "praise," or "worship." Frankly, that is how we are to live—to honor, praise, worship, and glorify Christ. Paul stated, "Whether you eat or drink, or whatever you do, do all to the glory of God" (1 Cor. 10:31).

Peter uses the word *dóxa* some eleven times in this epistle in encouraging us to recognize the glory of Christ and to seek to glorify Him in all we do. He presents the same teaching as John who declared, "We beheld His glory, the glory of the only begotten of the Father, full of grace and truth" (John 1:14).

With all of this wonderful resurrection power and glory of Christ, we should be those who live with our faith and hope in God (v. 21). As we know, faith is a very key word in Christian lifestyle. Without faith, it is impossible to please God (Heb. 11:6). "The just shall live by faith" is a command repeated four times in Scripture.

We come to Christ in faith, we are saved by faith (Eph. 2:8–9), and now we must live by faith. As we have seen in our study of James, faith is active obedience to Jesus Christ as Lord (see commentary on "How to Make Faith Work," p. 60). This faith is a gift from God.

But we are not only to live by faith, we are to live the life of hope. As we have seen, "hope" is one of the key words in the theology and teaching of James. Authentic hope came to mankind through the resurrection of Jesus Christ. Now we can live with hope within a world that is overcome with despair.

LOVING FROM THE HEART

22 Seeing you have purified your souls in obeying
the truth through the Spirit in unfeigned love of the
brethren, love one another fervently with a pure heart,

23 having been born again, not of corruptible seed
but incorruptible, through the word of God which lives
and abides forever,

24 because
"*All flesh is as grass,*
And all the glory of man as the flower of the
grass.
The grass withers,
And its flower falls away,
25 *But the word of the* Lord *endures forever.*"
Now this is the word which by the gospel was preached
to you.

1 Peter 1:22–25

Love is at the very center of Christian lifestyle. In fact, love is
the very character, the very essence of God (1 John 4:8). And Jesus
contended that it would be by this love that everyone would recognize
His disciples (John 13:35). Within this passage, Peter teaches us that
we should love in three specific ways.

1. *Love sincerely* (v. 22). To love sincerely is *anupókritos*, which means
"genuine" or "without hypocrisy." It is unfeigned love which is without pretense or without acting a part. To love sincerely is to love
authentically—like God Himself.

Jesus was the personification of love. He loved everyone whom
He met. He reached out to the sick, the blind, the crippled, the lonely,
the widows, the poor, the dishonest tax collector, the Roman officer,
the children—everyone whom He encountered, He loved!

His love was authentic. He disliked hypocrisy greatly, and He spoke
against hypocrisy directly. For example, in His Sermon on the Mount,
Jesus warned against sounding a trumpet before doing a charitable
deed as the hypocrites did in the synagogues and in the streets, that
they may have glory from men (Matt. 6:2). Or "when you pray,
you shall not be like the hypocrites. For they love to . . . be seen
by men" (Matt. 6:5). "Moreover, when you fast, do not be like the
hypocrites, with a sad countenance" (Matt. 6:16).

In order to have a sincere or unfeigned love, Peter points out two prerequisites. First, we must have "purified our souls" (v. 22). Under Levitical law, the act of purification required the slaying of a sacrificial animal and the sprinkling or pouring of the blood upon that which was to be cleansed including the altar (Lev. 8:15), all that was holy (1 Chron. 23:28), the priests and Levites, the rebuilt gates and walls, and even the people of God themselves (Neh. 12:30).

Peter is obviously referring us to the cleansing that we can experience through the precious blood of the Lamb without blemish and without spot who was foreordained before the foundation of the world (1 Pet. 19–20). That lamb is Jesus Christ.

If we are to love sincerely, we must be cleansed from our sins by Jesus Christ. We must be dead to self and alive to God. We must receive this unconditional love from Him in order to express it to others. He is the source of love and forgiveness and all that is good.

Second, we must be those who obey the truth through the Spirit (v. 22). Jesus Christ is the source of all truth. He is "the way, the truth, and the life" (John 14:6). And truth, love, and obedience all go together. Jesus said that those who authentically love Him are those who obey Him (John 14:15, 21, 23).

John reiterates that same truth in all three of his epistles. He summarizes the important teaching on the subject when he writes, "this is love, that we walk according to His commandments. This is the commandment, that as you have heard from the beginning, you should walk in it" (2 John 1:6).

2. *Love fervently* (v. 22). Peter teaches us that we should not only love one another sincerely or unfeigningly, but we should also love fervently. This word *"fervently"* (*ektenōs*) means to love deeply or intensely. To love fervently is to love with all of your strength.

This reminds us of the teaching of Jesus when He said, "And you shall love the Lord your God with all your heart, with all your soul, with all your mind, and with all your strength" (Mark 12:30). That is how we should first love God, and then love one another.

3. *Love with a pure heart* (v. 22). Men speak romantically about loving from the heart, but God speaks realistically about loving from a pure heart. The Proverb asks the question, "Who can say, 'I have made my heart clean, I am pure from sin'?" (Prov. 20:9). The answer is that no one can cleanse or purify himself or herself from sin. As Peter has just reminded us, only Christ can do that (vv. 19–20).

Just as our love must come from God, so must a pure heart come from God. This is what Paul writes to young Timothy, "Flee also youthful lusts; but pursue righteousness, faith, love, peace with those who call on the Lord out of a pure heart" (2 Tim. 2:22).

Peter proceeds to inform us that the quality of loving God sincerely, fervently, and with a pure heart flows from that marvelous and necessary experience of "having been born again, not of corruptible seed but incorruptible, through the Word of God which lives and abides forever" (v. 23). Earlier in chapter 1, he writes about our inheritance which is incorruptible and undefiled (see commentary, p. 115). And all of that is based upon the resurrection of Jesus Christ (vv. 3–4).

To illustrate his point, Peter quotes Isaiah 40:6–8 saying that "all flesh is as grass . . . the grass withers, and its flower falls away" (v. 24). In contrast, "the word of the Lord endures forever" (v. 24), or as Peter states it, ". . . *the word of God which lives and abides forever*" (v. 23). And this, says Peter, *"is the word which by the gospel was preached to you"* (v. 25).

The Word of God will endure forever, and so will love. We should not be surprised. For if God is love, and if God is eternal, so must love be eternal. Love never comes to an end (1 Cor. 13:8). Love goes on forever (1 Cor. 13:13).

NOTE

1. Copyright 1945, Norman J. Clayton. © Renewed 1973 Norman Clayton Publishing Company (a division of Word, Inc.). All rights reserved. International copyright secured.

CHAPTER TWO

What Christian Living Is All About

1 Peter 2:1–25

Christianity is not only to be believed; it must also be lived. Life begins with birth, and in the first chapter of this epistle, Peter has reminded us of the reality of the new birth—of being born again not of corruptible or temporary seed, but of incorruptible or eternal seed. God invites us to be born anew of the Spirit so that we might have life eternal (John 3:1–17).

Birth must be followed by nurture. And just as a natural baby requires milk in order to be nourished and to grow, so must a spiritual baby have the milk of God's Word in order to be nourished and to grow up in Christ. That is a contention which Peter makes so directly and plainly that none of us can miss it!

GROWING GOES BETTER WITH MILK

1 Therefore, laying aside all malice, all guile, hypocrisy, envy, and all evil speaking,

2 as newborn babes, desire the pure milk of the word, that you may grow thereby,

3 if indeed you have tasted that the Lord is gracious.

1 Peter 2:1–3

Mark Twain is quoted as saying, "Most people are bothered by those passages in the Bible which they cannot understand; but as for me, I always notice that the passages in the Scripture which trouble me the most are those which I do understand." His statement is a commentary of this passage. The question is, what are we going to do about it? Peter invites us to take three specific steps.

1. *Lay aside all evil* (v. 1). James shares the same counsel as Peter when he writes, "Therefore lay aside all filthiness and overflow of wickedness" (James 1:21). True repentance must always begin with putting off evil and turning from it. The verb used by both Peter and James is *apotíthēmi* which means "to get rid of" or "to cast it off."

That is the way we should always approach evil. The writer of Hebrews encourages us to "lay aside every weight, and the sin which so easily ensnares us, and let us run with endurance the race that is set before us" (Heb. 12:1). In order to repent, we must turn from every form of sin.

Do you realize how many of our problems would be resolved if we took that counsel seriously? If we would only flee from sin, our lives would be so much more full and blessed. Sin deprives us of God's best, and yet often we play games with sin. We try to get as close as possible without being burned. But sin is never without consequence. What we sow, we reap. "For he who sows to his flesh will of the flesh reap corruption" (Gal. 6:8).

The kinds of sin which we should lay aside or cast off include *"malice"* (*kakía*) which denotes depravity and wickedness, *"all guile"* (*dólos*) which means "deceit," and *"hypocrisy"* (*hupókrisis*) which depicts play acting. We should also lay aside *"envy"* (*phthónos*) which is "jealousy" or "ill will," and all *"evil speaking"* (*katalaliá*) which can be correctly translated much more strongly as "a defamation of character" or "slander of every kind."

All of these forms of sin deal with that which is untrue. Sin is always deceitful and untrue. God is the source of all truth and Satan is the source of untruth. From the time he tempted Adam and Eve in the Garden, Satan has shared lies, deception, and half-truths with mankind. If we are to enjoy the life of truth and love and fullness, we must cast off all the evil. The way that God liberates us from evil desire is to give us a vivid image of what Christ can do in our lives. The closer we come to Christ, the more He replaces our desires with His.

2. *"Desire the pure milk of the word"* (v. 2). To *"desire"* is *epipothéō* which means "to long for" or "to crave." As we turn away from evil, we must take the second step of repentance; we must turn to God. In

fact, we must not only turn to God, but we must do so with resolution and aggressiveness (Heb. 12:2).

The word *epipotheō* is used by the Apostle Paul in Romans 1:11 when he writes, "I long to see you" and when he writes to young Timothy, I am "greatly desiring to see you" (2 Tim. 1:4). There is the sense of deeply longing, even as a baby deeply longs or craves for milk.

That desire which God wants us to have should be for the pure milk of His Word. The word *"pure"* is *ádolos* which means "unadulterated," "undeceitful," or "sincere." In other words, the pure milk of God's Word is truth as opposed to the evil or non-truth which we are to put off. As newborn babes, we should have that craving desire for the pure milk of God's Word.

Paul refers to the Word of God as nourishing milk in his letter to the church at Corinth when he writes, "I fed you with milk and not with solid food; for until now you were not able to receive it" (1 Cor. 3:2). As babies need physical milk, so spiritual babies need spiritual milk so that they may grow up to maturity and begin to need and enjoy the nourishment of solid spiritual food.

3. *"That you may grow thereby"* (v. 2). God is concerned that we grow in the grace and knowledge of Jesus Christ—that we no longer be spiritual babes or children tossed about with every wind of doctrine. Instead, that we may grow up in all things into Him who is the head—Christ. And that we grow to become more and more like Him, measured by the stature of the fullness of Christ (Eph. 4:13–16).

That is what Peter is addressing. He wants us to "grow up" spiritually. The verb which Peter uses for grow is *auxánō* which he also uses in his second letter when he concludes, "But grow in the grace and knowledge of our Lord and Savior Jesus Christ" (2 Pet. 3:18). It is interesting to note that it was this verb which John the Baptist used when he said, "He must increase, but I must decrease" (John 3:30).

As Peter speaks about growing, he also speaks about tasting. Before one can crave or deeply desire spiritual milk, he or she must first taste and see that the Lord is gracious. Tasting precedes craving (v. 3).

Recently I was visiting with a missionary statesman who is a third generation missionary. He was born in the Orient and has spent most of his life in cultures where Christianity is very much a minority faith. During several decades of missionary service, he has discovered a marvelous and effective approach to those who are agnostic or opposed to Christ.

He simply encourages them to "taste" of the Word of God and what He has told them about Himself in Jesus Christ. His approach is very honest and logical. Before you reject Jesus Christ, you should at least explore His teachings and take a little taste of Him. Only then can you know whether He tastes good or bad. Only then can you authentically decide to follow Him or reject Him.

The results to this evangelistic approach have been most encouraging. In short, just as Peter is teaching, when we taste of the things of the Lord, we find that they are good and satisfying. Tasting leads to the deep desiring and craving for the pure milk of God's Word.

BUILDING WITH LIVING STONES

4 Coming to Him as to a living stone, rejected
indeed by men, but chosen by God and precious,
5 you also, as living stones, are being built up a
spiritual house, a holy priesthood, to offer up spiritual
sacrifices acceptable to God through Jesus Christ.
6 Therefore it is also contained in the Scripture,
"Behold, I lay in Zion
A chief cornerstone, elect, precious,
And he who believes on Him will by no means
be put to shame."
7 Therefore, to you who believe, He is precious;
but to those who are disobedient,
"The stone which the builders rejected
Has become the chief cornerstone,"
8 and
"A stone of stumbling
And a rock of offense."
They stumble, being disobedient to the word,
to which they also were appointed.

1 Peter 2:4–8

God has called us to the life of building, not destroying. After Peter has instructed us to rid ourselves of evil and to grow up in our salvation, he proceeds to tell us how to do that. After using the analogy of a baby who craves for milk, he now uses an analogy which is used frequently in the New Testament to illustrate the personal growth in one's spiritual life, or the building up of the Body of Christ—the church. It is the analogy of building a house.

As you will remember, Peter is writing primarily to Jewish Christians who have been dispersed throughout the world because of the persecution they have been suffering for their Christian faith. Therefore, Peter's analogy is more specific than merely building a house, it is the building of God's house—the temple. The original temple was built by King Solomon under the first covenant of God with His chosen people.

Under the New Covenant, the spiritual house or temple is being built by the Lord Himself. A spiritual temple requires a very specific kind of building material. It is to be built of living stones—the very lives of those who have become spiritually alive through faith in Jesus Christ. And such building must begin with Jesus Christ.

Jesus Christ—the Cornerstone (vv. 4–6). Peter begins his teaching on this important subject by referring to Jesus Christ as a *"living stone"* (v. 4). The word for living is *záō.* It is the same word used by Jesus when He told the Samaritan woman about living water (John 4:10) and when He told the Jews, "I am the living bread come down from heaven. If anyone eats of this bread, he will live forever" (John 6:51). Indeed, we need to come to Him, the living stone, that we might have life eternal.

In verse 6 Peter also contends that Jesus is the chief cornerstone as he quotes from Isaiah 28:16, *"Behold, I lay in Zion a chief cornerstone."* Paul agrees with Peter when he writes, "[You] having been built on the foundation of the apostles and prophets, Jesus Christ Himself being the chief cornerstone" (Eph. 2:20).

But many of us may ask, "What does that mean? What is a cornerstone?" Webster's dictionary will help us discover the basic answer by defining cornerstone in the following manner: "A stone which lies at the corner of two walls and serves to unite them; specifically, a stone built into a corner of the foundation of an important edifice as the actual or nominal starting point in the building."[1]

That is the role of Jesus in the Church. Paul states it in this way, "In whom (Christ) the whole building, being joined together, grows into a holy temple in the Lord, in whom you also are being built together for a habitation of God in the Spirit" (Eph. 2:21–22). Jesus is a lively stone and the chief cornerstone who seeks to be the master builder of our lives and who desires to build us together into a holy temple in the Lord—His Church.

Jesus Christ is also the elect (*eklektós*)—chosen by God (v. 4). Peter refers to the prophecy of Isaiah 28:16. Jesus Christ has not become the chief cornerstone by accident nor by His own initiative. He has been chosen by God.

This "chosen one" is also precious to God (vv. 4–6). To be *"precious"* (*éntimos*) is to be held in honor, to be prized. The word is used in the Gospel of Luke to describe the fact that a certain centurion's servant was "dear" or "precious" to him (Luke 7:2). Jesus is precious to God. He is His only begotten son (John 3:16).

The rejecters—who stumble (v. 7). Although chosen by God and precious to Him, Jesus Christ has been rejected by many. As Jesus said "that light has come into the world, and men loved darkness rather than light, because their deeds were evil" (John 3:19). Peter quotes from Psalm 118:22, *"The stone which the builders rejected has become the chief cornerstone"* (v. 7).

People not only reject Christ, but they stumble over Him. He is *"a stone of stumbling and a rock of offense"* (v. 8), states Peter, as he quotes from Isaiah 8:14. To every human being, Jesus will either be the chief cornerstone—the very Lord of his or her life—or He will be a stone of stumbling and a rock of offense. We cannot be neutral concerning Jesus. To ignore Him is to reject Him.

Have you ever noticed how our American society feels quite comfortable with us talking about God but becomes exceedingly uncomfortable at the mention of Jesus. Over the years, I have been invited to speak to many service clubs and civic organizations. Usually, my host has asked me not to mention the name of Jesus "because there are some here who would be offended." Indeed, the Light of the world has come into the darkness, and the darkness continues to resist.

That is the reason for the stumbling. Peter states, *"They stumble, being disobedient to the word"* (v. 8). When we disobey the Word of the Lord, when we reject Jesus Christ who is God's one gift of grace to save us from our sins and the darkness of sin, we will certainly stumble and fall.

Peter concludes by saying, "To which they also were appointed" (v. 8). Once again, we come to a passage in which it is difficult to distinguish between the sovereignty of God and man's free will. However, it is not difficult to understand that God has known from the beginning who would believe in Him and who would reject Him. Those who disobey God are destined to stumble and fall.

The accepters—who are living stones (vv. 5–6). However, Peter's instructions and encouragement are being directed primarily to the "accepters," not to the "rejecters." He writes, "You also, as living stones, are being built into a spiritual house." As we have seen, this "spiritual house" is the Church of Jesus Christ.

It is fitting for Peter to use the analogy of the living stones since Jesus had called him Cephas, which means "a stone" (John 1:42). And it was to Peter that Jesus said, "You are Peter, and on this rock I will build My church, and the gates of Hades shall not prevail against it" (Matt. 16:18). And Peter was the human instrument, the rock, that Jesus used to lay the foundation for His Church. Peter was filled with the Holy Spirit at Pentecost and preached in the streets of Jerusalem on the day of the birth of the church with some three thousand coming to faith in Christ on that very day (Acts 2:1–41).

Jesus Christ, "the living stone," invites us to become "living stones" so that He might use us to build His Church. We cannot live in spiritual isolation. We must be available to Him and to each other so that our Lord can use our lives to build the Kingdom of Christ.

Also, Peter states that we are being built into *"a holy priesthood"* (v. 5). Within the first covenant, the priesthood belonged to the sons of Aaron and the tribe of Levi. These priests had at least three distinctives. First, they had direct access to God. At appointed times they went into the Holy of Holies to communicate with God.

Second, the priests represented the people of Israel to God. And, third, they brought offerings to God for the people. It was an honor to be chosen as a priest within the first covenant.

Within the second covenant, states Peter, all believers are being built into a holy priesthood. The New Covenant provides for a priesthood of all believers. We no longer need others to represent us to God. We have direct access to Him through Jesus Christ (Heb. 10:1–25).

Thus, we are those who should be offering up spiritual sacrifices acceptable to God through Jesus Christ (v. 5). This should be a vital part of Christian lifestyle. The writer of Hebrews declares, "Therefore by Him let us continually offer the sacrifice of praise to God, that is, the fruit of our lips giving thanks to His name" (Heb. 13:15). It is always appropriate to praise God, and the sacrifice of praise is always acceptable to Him.

Peter summarizes this exciting teaching in verses 5–6: If we allow Christ to build us up into a spiritual house as living stones, and if we allow Him to build us into a holy priesthood, and if we continue to offer up spiritual sacrifices which are acceptable to God through Jesus Christ, and if we believe on Him, we will by no means be put to shame. Sin always brings ultimate shame, but the life of obedience will assure us that we will never stumble nor ever be put to shame. Instead, we are becoming a part of a spiritual temple which is eternal.

The Truth about Self-Image

9 But you are a chosen generation, a royal priesthood, a holy nation, His own special people, that you may proclaim the praises of Him who has called you out of darkness into His marvelous light;

10 who once were not a people but are now the people of God, who had not obtained mercy but now have obtained mercy.

1 Peter 2:9–10

No society in history has motivated its people to be more concerned about "self-image" than has contemporary American society. We have been led to believe that if our self-image is adequate, the remaining areas of our lives will become well-adjusted and successful.

This contention has resulted in a literal flood of books and magazine articles on the subject of self-image. One of the most popular teachings is called transactional psychology. Its major premise declares "I'm O.K. and you're O.K."

The Scripture also speaks to the challenge of self-image. It declares that our basic problem with a poor self-image is spiritual. Peter speaks very specifically about the need. Although he does not label it as "self-image," he teaches that the solution to enjoying an adequate self-image is in living a life that is authentic in order for the communication of self to be adequate.

As I mentioned previously, early in my ministry I had the privilege of ministering for several years with the Billy Graham Evangelistic Association. You can imagine that those were days of great growth and learning.

In a memorable meeting of the Billy Graham team, one of the team members shared a spiritual insight I have never forgotten. The topic of discussion was the "image" of Dr. Graham and his ministry. He summarized the subject by declaring, "Our need is not to create any kind of image for this ministry. It is our task to simply and honestly communicate the image God has created for Dr. Graham and his ministry!"

That is exactly what Peter is saying about self-image. We cannot create a self-image which does not authentically communicate what we really are or what our lifestyle actually is. We must communicate the real person and the actual lifestyle. If the self-image is to be good, the life and the lifestyle must be good. Anything less than that would be deception and hypocrisy. Peter reveals four specific characteristics of the Christian's life that should be lived and appreciated. In turn, they will make major positive contributions to our lifestyle.

1. *We are a chosen people* (v. 9). Within the Kingdom of our Lord, there is that wonderful mystery regarding whether we have chosen the Lord or He has chosen us. Anyone who has studied the subject carefully in the Scriptures realizes that both are true.

For example, in 1 Peter 1:2, Peter has reminded us that we are "elect according to the foreknowledge of God the Father." He proceeds to teach us to be holy in all our conduct, "as He who has called you is holy" (1:15). Indeed, God has called us and elected us to be His chosen people. We are members of His Body—the Church. He is the head, and we are the various parts of His Body.

Peter's primary audience was comprised of Jewish Christians who knew a great deal about the covenant which God made with the Children of Israel through Moses. "If you will indeed obey My voice and keep My covenant, then you shall be a special treasure to Me above all people: for all the earth is Mine" (Exod. 19:5).

Think of it. God has extended that covenant to all who will follow Jesus as Lord. We, through faith in Christ, are God's chosen people. As we sing in an old gospel hymn, "I'm a child of the King!" what that should do for our self-image!

2. *We are a "royal priesthood"* (v. 9). Whenever the church has been

spiritually alive and vital, there has been a rediscovery of one of the basic premises of the New Covenant—that is the priesthood of believers. Under the first covenant, there were the sons of Aaron and then the tribe of Levi to whom God entrusted the privilege of being His priests.

In the "new covenant" through Jesus Christ, He invites all of us to be members of His royal priesthood. All of us have been called to ministry (Eph. 4:11–13). All of us have both the joy and the responsibility of serving Christ and each other.

As we have seen earlier, within the first covenant the priests were given three major functions which have been passed on to all Christian believers. First, we have direct access to God through Jesus Christ. Jesus is our high priest, and we need none other (Heb. 4:14, 5:6). Second, God Himself in the person of the Holy Spirit makes intercession for us (Rom. 8:26). Third, the priest would bring offerings to God for the people. Now, we can bring those offerings directly to God.

The writer of Hebrews reminds us that the offerings which are most acceptable to God are those of praise and service. "Therefore by Him let us continually offer the sacrifice of praise to God, that is, the fruit of our lips, giving thanks to His name. But do not forget to do good and to share, for with such sacrifices God is well pleased" (Heb. 13:15–16).

3. *We are citizens of a "holy nation"* (v. 9). From the very beginning of his first epistle, Peter is reminding his readers that we are citizens of a holy nation. He refers to Christians as "pilgrims [strangers, aliens] scattered throughout the world" (1:1) (see commentary, p. 112). He also refers to believers as those who are "sojourning here" (1:17) (see commentary, p. 127).

To belong to Christ is to belong to His Kingdom. Most of you who are reading this commentary are citizens of one of the nations of the world such as the United States of America, Canada, or India. But Peter is writing about a spiritual citizenship that transcends all geographical borders or political differences. If we belong to Christ, we are citizens of His holy nation which is eternal. "Now, therefore, you are no longer strangers and foreigners, but fellow citizens with the saints and members of the household of God" (Eph. 2:19).

4. *We are "His own special people"* (vv. 9–10). Peter reminds us of the awesome and wonderful truth that once we were not a people,

but now we are the people of God (v. 10). This marvelous fact has not come to reality by mere chance; it has been the plan of God for ages.

Paul shares this fact in Romans 9:25 when he quotes from the prophet Hosea, "I will call them My people, who were not My people, and her beloved, who was not beloved" (Hos. 2:23). And, in the following verse, Romans 9:26, he quotes Isaiah, "And it shall come to pass in the place where it was said to them, 'You are not My people.' There they will be called sons of the living God" (Hos. 1:10).

Paul shares that same truth in 2 Corinthians 6:16–17 as he quotes from Leviticus 26:12, Jeremiah 32:38, and Ezekiel 37:27. In addition, the writer of Hebrews communicates about the wonderful fact that those who were not the people of God in the first covenant have become the people of God through the New Covenant (Heb. 8:7–13, Jer. 31:31–34).

In summary, we are a chosen generation, a royal priesthood, a holy nation, and God's own special people who were once not a people but are now the people of God. That description should enhance the self-image of all of God's people. The key to a good self-image is found in the image of what we are in Jesus Christ. It is His image that is available to us as we trust in Christ Jesus. As the Apostle Paul wrote, "I have been crucified with Christ; it is no longer I who live, but Christ lives in me" (Gal. 2:20).

As a result of becoming the people of God, we should be proclaiming or communicating the praises of God who has called us into His marvelous light (v. 9). And, we who had not obtained mercy, have now obtained mercy (v. 10). What marvelous contributions to a healthy and good self-image.

GOODNESS, FREEDOM, AND SERVANTHOOD

11 Beloved, I beg you as sojourners and pilgrims, abstain from fleshly lusts which war against the soul,

12 having your conduct honorable among the Gentiles, that when they speak against you as evildoers, they may, by your good works which they observe, glorify God in the day of visitation.

13 Therefore submit yourselves to every ordinance of man for the Lord's sake, whether to the king as supreme,

14 or to governors, as to those who are sent by him
for the punishment of evildoers and for the praise of
those who do good.

15 For so is the will of God that by doing good
you may put to silence the ignorance of foolish men—

16 as free, yet not using your liberty as a cloak for
vice, but as servants of God.

17 Honor all people. Love the brotherhood. Fear
God. Honor the king.

1 Peter 2:11–17

Once again, Peter refers to his readers as sojourners and pilgrims.
He uses those same terms in chapter 1, verses 1 and 17 (see commentary on pp. 112 and 127). His instructions and encouragement fall
into three specific areas of Christian lifestyle.

1. Live good lives (vv. 11–15). Peter shares three specific steps
which we should follow in living good lives before God, the world,
and one another.

"Abstain from fleshly lusts" (v. 11). Godly living always begins with
the forsaking of sin. The word "abstain" (*apéchomai*) is the same word
which Paul used when he wrote, "Abstain from every form of evil"
(1 Thess. 5:22). These fleshly lusts are literally at war with our souls
(*psuchē*)—the spiritual part of us. If we are to live good, godly lives,
we must forsake those fleshly lusts.

"[Have] your conduct honorable among the Gentiles" (v. 12). Peter returns
to one of the basic themes of this epistle—that of holy conduct.
He reminds us vividly that God is not merely concerned with our
profession; He is concerned with our possession—our lifestyle. He
desires that we live holy and honorable lives; that our *"conduct"*
(*anastrophē*) may be observed as good by outsiders (see commentary
on 1 Pet. 1:15, p. 125).

In fact, they should not only see our good works, our honorable
(honest) conduct should result in their glorifying God. As Jesus said,
"Let your light so shine before men, that they may see your good
works and glorify your Father in heaven" (Matt. 5:16).

"Put to silence the ignorance of foolish men" (v. 15). As Peter continues
on the theme of living good lives before others, he provides a list
of specific examples of how that kind of lifestyle should be carried
out in day-to-day living.

He begins by saying that we should submit ourselves to every ordinance of man for the Lord's sake (v. 13). This should be done in response to a leader of civil government when he is supreme, to governors, or to the representatives of the supreme ruler who are sent to punish evildoers and to praise those who do good.

Of course, Peter is writing within the context of the reign of Nero, the emperor of Rome. He is stating clearly that we should do all that we can to obey civil authorities. However, this does not mean that we violate the "higher laws" of God nor the lordship of Jesus Christ. It was Peter himself when standing on trial before the Sanhedrin who said, "We ought to obey God rather than men" (Acts 5:29).

When man's laws come into conflict with God's laws, we must always go with God. Lordship sometimes requires civil disobedience. He is our Lord and King. We are His servants. We are citizens of His kingdom.

2. *Live as free persons* (v. 16). Jesus Christ has invited us to enjoy the life of freedom. Only in Christ can we be truly free. When we know Him, we know truth personified and the truth will make us free (John 8:32). But, the freedom that comes from Jesus Christ is not to be used as *"a cloak for vice"* (v. 16)—an excuse for sin. As Paul wrote, "For you, brethren, have been called to liberty; only do not use liberty as an opportunity for the flesh" (Gal. 5:13). In fact, the freedom or liberty which comes from Christ cannot be used as an excuse for sin. As soon as we misuse it for those ends, we shall lose it and once again we are entangled with the slavery to sin. Authentic freedom is ours only when we walk in the Spirit; only when Jesus Christ is reigning as the Lord of our lives.

The highest calling of life is to use our liberty as servants of Jesus Christ (v. 16). The freedom and liberty which come from Him continue to flow as we serve Him and others—as we continue in the flow of the fellowship of the Holy Spirit. Liberty misused is like a mighty river flooding its banks and bringing terrible destruction upon all in its path. Liberty used as service is like a mighty river flowing within its banks bringing life and refreshment to all who drink of its waters.

Love is central to this kind of lifestyle. As Paul wrote, "Do not use liberty as an opportunity for the flesh, but through love serve one another. For all the law is fulfilled in one word, even in this: 'You shall love your neighbor as yourself' " (Gal. 5:13–14).

3. *Live as servants of God* (vv. 16–17). Peter continues his teaching on the important subject of being servants of God by listing several

specific examples of how we must do that. Again, he is writing within the context of acute suffering by Christian brothers and sisters at the hand of Rome and at the hand of the established religious rulers of Israel.

"Honor all people" (v. 17). The word honor (*timáō*) is the same word Jesus uses in telling us to honor our father and mother (Matt. 15:4), and that we should honor the Son even as we honor the Father (John 5:23). This is a mark of authentic Christian lifestyle—that we honor all people as our Lord does. We never violate others nor use them as objects. We are to love and honor them.

"Love the brotherhood" (v. 17). *Agapē* love must flow freely and generously from the lives of true Christians. It is another mark of authentic Christian lifestyle that we love one another. As Jesus said, "By this all will know that you are My disciples, if you have love for one another" (John 13:35).

"Fear God" (v. 17). To fear God (*phobéomai*) is "to revere or reverence Him"—"to be in awe in His presence." It means "to be put in fear or fright," "to be afraid." It is the word which describes the fear of the disciples when the storm arose, and they were alone in the boat (John 6:19).

To appropriately fear God is one of the greatest needs of the contemporary Church. We have made Him all too familiar. We have tended to create Him in our own image as "the man upstairs," "the good guy," or "the good Lord." We need to see the Lord high and lifted up in all of His glory and might, and then to bow in awe in His presence, to revere and worship Him.

"Honor the king" (v. 17). The same word is used here for honor (*timáō*) as is used earlier in verse 17 in encouraging us to honor all people. It is natural for us to honor a good king or a ruler whom we respect. However, Peter is asking his readers to honor no one less than Nero himself. That is another mark of authentic Christian lifestyle—to love and honor even the tyrants of our society, those who would abuse and persecute us (Matt. 5:44).

CALLED TO BE SERVANTS

18 Servants, be submissive to your masters with all fear, not only to the good and gentle, but also to the harsh.

19 For this is commendable, if because of conscience toward God one endures grief, suffering wrongfully.

20 For what credit is it if, when you are beaten for your faults, you take it patiently? But when you do good and suffer for it, if you take it patiently, this is commendable before God.

21 For to this you were called, because Christ also suffered for us, leaving us an example, that you should follow His steps:

22 *"Who committed no sin,*
   Nor was guile found in His mouth";

23 who, when He was reviled, did not revile in return; when He suffered, He did not threaten, but committed Himself to Him who judges righteously;

24 who Himself bore our sins in His own body on the tree, that we, having died to sins, might live for righteousness—by whose stripes you were healed.

25 For you were like sheep going astray, but have now returned to the Shepherd and Overseer of your souls.

1 Peter 2:18–25

Peter continues to address the vital subject of servanthood which is central to Christian lifestyle. Not long ago, I was leading a small group of professional people in a Bible study on the Book of James. Within that context, I shared a word study on the word "faith" which is so central to the message of James. I contended that an appropriate Biblical definition for faith is "active obedience," and shared that God has called us to be His obedient servants. The initial response of those in the group was surprise and resistance.

Like many of us, they had fallen into the self-centered lifestyle. They did not wish to be servants of anyone nor were they excited about the lifestyle of obedience. Instead they preferred for God to fall into the flow of their lives and to subscribe to their wishes.

Of course, they were challenging one of the basic requirements of being a true Christian. To follow Jesus Christ as Lord in obedience and to serve Him is not an option for authentic Christian lifestyle; it is imperative. And, as we serve Christ, we must also serve others. It is this teaching which Peter now expands.

"Servants, be submissive to your masters" (v. 18). The statement is clear. Christians are not free to merely do their own thing nor to simply

follow Christ without carrying on their responsibility to their masters. To submit (*hupotássō*) is to be subject. Christian servants are to be subject to their masters (v. 18); all Christians are to be subject to every ordinance of man for the Lord's sake (2:13). Christian wives are to be subject to their husbands (3:1); younger Christians are to be subject to their elders (5:5); and all Christians are to be subject to one another (5:5).

In verse 18 Peter implies that it is quite easy and natural for us to be submissive and obedient to employers who are good to us and gentle with us. In fact, it is a very real temptation to take advantage of such employers.

Paul's instructions to the Ephesian believers are appropriate for us as we consider this passage. "Servants, be obedient to those who are your masters according to the flesh, with fear and trembling, in sincerity of your heart, as to Christ; not with eyeservice, as menpleasers, but as servants of Christ, doing the will of God from the heart" (Eph. 6:5–6).

Paul continues by reminding us that when we work for others, we should not do more merely to please them but rather we should work as unto the Lord Himself. In other words, we should not merely "get by" with what is expected of us by kind and gentle employers. We should do our very best in a way that will please God. When we please God, we will be pleasing to our employers. Excellence for God usually brings the approval and admiration of God from employers.

To submit to employers who are good and gentle is not difficult, but verse 18 also instructs us to submit to masters who are harsh. To be whipped or beaten into submission is one thing, but to submit by one's own free will to a harsh master is quite improbable or even impossible without the Lord's help. However, Peter is not talking about the natural; he is counseling us to enjoy and to practice the life of the Spirit—the supernatural.

He contends that such conduct is *"commendable"* because it requires that our conscience toward God is the motivation for such behavior (v. 19). We endure grief and suffer because our deepest commitment is to Jesus Christ, and the ultimate purpose of our work is to please Him—to do all to His glory (1 Cor. 10:31).

This conduct is also commendable because it is pleasing to God (v. 20). Peter writes with directness and honesty when he asks the rhetorical question, "For what credit is it if, when you are beaten

for your faults, you take it patiently?" (v. 20). His inference is clear—
that response is expected of us by our earthly masters and by our
society.

However, there is a dimension of Christian behavior which goes
far beyond that which is expected by others, and it is pleasing to
God. That is when we do good and suffer for it, and take it patiently.
This behavior is commendable before God (v. 20). This kind of behavior not only brings glory to God, but it also has the potential of
ministering to our masters and to others around us.

In fact, most of us have seen the power of that kind of behavior
affect the lives of others. For example, a number of years ago, I met
a man who had come to personal faith in Christ through the influence
of his teenage son who had personified this kind of behavior to his
father.

The young man had been stricken with polio at an early age and
was badly crippled in both of his legs. His father had become very
bitter over this malady which had afflicted his only son. He became
an alcoholic and began to badly mistreat his wife and son.

Life became literally "hell on earth" for his family. However, within
this context, the mother and son began to attend church and both
received Christ as Savior and Lord. Their hatred and resistance to
the man's cruelty was changed to love and concern. One evening,
after the father had beaten the boy badly, he realized that the boy
was expressing love to him rather than fear and hatred.

He was deeply touched by that response even in his stupor. He
asked the boy why he was responding so strangely, and the young
man replied, "It's because I love you, Daddy. God loves you, and
so do I!"

During the coming months, as he continued to abuse his wife and
son, that simple message kept coming back to him, "God loves you,
and so do I!" The more hatred and bitterness he directed toward
his family, the more love they returned to him. And one evening,
he could stand it no longer. He was so convicted by the Holy Spirit
through the love of his own son, he blurted out to the young man,
"I want to love you and your mother and God! How can I do it?"

That night, his twelve-year-old son explained how he could come
to know God through personal faith in Jesus Christ as Savior and
Lord. The boy led his father to Christ. That is the potential power
of "supernatural" living in relationship to harsh masters, bitter parents, and to all of those outside the Kingdom of God.

The kind of behavior to which we have been called (v. 21) is not an option to the believer; it is expected of us by our Lord. Yet we do not need to live that kind of lifestyle without help or without an adequate example. Jesus Christ is the source for both our help and our example. Peter reminds us that He also suffered for us *"leaving us an example, that [we] should follow His steps"* (v. 21). Peter then quotes from Isaiah 53:9, *"Who committed no sin, nor was guile found in His mouth."*

To disobey even a harsh master is to sin. To obey with bitterness or anger or accommodation as our motive is also sin. Love is the only motive which is acceptable to God for any and all of our behavior (1 Cor. 13:1–3). Indeed, we should follow the steps of Christ who did everything with the motive of love.

What a difference that makes in our attitude and conduct. For example, because Christ loved, He did not revile in return when He was reviled; when He suffered unjustly at the hands of others, He did not threaten them. He simply loved them and committed Himself to His Father (v. 23).

His love for us and for all people motivated Him to bear our sins in His own body on the cross that we might be forgiven of our sins and live for righteousness (v. 24). That is the ultimate of love—to give our bodies, our very lives, for the unrighteous.

The marvelous result of Christ's love for us is that we were once like sheep going astray but have now returned to the Shepherd and Overseer of our souls (v. 25). This is the ultimate example of love, given to us by Jesus Christ. Martin Luther summarized the example of Christ well when he wrote, "When I consider my crosses, tribulations, and temptations, I shame myself almost to death thinking what are they in comparison to the sufferings of my blessed Savior Christ Jesus."

As Christ has so lived for us, we are able to live for Him and for others. And as we do, we are enabled to give an answer to those who ask, "Why do you have such hope and such love? Why are you so good to me when I am so bad to you? Why do you love me when I abuse you?" We should be ready to tell them about Jesus (1 Pet. 3:15).

NOTE

1. *The Living Webster Encyclopedic Dictionary* (Chicago: The English Language Institute of America, 1975).

CHAPTER THREE

What Being Good Is All About

1 Peter 3:1–22

God is the source of all that is good! As James declares, "Every good gift and every perfect gift is from above, and comes down from the Father . . ." (James 1:17). If God is the source of our new life in Christ, we must be living good lives and doing good things. And so Jesus said, "Let your light so shine before men, that they may see your good works and glorify your Father who is in heaven" (Matt. 5:16).

John Wesley had a marvelous rule concerning being good and doing good. It was simply this:

> Do all the good you can,
> By all the means you can,
> In all the ways you can,
> In all the places you can,
> At all the times you can,
> To all the people you can,
> As long as ever you can.

As Peter has written about the important subjects of "What Salvation Is All About" and "What Christian Living Is All About," he now turns to the important subject of "What Being Good Is All About." And he begins with the important subject of how to be a good wife.

How to Be a Good Christian Wife

1 Likewise you wives, be submissive to your own husbands, that even if some do not obey the word,

they, without a word, may be won by the conduct
of their wives,

2 when they observe your chaste conduct
accompanied by fear.

3 Do not let your beauty be that outward adorning
of arranging the hair, of wearing gold, or of putting
on fine apparel;

4 but let it be the hidden person of the heart, with
the incorruptible ornament of a gentle and quiet spirit,
which is very precious in the sight of God.

5 For in this manner, in former times, the holy
women who trusted in God also adorned themselves,
being submissive to their own husbands,

6 as Sarah obeyed Abraham, calling him lord,
whose daughters you are as long as you do good and
are not afraid with any terror.

1 Peter 3:1–6

An ancient Jewish proverb states, "God could not be everywhere,
and so He made mothers." Of course, that is not to deny His omni-
presence, but rather to acknowledge that in the present age, God
has chosen to live in and through the lives of His people. And for
many of us, He has expressed Himself indelibly through the lives
of our Christian mothers.

An eight-year-old girl wrote the following letter to a local newspaper. Although her spelling and punctuation could be improved, little
Nicole has written what many of us have experienced in our own
lives—a mother who has done so much good for us and for others:
"My mom's the most because she never spoils me. She says I can
have friends over when she raises me excellent and when I want
somebody for I ask her well most of the time she doesn't let me go
any comfort, and to love up. My mom takes care of were alone because
I might get kidnapped she is a good mother. She has seven daughters
and that is why it is hard for her to be nice to all of us but she is.
I had an operation on my eyes and she was with me every second
ecsept for in the operation room she rubbed my head and told me
it would be okay I love my mom so much she is so kind to me."

Indeed, our Lord has lived in and through the lives of many of
our mothers and wives and other significant women who have touched
us deeply for good and for God. It is to this important subject which
Peter is writing. How can one be a good and godly wife? Peter shares

three specific attributes of a good Christian wife which are appropriate not only for the Christian wife, but for all women who would please God by their good lives.

First, verses 1 and 2 describe the quality of conduct or behavior which is most pleasing to God. Earlier in this letter, Peter has written, "As He who has called you is holy, you also be holy in all your conduct" (1 Pet. 1:15). God calls all of us to the life of holy behavior.

Such a lifestyle releases great influence upon the lives of others. Peter contends that this kind of living is much more important than what we say. In fact, he asks that Christian wives so live that husbands who do not obey the Word may be won by the conduct of their wives.

Several years ago, an attractive young wife came to personal faith in Christ through the ministry of the church which I was serving as pastor. Prior to her conversion, she and her husband had been involved in a very immoral lifestyle.

Shortly after becoming a Christian, she came to me for counsel regarding how she could best influence her husband so that he might come to new life through Jesus Christ. In response to her question, I shared these verses from 1 Peter, chapter 3, and then I made the following suggestion: "At a proper time, tell your husband what has happened to you. Tell him about the love and forgiveness of Christ, and what a difference He is making in your life. Then, never mention another word about God or Christ or the Gospel again until he asks you or until the Holy Spirit prompts you to speak. In the meantime, live for Christ in all that you do. Allow Him to fill you with the Holy Spirit and to give you the fruit of the Spirit of love and joy and peace and so on."

We prayed together, and then she went home to live for Christ and to love her husband as only Christ could enable her to do. Some three months later, I had the privilege of leading her husband to Christ. At that time I asked him, "What influenced you most for Christ?"

Without a moment's hesitation, he responded. "It has been my wife. Several weeks ago she told me of how she had come to know Christ personally. She said that she hoped that I would also come to Christ, but that she would not bug me. Whenever I had a question or whenever I was ready to know more, she would share with me. She was a changed woman. She did not nag me or preach to me;

she only loved me! I know that whatever she has is what I want and need. And I believe that it is Jesus Christ."

The message of Peter worked in that husband's life and it has been used of God in countless others. It is not a message of compromise or nonchalance; it is a message of holy and godly living. It is a reminder that we seldom "talk" or "argue" people into the Kingdom; we love and pray and influence them by our holy living. This allows the Holy Spirit to minister through us and to draw people to Christ!

In fact, Peter goes on to say that this holy living must be done with chaste conduct and with fear. The Greek word "chaste" is *hagnós*, which comes from the root *hágios*, "holy." It is the word often translated in the New Testament as "pure." For example, in 1 Timothy 5:22, Paul instructs us to keep ourselves pure.

The word fear is *phóbos*. A better translation is "reverence." Peter uses this word several times in this epistle including chapter 1, verse 17, chapter 2, verse 18, and chapter 3, verse 15. In summary, his teaching is simply this, that we should live the holy life of purity and reverence so that we might influence those outside the faith by our godly behavior.

The second attribute of a good Christian wife is found in verses 3 and 4. There is a form of beauty which comes from the outward adorning of the body such as the arranging of the hair, wearing jewelry, or putting on fine apparel. Peter asks for Christian women to recognize that there is a beauty which is far more vital and important. He does not suggest that it is wrong to dress beautifully. In fact, the godly woman described in Proverbs 31 has clothing of silk and purple.

But there is a beauty which is much deeper and of a much higher priority. It is the beauty of the inner person which Peter describes as the hidden person of the heart. This person should be adorned with the incorruptible ornament or unfading beauty of a gentle and quiet spirit, which is very precious in the sight of God.

This is a beauty which never fades. It is spiritual beauty. It is the kind of beauty described in the old hymn:

> Let the beauty of Jesus be seen in me,
>   All His wonderful passion and purity;
>   O Thou Spirit divine, all my nature refine,
>   'Till the beauty of Jesus be seen in me!

The third of the attributes Peter describes is submission (vv. 5–6), a subject that is never popular. At the very center of our sinful nature is the deep desire to go our own way, to do our own thing, to be "number one." The only way we can come to God is to submit to Him. But that submission is not based upon rebellion or legalism or "doing it because we have to."

Love is at the root of the Biblical understanding of submission. The Scripture tells us that Jesus submitted to the Father because of His deep love for Him, and that He submitted to the cross because of His deep love for us.

To submit is not to be inferior. To the contrary, Jesus was equal with God but He emptied Himself in submission by becoming a servant and He humbled Himself and became obedient to the point of death, even death on the cross.

Within the Kingdom of God, the servant is greater than the master. He or she who serves is to be the greatest in the Kingdom. The leader in the church should not lord over the flock, but should serve them. "Just as the Son of Man did not come to be served, but to serve, and to give His life a ransom for many" (Matt. 20:25–28).

A Christian marriage is predicated upon the same principles. A woman is not inferior or superior to a man in marriage. In Christ "there is neither male nor female; for you are all one in Christ Jesus" (Gal. 3:28). Submission of the wife to the husband is not a matter of inferiority; it is simply a matter of love. She does it because she loves Christ, because she loves her husband, and because she is obeying the Word of the Lord.

But we must also remember that the husband is also to serve the wife. "Husbands, love your wives, just as Christ also loved the church and gave Himself for it" (Eph. 5:25). The teaching is clear: Christian husbands are to give themselves for their wives in the same way in which Christ gave Himself for the Church.

And then there is the matter of mutual submission within the Body of Christ which is even a higher principle. It is the key to Christian marriage. Paul declared that we should submit to one another out of reverence for Christ (Eph. 5:21). That is a basic principle of the Christian faith. We should live under the lordship of Christ as willing servants and joyfully submit to each other as servants of Christ and of one another.

With the understanding of this basic Christian principle, we can better understand what Peter is teaching to the leaders of the church in the first verses of chapter 5 and what he is teaching Christian wives in this portion. Christian wives should be submissive to their own husbands as Sarah was to Abraham.

How does one do that? Peter gives us two practical answers. First, a Christian wife should do what is right, and then she should not give way to fear nor be afraid with any terror (v. 6).

To do what is right, or what is good, is to keep the commandments of the Lord. And what are those commandments which our Lord has given to us? Jesus said, "And you shall love the Lord your God with all your heart, with all your soul, with all your mind, and with all your strength. . . . You shall love your neighbor as yourself" (Mark 12:30–31).

To do good is to obey the Lord's commandments. And all of His commandments are summarized in these two. A wife that is doing good is a wife that is loving God and loving her husband and loving her family. She is a "lover" in the Biblical sense of the word.

Second, she must not give way to fear. And how does one overcome or escape fear? The Biblical answer is clear, "There is no fear in love; but perfect love casts out fear, because fear involves torment. But he who fears has not been made perfect in love" (1 John 4:18).

Once again, the answer is love. It is not difficult to submit to a God we love and then to serve Him. It is not difficult to submit to a husband we love and then to serve him. It is not difficult to give ourselves for a wife whom we love as Christ loves the Church and gave Himself for it. To serve is to love—and Christ is our model.

How to Be a Good Christian Husband

> 7 Likewise you husbands, dwell with them with
> understanding, giving honor to the wife, as to the
> weaker vessel, and as being heirs together of the grace
> of life, that your prayers not be hindered.
>
> *1 Peter 3:7*

As we might have suspected, Peter does not merely speak to wives concerning how they should live; he gives some very helpful and practical advice to the husbands. In short, he tells us how we should live with our wives as Christian husbands.

Peter tells husbands that they should begin by living with their

157

wives with understanding (v. 7). The word for understanding is *gnōsis*, which is usually translated as knowledge. If we are to be understanding or considerate to our wife, we must know her. That is one of the greatest challenges of the marriage relationship or of any close interpersonal relationship. In order to be able to love deeply, we must know each other profoundly. If we are to lovingly respond to the needs of another, we must know what they are.

To know another requires time, honesty, mutual openness, patience, sensitivity, and above all, **love.** Husbands should be getting to know their wives better and better day by day as they love them, share with them, engage in honest communication, and become deeply intimate.

Peter also teaches that husbands should give honor and respect to their wives, as weaker vessels (v. 7). The word for honor is *timē* which is sometimes translated as price or precious. It denotes value and esteem.

Indeed, a wife should be treated as someone very precious, of great value and to be highly esteemed.

A woman writing to a newspaper columnist expressed it in the following way:

> Woman was created from the rib of a man.
> She was not made from his head to top him,
> Nor out of his feet to be trampled upon.
> But out of his side to be equal to him,
> Under his arm to be protected,
> And near his heart to be loved.

The Lord has not given more of His grace of life to either the husband or the wife. Together, a man and his wife are the children of God and, therefore, heirs of God and joint heirs with Christ (v. 7, Rom. 8:17). What grace! That God should extend His love to us in such great measure that we should enjoy all the benefits of being His children.

Husbands and wives are neither inferior or superior to one another. We are encouraged to love each other, to serve each other with the love and spirit of Christ, and to live as heirs together of the grace of life. In other words, we should live in communion with God and with each other.

Peter underscores the importance of living in a vital communion with each other when he states, "that your prayers not be hindered." There is only one thing that hinders prayers, and that is sin.

And Jesus spoke about the very special sin which will hinder our prayers. It is the sin of being unforgiving. As Jesus taught His disciples and us how to pray in His Sermon on the Mount, He concluded His teaching on prayer by saying, "For if you forgive men their trespasses, your heavenly Father will also forgive you. But if you do not forgive men their trespasses, neither will your Father forgive your trespasses" (Matt. 6:14–15).

I believe that Peter is focusing on that basic teaching when he instructs husbands to so treat their wives that their prayers not be hindered. They must be living in a loving, open, sensitive, forgiving relationship. Nothing should separate their love, fidelity, and commitment.

Shortly before my wife, Jeannie, and I were married, some friends held a bridal shower for her. One of the highlights of the evening was a time when each of the ladies shared a word of advice or counsel for the young bride-to-be. There was a wise Christian lady who shared some advice which has been of great help to us over the years of our marriage. It was simply this: "Never go to sleep at night without forgiving each other for anything that needs forgiving."

That is exactly what Peter is saying. Love your wife in the same way in which Christ relates to the Church. Let love prevail. Treat your wife with understanding and honor as one who is very precious. Live together as heirs of the grace of God in its many and varied forms. And keep forgiving her and loving her and living in vital union with her.

Paul summarized these important truths as follows: "And be kind to one another, tenderhearted, forgiving one another, just as God in Christ also forgave you" (Eph. 4:32).

Repaying Evil with Good

8 Finally, all of you be of one mind, having
compassion for one another; love as brothers, be
tenderhearted, be courteous;
9 not rendering evil for evil or reviling for reviling,
but on the contrary bless, knowing that you were called
to this, that you may inherit a blessing.

10 For

    "He who would love life
    And see good days,
    Let him refrain his tongue from evil,
    And his lips that they speak no guile;

11 *Let him turn away from evil and do good;*
    Let him seek peace and pursue it.

12 *For the eyes of the* LORD *are on the righteous,*
    And his ears are open to their prayers;
    But the face of the LORD *is against those who*
      do evil."

                                    1 Peter 3:8–12

After giving instruction to us regarding how we should live in relationship to outsiders (2:11–12), to government (2:13–17), to masters (2:18–25), to husbands (3:1–6) and to wives (3:7), Peter now gives a summary of the qualities which we should express in our relationships with every person who comes into our lives—especially those who are brothers and sisters in Christ.

1. *"Be of one mind"* (v. 8). A better translation of this word of instruction would be, "Live in harmony with one another!" The word translated as "one mind" or "harmony" is *homóphrōn,* which literally means "harmony," "unity," "akin," or "together." Although this is the only place in Scripture where this particular word is used, it comes from a family of words which is used often to denote the oneness or harmony of the Body of Christ.

For example, in the Book of Acts we read, "Now when the Day of Pentecost had fully come, they were all with one accord in one place" (Acts 2:1). The word translated as "one accord" is *homothumadón* which is used some seven times just in the Book of Acts to describe the oneness and the harmony of the early believers who comprised the church.

God has called His sons and daughters to live in harmony with Him and with one another. It is His desire for us to be growing continually into a unity of the faith and a unity of the knowledge of Jesus Christ so that we may grow into maturity to become more and more like Jesus Christ Himself (Eph. 4:13).

All of us have witnessed the harmony of an orchestra when all the instruments are in tune and all the musicians are following the lead of the conductor. And many of us have been thrilled to watch an athletic team which is playing together with perfect unity as opposed to each player doing his or her own thing.

This should be the experience of our lives and of our churches. The oneness and the harmony which our Lord desires for the Church must begin with us. The Church is people—the people of God. When we are living under the lordship of Jesus Christ and are in tune with Him, we are in harmony with our brothers and sisters in Christ. When there is disharmony and disunity in the Church, sin is present. The solution is spiritual not organizational. We must seek the will of the Lord together—and do it. Then there will be harmony.

2. *Have compassion for one another* (v. 8). The Greek word translated as "compassion" is *sumpathēs* from which we get our English word "sympathy." Peter instructs us to be sympathetic or compassionate toward one another.

As a pastor, I have discovered that on a given Sunday, there are a certain number of people in our worshiping congregation who are hurting and who need our sympathy and compassion. The ministry of reaching out in love to those dear people needs to be a part of our worship experience. And, of course, it needs to be a vital part of our personal ministry within the Body of Christ.

The people of God should always be able to share their needs and hurts with one another. And we who are pastors of the flock of God should make certain that the right atmosphere and opportunities to share are provided.

In my opinion, that is why small groups are so important within the life of a church family. They provide the atmosphere of love and trust which encourages the participants to share personal needs and to "bear one another's burdens, and so fulfill the law of Christ" (Gal. 6:2).

Paul reminds us that within the Body of Christ, when one member suffers, we all suffer (1 Cor. 12:26), and that we should rejoice with those who rejoice and weep with those who weep (Rom. 12:15). Indeed, that is the ministry of sympathy and compassion—the very spirit of Christ.

3. *"Love as brothers"* (and sisters) (v. 8). The word used in this text for *"love"* is not *agapē* but rather is the compound word *philádelphos* which is best translated as "brotherly love." Of course, that is why the city of Philadelphia is known as the city of brotherly love.

Peter is certainly not suggesting that we should love one another within the church with a quality of love which is secondary to, or less than the quality of *agapē.* Instead, he is using "family vocabulary" which is so central to the teaching of the New Testament. We are members of the "family of God" and are brothers and sisters in Christ with God as our Father.

Our instructions to love one another as brothers and sisters in Christ are numerous in the New Testament including the instruction of Paul to "be kindly affectionate to one another with brotherly love" (Rom. 12:10). The writer of Hebrews encourages us to "let brotherly love continue" (Heb. 13:1). In other words, *philadelphos* should be our continual lifestyle for brothers and sisters in Christ.

4. *"Be tenderhearted"* (v. 8). To be *"tenderhearted," eúsplanchnos,* is to be "kindly" or "pitiful." Again, it denotes the very Spirit of Christ. If we are to live for Christ, or if we are to allow Him to live in and through us, we must be tenderhearted. Our hearts need to be broken with the things that break the heart of our Lord.

One of the first Scripture verses that many of us learned as children was, "And be kind to one another, tenderhearted, forgiving one another, just as God in Christ also forgave you" (Eph. 4:32). Of course, we must not only believe the message of that verse—we must live it.

Unfortunately, there is often a great gulf between our Biblical knowledge and our lifestyle, between our theology and our actions. I witnessed a vivid example of this discrepancy while I was a student in a Chicago theological seminary in the mid-1960s during the time in which the infamous "God is dead" movement was taking place in the church.

One of the noted "God is dead" theologians was invited to our campus to debate one of the leading evangelical scholars of our nation. The evangelical theologian easily won the debate in terms of content and spiritual truth. However, in my opinion, he lost the debate in another vital area—that of personal conduct.

The "God is dead" theologian was a gracious, kind man who shared his material with an open spirit, while the evangelical theologian was a critical, negative, unkind, and sarcastic man who fought, attacked, and condemned. His lifestyle loudly contradicted all the truth he verbalized. (How tragic it is to know the truths of God and to live like the devil.) Christ is calling us to be compassionate and loving and tenderhearted and courteous—like Christ Himself.

5. *Be courteous* (v. 8). This word translated as "courteous" is *philóphrōn,*

from the same root word as *philadelphia*—*philos,* or friend. It means literally to be "friendly of mind" or to be "courteous in our attitude."

Again we are reminded that we are not merely to love those who love us, but to be loving and courteous to all who come into our lives—like Christ. The challenge is to treat others with the same courtesy and love that we would extend to a dear friend. And this must not be done merely mechanically or as a religious duty. It must begin with a "courteous" or "friendly" attitude.

6. *Be a blessing* (vv. 9–12). We who belong to Christ and are possessed by Him should bring blessing wherever we go and through whatever we do. To be sure, we live in a world in which we are often confronted by evil. Our natural response is to do evil to those who do evil to us. But Peter reminds us of the basis of Christian ethics and lifestyle: we should not render evil for evil or reviling for reviling, but on the contrary, we should do good to those who do evil. In fact, bringing blessing to others is a part of our Christian calling (v. 9).

The *New English Bible* has a marvelous translation of those important instructions: "Do not repay wrong with wrong, or abuse with abuse; on the contrary, retaliate with blessing" (1 Pet. 3:9). What a marvelous ministry God has entrusted to us. We should be on the offensive in bringing blessing to our society, and we should be especially aggressive in bringing blessing to those who do evil to us and to others.

Peter reminds us next of the fact that when we bring blessings to others, we are blessed ourselves. The goodness of God is a blessing to everyone. He quotes from Psalm 34:12–16, which in verses 10–12 encourages us to turn away from evil and to do good. That is a wonderful way to live—like Christ.

SHARING THE HOPE

13 And who is he who will harm you if you become followers of what is good?

14 But even if you should suffer for righteousness' sake, you are blessed. *"And do not be afraid of their threats, nor be troubled."*

15 But sanctify the Lord God in your hearts, and always be ready to give a defense to everyone who asks you a reason for the hope that is in you, with meekness and fear;

16 having a good conscience, that when they speak

> evil of you as evildoers, those who revile your good
> conduct in Christ may be ashamed.
>
> *1 Peter 3:13–16*

In the previous verses, Peter has encouraged us to do good to others even when they do evil to us; in so doing, they will be blessed and we will be blessed. He continues in verse 13 by posing the rhetorical question, "And who is he who will harm you if you become followers of what is good?"

In other words, Christians have an incredible contribution to make to the society in which they live by breaking the cycle of people returning evil for evil. As we begin to do good, most people will return that good by doing good. What a marvelous ministry—with very immediate and measurable results. Just as people tend to return evil for evil, they usually return good for good. Indeed, when you do good, blessing comes to everyone involved.

However, Peter also recognizes the reality of a sinful society. There are times when even as we do good and our motive is love, we will suffer for it. As Peter reminds us later in this chapter, that is exactly what happened to Jesus Christ who only loved and only did good. He suffered for His good deeds to the ultimate by being put to a criminal's death on the cross.

We, too, will sometimes suffer for doing good just as our Lord did. Jesus told us that it would be so, "A servant is not greater than his master. If they persecuted Me, they will also persecute you" (John 15:20).

That is the challenging news. But there is also the good news which should be of great encouragement to us. Peter shares it with a suffering church and with all of us who might experience suffering in response to our doing good. He writes, "But even if you should suffer for righteousness' sake, you are blessed" (v. 14). Indeed, we are called to the marvelous ministry of retaliating with blessings, and as we do, we will be blessed of God regardless of the response of the other persons. We are blessed people!

Within this context, Peter encourages us to share the blessings of God with others. The "good life" is never to be kept for ourselves; it is to be shared with others. Peter suggests three steps we should follow in sharing the good life:

1. *"Sanctify the Lord God in your hearts"* (v. 15). To sanctify, *hagiázō,* is to "set apart." The Christian faith makes no sense nor does Christian

lifestyle ever work until and unless we "set apart" our lives to allow Jesus Christ to be Lord. The word "sanctify" comes from the same root word as holy (*hágios*).

Peter writes a great deal about the life of holiness in his first letter. As we have seen, he instructs us to "be holy in all your conduct, because it is written, 'Be holy, for I am holy' " (1:15–16). Holy living is possible only as we "sanctify the Lord God in our hearts."

Also, Peter refers to Christian believers as "a holy priesthood" (2:5) and as "a holy nation" (2:9). To be holy is to be different. It is to be like the Lord who is the personification of holiness. To sanctify Christ as Lord in our hearts enables us to live the life of holiness. In the truest sense, it allows Christ to live His life of holiness in us and through us.

Lordship is the key to godly living. Jesus asked the question, "But why do you call Me 'Lord, Lord,' and not do the things which I say?" (Luke 6:46). Authentic lordship must be lived out in obedience to Christ. If He is to be my Lord, He must control and rule my life. He must be at "master control." He must "call the plays" of my life moment by moment.

Samuel Wilberforce once said that lordship could be defined in four words: admit, submit, commit, transmit. Indeed, we must admit our sin and need of a savior; we must forsake sin and submit our lives to Christ as Lord; we must commit our way to the Lord day by day; and we must transmit or share His love and goodness with others. Peter proceeds to discuss the importance of transmitting.

2. *"Always be ready to give a defense to everyone who asks you a reason for the hope that is in you"* (v. 15). The word *"defense"* is *apología* from which we get our English word apologetics. Paul used this word when he made his defense before the Jews in Jerusalem (Acts 22:1) and when he made his defense to King Agrippa (Acts 25:16). To give an *apología* means simply to give reasons or a rationale for what you believe or for what you are communicating through your lifestyle.

Peter uses the example of giving a defense for the hope that is being communicated through us in the way we live and act. Of course, this instruction is based upon the basic assumption that we are living the life of hope. And that is based upon the lordship of Jesus Christ.

In writing to a suffering church and its hurting people, Peter speaks about the life of hope. Outwardly, those people had little reason to rejoice or to have hope. But because of Christ living in them, they were displaying hope in their lives even when outward circumstances seemed very hopeless. No wonder people would ask them, "Why are you so filled with hope?"

Peter is telling them and us that when such questions are posed to us, we should not be surprised. In fact, we should always be ready to give them the answer—the defense or apologetic for our Christian faith. Needless to say, hope is not the only expression of authentic Christian lifestyle. All of the fruit of the Spirit of love, joy, peace, longsuffering, kindness, goodness, faithfulness, gentleness, and self-control will communicate to outsiders. We need to be prepared to tell them that such qualities of life do not come from us but rather that they come from the Holy Spirit who dwells within us as we allow Jesus to be the Lord of our lives.

Many of us resist the exciting ministry of sharing with others. We are like Charlie Brown's little sister, Sally, who once said to Charlie, "I'm doomed! I need to write a report on rivers, and it's due next week, and I know that I'm going to fail!" To that, Charlie Brown responded, "Well, why don't you work real hard and turn in the best report you can possibly write?" With that, Sally meekly replied, "You know, that never even occurred to me!"

That is how many of us have lived the Christian life for a long time. We are afraid that someone is going to find out about it. Recently I was visiting with a pastor friend from one of the major cities in the United States. He shared a marvelous story with me.

One of the Christian businessmen from his church was leading a weekly Bible study for presidents of major corporations located in that particular city. The president of a large corporation became a Christian through the impact of the study. He was faithful to the study, but he remained a "secret Christian." He didn't want anyone to find out about his Christian commitment.

As he began to grow spiritually, he found it more and more difficult to hide the fact that he was a Christian. His life began to change outwardly, and the influence of Christ was affecting his lifestyle. His associates and friends were asking what was happening to him. Why was he different?

One day, in desperation, he asked his friends in the Bible study group, "Isn't it possible to live the Christian life in secret?" To that question, one of his wise friends replied, "Friend, it is impossible for you to have Jesus living within you without some of Him leaking out!"

That is exactly what Peter is teaching. Allow the love, joy, peace, and hope of Jesus Christ to "leak out" of your life. And when that happens, be ready to give an answer to those who ask you about it. In other words, share the love, joy, peace, and hope of Jesus Christ with others. Don't resist it; don't hide it; don't ignore it; share the good life!

3. *Share it with meekness and fear and a good conscience* (vv. 15–16). As we share the good life with others, we must do so with the spirit of Christ—with gentleness and respect and a clear conscience.

The word for "meek" is *praútēs*, which is sometimes translated as "gentleness." Jesus shared in His beatitudes, "Blessed are the meek, for they shall inherit the earth" (Matt. 5:5).

To be meek is to be gentle, kind, and gracious. It is the opposite of being rude, insensitive, and uptight. To be meek is to be like Christ as He lovingly met people at the point of need or hurt. To be meek is to have the spirit of "one beggar sharing a piece of bread with another."

To respond with *"fear"* (*phóbos*) is to respond with "respect." We should not "talk down" to others. Effective sharing and witnessing always takes place on eye level with others. We are not better than others. We have been forgiven by Jesus Christ and are enjoying the benefits of the good life which comes from living under His lordship.

We need to respond to others with the same respect which Jesus has for all persons. Our Lord never violates people or ever forces His way into their lives. He is gentle and respectful and loving. We need to have that kind of respect for others. But we will have it only when we have adequate respect for God. We must respect the Creator before we can truly respect His creations (see commentary on 1 Peter 2:18, p. 148).

Peter recognizes that it is vitally important for a Christian to have a clear conscience (*suneídēsis*) if he or she is to be used of God effectively in sharing the good life with others. The Christian does not have the option of living a "double life" or a "secret life."

God has called us to a life of transparency and authenticity. To "sanctify the Lord God in our hearts" means to be possessed by the Holy Spirit. The Spirit and the flesh are opposed one to another. One cannot walk honestly before God and others with a clear conscience unless he or she forsakes the works of the flesh and walks in the Spirit.

In practical terms, Peter refers to us having a clear conscience in relationship to our masters (2:19) and in our relationship to God

(3:21). To have a clear conscience requires having our sins forgiven by our Savior and Lord, Jesus Christ. To be "clear" is to be forgiven.

Responding to others in gentleness and respect and with a clear conscience has some wonderful benefits for everyone who is involved. When we have done good to others, and they have spoken evil of us and have reviled our good conduct in Christ, they will be ashamed. In other words, the Holy Spirit will use our good conduct as a means for conviction in the lives of others. Light will come into the darkness—and the darkness will have the opportunity to respond! We have the wonderful opportunity to be light and salt and leaven to a hurting, dark world.

SUFFERING FOR DOING GOOD

17 For it is better, if it is the will of God, that you suffer for doing good than for doing evil.

18 For Christ also has suffered once for sins, the just for the unjust, that He might bring us to God, being put to death in the flesh but made alive by the Spirit,

19 by whom also He went and preached to the spirits in prison,

20 who formerly were disobedient, when once the longsuffering of God waited in the days of Noah, while the ark was being prepared, in which a few, that is, eight souls, were saved through water.

21 There is also an antitype which now saves us, namely baptism (not the removal of the filth of the flesh, but the answer of a good conscience toward God), through the resurrection of Jesus Christ,

22 who has gone into heaven and is at the right hand of God, angels and authorities and powers having been made subject to Him.

1 Peter 3:17–22

As we have seen, Peter is writing to a suffering church. These believers have been persecuted for their faith in Christ and have been dispersed throughout the world. The subject of suffering is a recurring theme in this letter. In this section, Peter focuses upon the challenge of suffering for doing good. But first he comments on suffering on account of our sin.

There is the kind of suffering which comes into the life of the Christian simply because we have done evil by missing the mark or disobeying God. Peter warns against this kind of suffering when he writes, "But let none of you suffer as a murderer, a thief, an evildoer, or as a busybody in other people's matters" (4:15).

This kind of suffering is simply the logical consequence of sin. It is a good example of the way cause and effect works in our lives. It is reaping what we have sowed. As Paul stated, "Do not be deceived, God is not mocked; for whatever a man sows, that he will also reap. For he who sows to his flesh will of the flesh reap corruption, but he who sows to the Spirit will of the Spirit reap everlasting life" (Gal. 6:7–8).

All of us have experienced that kind of suffering at one time or another in our lives. For example, if we have placed our hand on the burner of a hot stove, we have been burned. We have reaped what we have sowed. We have experienced the logical results of our actions.

Recently I was invited to serve as a guest host on a talk program on a major Los Angeles religious radio station. I had a wonderful time in counseling with many hurting people. As the three hours of our air time came to a close, God opened my eyes to a basic common denominator which was being revealed through the lives of most of the callers.

It was simply this—most of the callers were suffering in a given area of life because they had disobeyed the Lord in some specific way. The solution for this kind of suffering is simple. We need to repent of our sins and turn to Christ to receive His forgiveness. Then we need to begin to follow Him in obedience as the Lord of our lives. As Peter has said, we need to sanctify the Lord God in our hearts (v. 15).

Suffering for doing good seems to be much more of a challenge in most of our lives than suffering for doing evil. By our very human nature we seem to be surprised by it, and we tend to resist it in every possible way. Peter tells us not to be surprised by it (4:12), and in these verses he reveals that we should not resist it but instead we should enjoy the benefits of suffering for doing good.

As we have seen in verse 14, we are blessed by the Lord when we suffer for doing good (also see commentary, p. 164). Jesus said, "Blessed are you when they revile and persecute you, and say all kinds of evil against you falsely for My sake. Rejoice and be exceedingly glad, for great is your reward in heaven, for so they persecuted the prophets who were before you" (Matt. 5:11–12).

Peter has reminded us that we are strangers and pilgrims in this world. Our king is Christ and our citizenship is in the Kingdom of God (see commentary, p. 127). Suffering is only temporary, and "the sufferings of this present time are not worthy to be compared with the glory which shall be revealed in us" (Rom. 8:18). And so we can rejoice, be glad, and be blessed in the midst of suffering for doing good.

Suffering for doing good may be God's will (v. 17). Doing the will of God is not always easy, but it is always best. Peter states that it is better to suffer for doing good "if it is the will of God." God is not the source of evil or suffering, but He allows suffering to come into our lives even as He allowed it to come into the life of His dear Son, Jesus Christ, and into the life of His servant, Job.

As the Lord allows suffering to come into our lives, He uses it for our good. "And we know that all things work together for good to those who love God, to those who are the called according to His purpose" (Rom. 8:28). God uses even suffering for our good.

That was the insight which Joseph shared with his brothers after they had sold him into slavery. He had become the prime minister of Egypt and was used of God to rescue his father and brothers and their families from starvation. Joseph said to them, "You meant it for evil against me; but God meant it for good" (Gen. 50:20). That is the grace and goodness of God. When we commit our lives to Him, He uses everything for our benefit.

Recently, I received a letter from a dear friend who was going through a time of great suffering. He wrote, "It's amazing to me that I had once entertained the notion that I would get through life without being severely tried. The last three years have been a nightmare. As a matter of fact, I have tears in my eyes right now as I type this paragraph." Then he went on to write, "The weird part about it is: If you asked me why, I couldn't give you an answer." My response to this dear, aching friend and to you is this: God has not promised to always answer "why" but He will always help us with the "what." We can be sure that all of our sufferings and trials will be used for our good and our growth as we entrust ourselves to our good and faithful Father.

Over the years, I have discovered that most people whom God is using significantly have gone through a period of suffering and testing similar to the one my friend has been experiencing. God has taken me through times like that in my own life. They have been difficult times, but they have also been times which resulted in great blessing and major spiritual growth. Nothing is wasted when it is given to God—not even suffering.

Suffering for doing good allows us to identify more closely with Jesus Christ (vv. 18–22). Peter reminds us that Christ also has suffered once for sins, the just for the unjust. He has done this so that He might bring us to God, being put to death in the flesh but made alive by the Spirit (v. 18).

This reinforces the teaching that Peter shared earlier when he wrote, "For what credit is it if, when you are beaten for your faults, you take it patiently? But when you do good and suffer for it, if you take it patiently, this is commendable before God. For to this you were called, because Christ also suffered for us, leaving us an example, that you should follow His steps" (2:20–21). Indeed, Jesus Christ is our example in suffering for good, and when we suffer for doing good, He is our example and enabler; we can identify with Him!

This prompted Peter to write, "If anyone suffers as a Christian, let him not be ashamed, but let him glorify God in this matter" (4:16). This identification with Christ is not only in the present tense, but also in the future. Paul wrote, "We are children of God, and if children, then heirs—heirs of God and joint heirs with Christ, if indeed we suffer with Him, that we may also be glorified together" (Rom. 8:16–17).

The friends who are the closest to us are those with whom we have suffered and hurt and prayed and then mutually encouraged. And so it is with our Lord. As we suffer with Him, we love Him more deeply and trust Him more fully. And the glory—both present and future—far exceeds the pain.

Peter then proceeds to some teaching which requires deep and thorough study. In short, Peter contends that Jesus went in the Spirit to preach to the contemporaries of Noah who had refused to respond to His preaching. Then Peter proceeds to discuss the practice of water baptism which, he states, signifies not merely the removal of dirt from one's body, but is the solution to providing a good conscience toward God. He is referring to the forgiveness of sins and the subsequent cleansing of the conscience. This wonderful salvation comes to us through the resurrection of Jesus Christ who has gone into heaven and is at the right hand of God with angels and authorities and powers having been made subject to Him (vv. 19–22).

The summation of Peter's teaching on the benefits of suffering for good, is found in the fourth chapter. "Therefore, let those who suffer according to the will of God commit their souls to Him in doing good, as to a faithful Creator" (4:19). May it be so in the lives of each of us.

CHAPTER FOUR

What Suffering Is All About

1 Peter 4:1–19

Peter's helpful and encouraging teaching on the subject of suffering reaches a climax in this chapter. Throughout the letter, the focus on suffering is balanced with the centrality of hope within the life of the Christian. This is blended with the fact that life on this earth is only temporary. Our true citizenship is in the Kingdom of God. Ultimate victory lies just ahead as we trust in Jesus Christ as Lord!

And we are never alone. Christ is with us in every circumstance of life into which we invite Him. We never need to suffer alone. He has suffered for us in the past and He will be with us in our sufferings in the present and future. We need not be fearful of the future—Christ will be with us always. He will never leave us nor forsake us (Heb. 13:5). And so "we may boldly say: 'The Lord is my helper, and I will not fear. What shall man do to me?' " (Heb. 13:6).

LIVING FOR THE WILL OF GOD

1 Therefore, since Christ has suffered for us in the flesh, arm yourselves likewise with the same mind, for he who has suffered in the flesh has ceased from sin,

2 that he no longer should live the rest of his time in the flesh for the lusts of men, but for the will of God.

3 For it should be sufficient that we did the will of the Gentiles in the former time of our lives—when we walked in licentiousness, lusts, drunkenness, revelry, drinking parties, and abominable idolatries,

4 in which they think it strange that you do not
run with them in the same flood of dissipation,
speaking evil of you.

5 They will give an account to Him who is ready
to judge the living and the dead.

6 For this reason the gospel was preached also to
those who are dead, that they might be judged
according to men in the flesh, but live according to
God in the spirit.

1 Peter 4:1–6

Suffering does not take place in a void nor does it take place without purpose in the life of the believer. To ignore suffering or to resist it would be natural, but these are not options for the committed Christian. We have the confidence that all things work together in our lives if we are trusting in Christ Jesus (Rom. 8:28).

And we know that if we trust in the Lord with all of our heart and lean not upon our own understanding, but instead, if we acknowledge the Lord in all our ways, He has promised to direct our steps (Prov. 3:5–6). As we have seen in our commentary on chapter 3 of 1 Peter, sometimes our Lord allows suffering to come into our lives. Just as it was His will for Christ to suffer for doing good, it is sometimes His will for His children to suffer for doing good (1 Pet. 3:17).

As Peter closes the third chapter by sharing some benefits which come to us as we suffer for doing good, he continues in the opening verses of this chapter to identify some additional benefits of suffering for Christ.

"Arm yourselves with the same mind [*as Christ*]*"* (v. 1). The word translated as *"mind"* is *énnoia* which can also be translated as "intent" or "attitude." As we know, our conduct is greatly determined by our mind or attitude. When our attitude is right, our conduct is usually right.

If we were to have the mind or attitude of Christ, what a difference it would make in the way in which we live day by day. Peter's teaching is clear. Since Christ suffered in the flesh for us, we should be prepared to suffer for Him. Jesus said, " 'A servant is not greater than his master.' If they have persecuted Me, they will also persecute you. If they have kept My word, they will keep yours also. But all these things they will do to you for My name's sake, because they do not know Him who sent Me" (John 15:20–21).

As Peter has shared in the previous chapter, there is a kind of suffering which comes from doing good—from being identified with Christ (see commentary, pp. 168). To face such sufferings, we need to have the attitude of Christ such as He had when He agonized in prayer in the Garden of Gethsemane when He prayed, "O My Father, if it is possible, let this cup pass from Me; nevertheless, not as I will, but as You will" (Matt. 26:39). To entrust ourselves to our Father and to His will is always right and always best.

Also in verse 1, Peter encourages us to cease from sin. Peter shares a very interesting relationship between suffering for Christ's sake and for righteousness' sake. It is natural for us to sin. We have all sinned and come short of the glory of God (Rom. 3:23). We have sinned by choice and by inheritance. No one had to teach us how to sin.

Since all of those things are true according to the Word of God, what could Peter mean when he says, "for he who has suffered in the flesh has ceased from sin"? (v. 1). I believe he means that the forsaking of sin, or repenting of sin, requires two specific steps. First we must, by an act of our will, turn from that sin.

But there is also a second step. When we turn from sin, we must turn to Christ. We must receive Him as Savior and then follow Him as Lord. As we follow Him and allow Him to live in and through us in the person of the Holy Spirit, we receive the fruit of the Spirit (Gal. 5:22–23), and the Lord enables us to do good. When we live lives that are good, and when we do good things for others, we will sometimes suffer for that good behavior (3:13–18).

Therefore, when you suffer in the flesh for doing good and for doing the will of God, it is an outward symbol of the fact that you have turned from sin or ceased from sin to follow after Jesus. It does not mean that you never stumble or slip into sin; it does mean that the major orientation and direction of your life is to follow Jesus. And it is often true that when we become serious about following Jesus as Lord, Satan becomes serious about attacking us. Indeed, we are engaged in spiritual warfare. But the Lord has promised us victory as we submit to Him and resist the devil (James 4:7–8).

Now Peter gets to the very heart of his teaching. That is, the focus of our living should be to do the will of God (vv. 2–6). Doing the will of God must begin with putting off the old life of walking in the flesh. Such a lifestyle is contrary to the will of God and to the life of walking in the Spirit. In verse 3, Peter reminds his readers of the post-Gentile ways that are no longer to be practiced:

(1) *"licentiousness"* (*asélgeia*): "without self-restraint, debauchery, filthiness, license." (2) *"lusts"* (*epithumía*): "evil desires, a longing for that which is forbidden." (3) *"drunkenness"* (*oinophugía*): "an excess or surplus of wine." (4) *"revelries"* (*kōmos*): "carousing, rioting, orgies." (5) *"drinking parties"* (*pótos*): "banqueting, drinking bouts." (6) *"abominable idolatries"* (*eidōlolatría*): "the forbidden worship of idols."

Those who still live that way respond to us and the Lord by thinking it strange that we don't run with them in the same flood of dissipation (v. 4) and by speaking evil of us (v. 4). However, they will have to give an account of themselves to the Lord (vv. 5–6).

Peter shares some insights regarding "how to live for the will of God" in the succeeding verses, particularly verses 7–11 in chapter 4. The contrast between doing the will of God and living in the Spirit and doing the will of the pagans and living in the lusts of the flesh is vivid. The two are diametrically opposed to one another. It is the difference between light and darkness, between life and death. Let us examine the truths of the following verses.

THE END IS AT HAND

7 But the end of all things is at hand; therefore
be serious and watchful in your prayers.
8 And above all things have fervent love among
yourselves, for *"love will cover a multitude of sins."*
9 Be hospitable to one another without grumbling.

1 Peter 4:7–9

Peter sounds a note of warning and motivation—the end is at hand! And because of this contention, there are some specific ways we should be living in order to do the will of God. Peter leaves the major theme of this chapter, suffering, to share some practical counseling regarding Christian living and ministry. Within these verses, we find three specific commands.

1. *"Be serious and watchful in your prayers"* (v. 7). Prayer is always appropriate for the Christian. It is the vital communication vehicle between a believer and his or her Lord. To pray is not merely to talk at God but it is to commune with God. Authentic prayer includes listening to God and responding to Him. In his book *Prayer*, O.

Hallesby gives the most helpful definition of prayer I have ever found. "To pray," he says, "is to let Jesus into your heart!"[1]

The word translated in verse 7 as *"serious"* is *sōphroneō*, which means "sober," or of "sound mind," or to be "clear-minded." This is the word that Paul uses in his letter to the Romans when he instructs them not to think of themselves "more highly than [they] ought to think, but to think soberly, as God has dealt to each one a measure of faith" (Rom. 12:3).

Prayer should never become something we do nonchalantly. Our spiritual vitality, to a great degree, depends upon our prayer lives. When Paul encourages us to "pray without ceasing" (1 Thess. 5:17), he is talking about Christian lifestyle. We must take prayer seriously. We need to live in a constant attitude of prayer—in continual communion with God.

We should seek to keep that flow open and constant. John Bunyan said, "Prayer is a sincere, sensible, affectionate pouring out of the soul to God, through Christ, in the strength and assistance of the Spirit, for such things as God has promised." Andrew Murray had this insight: "Prayer is not monologue, but dialogue; God's voice in response to mine is its most essential part. Listening to God's voice is the secret of the assurance that He will listen to mine." No wonder we should take prayer seriously.

Of course, all of this relates to doing the will of God. D. L. Moody once stated, "Spread out your petition before God, and then say, 'Thy will, not mine, be done.' The sweetest lesson I have learned in God's school is to let the Lord choose for me."

I have found it to be so in my own prayer life. How good it is to go to God with needs and then to allow Him to give the solutions according to His loving will! He is to be trusted.

The writer of Hebrews gives us great encouragement to be involved seriously in the lifestyle of prayer, "For we do not have a High Priest who cannot sympathize with our weaknesses, but was in all points tempted as we are, yet without sin. Let us therefore come boldly to the throne of grace, that we may obtain mercy and find grace to help in time of need" (Heb. 4:15–16).

The word translated in verse 7 as *"watchful"* (*nēphō*) is to be "sober" or "self-controlled." Paul shares some similar words of encouragement when he writes, "Therefore let us not sleep, as others do, but let us watch and be sober" (1 Thess. 5:6).

As Peter shares these words of encouragement, it is very possible that he was thinking back to his experience on the night in which Jesus was betrayed. As you will remember, Jesus took the eleven disciples to the Garden of Gethsemane to pray with Him. He invited Peter, James, and John to go deeper into the garden with Him. As He prayed, they fell asleep. He awakened them with the words, "What, could you not watch with Me one hour? Watch and pray lest you enter into temptation. The spirit indeed is willing, but the flesh is weak" (Matt. 26:40–41).

Peter is now sharing that same counsel with us. We must be sober and watchful, for these are crucial days. The end is at hand. He shares that warning not only in this passage but again in chapter five when he writes, "Be sober, be vigilant; because your adversary the devil walks about like a roaring lion, seeking whom he may devour" (5:8). Indeed, let us be serious and watchful in our prayers.

2. *"Have fervent love for one another"* (v. 8). As we have seen, *"love"* (*agapē*) is the mark of authentic Christian lifestyle. Jesus said that it was by this love that others would recognize us as His true disciples (John 13:35). Peter tells us not only to love, but to love fervently. The word "fervent" is *ektenēs,* which means intense or without ceasing. The *New English Bible* translates this phrase in a refreshing and helpful way: "Keep your love for one another at full strength."

This fervent love for one another should be a top priority of Christian lifestyle. Verse 8 says that our love should be *"above all things."* We cannot afford to let it slip or slide. This love must flow without ceasing. The faucet of love should never be turned off or even partially restrained. It should be flowing at full strength. This is the will of God for us.

How many problems which take place in our lives, in our families, in our churches, and in our communities could be easily resolved if Christians kept their love for God and each other at full strength. "There is nothing love cannot face; there is no limit to its faith, its hope, and its endurance" (1 Cor. 13:7, NEB).

After speaking about the priority of love, Peter now contends for the power of love. This quality of love can cover over all kinds of sins (v. 8). He appears to be quoting from the proverb which declares, "Hatred stirs up dissension, but love covers all wrongs" (Prov. 10:12, NIV). The word "cover" is *kalúptō,* which means "to cover up or to hide." This teaching does not suggest that love ignores the reality of sin nor justifies or condones sin. To the contrary, the only solution for sin is forgiveness—and love motivates us to forgive. In addition, love builds up rather than tears down (1 Cor. 8:1). Love focuses upon affirming strengths rather than criticizing weaknesses. It bears one another's burdens and so fulfills the law of Christ (Gal. 6:2).

I have discovered this Biblical principle to be exceedingly helpful in my own life. When I find myself becoming critical of one of my brothers or sisters in Christ, I ask the Lord to help me love that person with true *agapē* which is totally unconditional and which flows only from Him. What a difference takes place in my life and in my attitude. It is the difference between living in the flesh or living in the Spirit. The flesh criticizes and tears down, while the Spirit loves and builds up!

3. *"Be hospitable to one another without grumbling"* (v. 9). Authentic love must show itself in action in practical ways, and hospitality is one of the options. The Greek word for "hospitality" is *philóxenos,* which means to be fond of guests or to be a lover of hospitality. To be hospitable means to share what God has given to us with others including our home, our meals, our resources, and our very lives.

The early church was comprised of Christian brothers and sisters who loved to share with one another. Luke's description of that life-style of hospitality tells us, "They met constantly to hear the apostles teach, and to share the common life, to break bread, and to pray. . . . With one mind they kept up their daily attendance at the temple, and, breaking bread in private houses, shared their meals with unaffected joy, as they praised God and enjoyed the favour of the whole people" (Acts 2:42–47, NEB).

What a wonderful lifestyle—sharing all they had with one another as they praised God. This is in contrast to the spirit of selfishness and the human desire to protect what we have and keep it for ourselves. That is our mentality when we seek to run our own lives.

The ministry of hospitality continued to be very important in the early church. For example, the qualifications for a bishop or an overseer included the requirement of being hospitable (1 Tim. 3:2; Titus 1:8).

Peter not only instructs us to carry on this wonderful ministry of love and sharing, but we should do so without grumbling. There is the kind of Christian lifestyle that some practice in which one merely does what he or she is expected to do. It is usually done with grimness and with a legalistic spirit which is devoid of love or joy.

That is not authentic Christian lifestyle; it is hypocrisy and it is religious slavery in its worst form. How tragic it is to try to live for Christ and others merely out of a sense of religious duty. The fruit of the Holy Spirit can be flowing freely only when we are hospitable out of the motive of love and only when we delight to share the good things which God has entrusted to us.

YOU ARE CALLED TO MINISTRY

> 10 As each one has received a gift, minister it to one another, as good stewards of the manifold grace of God.
> 11 If anyone speaks, let him speak as the oracles of God. If anyone ministers, let him do it as with the ability which God supplies, that in all things God may be glorified through Jesus Christ, to whom is the praise and the dominion forever and ever. Amen.
>
> *1 Peter 4:10–11*

Peter is concerned about ministry. He has written about such important subjects as being serious and watchful in our prayers, practicing hospitality, and above all things, sharing fervent love with one another. Peter now turns his attention to the important area of practical ministry within the Body of Christ. His teaching is both clear and practical.

Verse 10 says we are to minister to one another *"as each one has received a gift."* The word translated as *"gift,"* chárisma, denotes a very special kind of gift. It comes from the root word cháris which means grace. Peter is writing about a "grace gift" or a spiritual gift which comes from the Lord.

There are four major passages in the New Testament that teach us about the important subject of spiritual gifts. They are Romans 12, 1 Corinthians 12–14, Ephesians 4, and this passage, 1 Peter 4. In addition, Paul encourages young Timothy to be faithful in using his spiritual gifts in 1 Timothy 4:14 and in 2 Timothy 1:6.

Peter contends that each of us has received at least one spiritual gift when he states, "As each one has received a gift." These gifts of grace are to be distinguished from natural talents which have been given to all of us through our natural birth.

In contrast, spiritual gifts are grace gifts of the Holy Spirit given only to those who have been born again of the Holy Spirit. The gifts are not static. Like the Holy Spirit, they are dynamic. The Spirit gives them as He wills (1 Cor. 12:3–11).

The logical questions that we might be asking may include: Why does God give spiritual gifts? What is the purpose of such gifts? How should they be used? Peter answers those questions very directly in his next statement: *"Minister it to one another"* (v. 10). The Greek word for *"minister"* is *diakoneō*, which means "to serve" or "to minister." From it we get our word "deacon." As you will remember, the deacons were appointed by the early church to serve the Body of Christ (Acts 6:2–4).

In summary, that is the purpose of spiritual gifts—to be used in ministry to one another. They are not given to us so that we will have a spiritual superiority complex nor to draw attention to us. None of us can ever say that he is more spiritual than a Christian brother or sister simply because God has given us a gift which they do not possess.

Paul states that the weaker gifts often receive more honor (1 Cor. 12:23–25). Fortunately, he doesn't identify the weaker gifts so that we cannot argue about who has the weaker or the most significant gifts. The Lord grants the gifts as He wills for the common good, or for the mutual benefit, of the Body (1 Cor. 12:1–7).

Spiritual gifts are functional only as we use them in ministry to one another. None of us receives all of the gifts to minister to each other. This is how the Body of Christ is built and how we all grow to become more and more like Christ (Eph. 4:11–13).

One of the questions I am often asked is, "How many ministers do you have at Lake Avenue Congregational Church?" I love to reply with an unexpected answer, "Oh, we have about three thousand ministers in our church." You see, I am giving a Biblical answer. We do have approximately three thousand members in our church. All of them have been called to ministry. Each of them has been given at least one spiritual gift which should be used in ministry to one another.

Do you realize how exciting it would be to be a part of a church which took this teaching seriously? Can you imagine what it would be like to have people spontaneously reach out with the loving attempt to minister to each other? That's the kind of church which God desires, and that's the kind of church which I want to pastor by using the spiritual gifts which God has entrusted to me. And I want and need to be ministered to by my brothers and sisters who are a part of the Body.

But how should we carry on that kind of ministry? What should be our approach and our attitude? As you might suspect, Peter answers those important questions as well.

"Minister . . . as good stewards of the manifold grace of God" (v. 10). In the day in which Peter lived, a steward was a slave. His life did not belong to himself. He belonged to his master. His purpose in life was to please his master. He owned nothing. He dispensed the goods of his master.

The *New English Bible* has a marvelous translation of this passage, "Like good stewards dispensing the grace of God in its varied forms" (1 Peter 4:10b). That is the highest calling of the Christian—to so live under the lordship of Jesus Christ that we acknowledge that He alone is our Master. Then we are called to serve Him and His people. We are the willing servants of Christ who have the delight of dispensing His grace in its varied forms. We minister to each other and build up the Body of Christ by using the grace gifts that God has entrusted to us.

Peter gives us two specific examples of the way in which these gifts of grace should be used within the Body. They are practical illustrations of how we should be involved in ministry to one another.

"If anyone speaks, let him speak as the oracles of God" (v. 11). In other words, if God has given us the gift of speaking, we should speak in the power of the Holy Spirit. We should speak as if God were speaking—the very words of God Himself.

"If anyone ministers, let him do it as with the ability which God supplies" (v. 11). We do not need to minister or serve in our own strength. We should do it in the strength and ability which God supplies.

This is true of every spiritual gift. A spiritual gift can never be administered in the flesh. It must always be used in the Spirit by allowing the Holy Spirit to minister through us. This is not a ministry which we carry on for God. Instead, it is a ministry which we must allow God to carry on through us.

What is the end result of such ministry? Peter also answers that question for us when he declares *"that in all things God may be glorified through Jesus Christ, to whom belong the glory and the dominion forever and ever. Amen"* (v. 11).

How exciting that is! As we allow the Holy Spirit to dwell within us, and as we allow Him to minister through us and the spiritual gifts which God has given to us, we are fulfilled and God is glorified. Does that not remind you of the answer to the first question in the Westminster catechism: "The chief end of man is to enjoy God and glorify Him forever"?

When we are living in the flow of the Spirit, and when we are using our spiritual gifts in the power of the Spirit, God is glorified through Jesus Christ our Lord. He is the One worthy to receive glory and praise forever and ever!

SUFFERING AS A CHRISTIAN

12 Beloved, do not think it strange concerning the fiery trial which is to try you, as though some strange thing happened to you;

13 but rejoice, insofar as you are partakers of Christ's sufferings, that when His glory is revealed, you may also be glad with exceeding joy.

14 If you are reproached for the name of Christ, blessed are you, for the Spirit of glory and of God rests on you. On their part He is blasphemed, but on your part He is glorified.

15 But let none of you suffer as a murderer, a thief, an evildoer, or as a busybody in other people's matters.

16 Yet if anyone suffers as a Christian, let him not be ashamed, but let him glorify God in this matter.

17 For the time has come for judgment to begin at the house of God. And if it begins with us first, what will be the end of those who do not obey the gospel of God?

18 And

"If the righteous one is scarcely saved,
Where will the ungodly and the sinner appear?"

19 Therefore let those who suffer according to the will of God commit their souls to Him in doing good, as to a faithful Creator.

1 Peter 4:12–19

Once again, Peter returns to his central theme of suffering. And once again, he focuses upon the positive aspects or benefits of suffering as a Christian. Suffering for the Christian must always be seen in the perspective of eternity. The glory of the Lord always lies ahead.

The first president of Columbia Bible College, Robert C. McQuilkin, once wrote, "It is suffering and then glory. Not to have the suffering means not to have the glory."

Many Christians are surprised or shocked when the trials and sufferings of Christ come into their lives. There is a popular theology which is espoused by some which suggests that the sun always shines upon the Christians, that our grass is always green, and that the spiritual temperature around us is always ideal.

Peter is reminding us that such teaching is simply not true. In fact, as we have seen, Christians will often suffer for doing good (3:13–18). We should not be surprised when the fiery trials come our way. We are at spiritual war with Satan himself. It is not a strange or unusual thing. Christians have faced trials and have suffered for their faith from the beginning of the church.

Peter himself suffered greatly for his Christian faith. Tradition tells us that he was crucified on a cross upside down because he felt unworthy to die in the same way as did his Master, Jesus Christ.

Nevertheless, Peter goes on to say, *"Rejoice insofar as you are partakers of Christ's sufferings"* (v. 13). Again, Peter refers to the identification we have with Christ and He has with us in His suffering for us. As we have seen, there is a kind of suffering which comes because we disobey the Lord—we reap what we sow. But in this context, Peter is obviously talking about another kind of suffering—that which comes from our identification with Christ (see commentary, p. 170). Peter reminds us of the day of the Lord when His glory shall be revealed. At that day, we shall truly rejoice and give God thanks for the privilege of suffering for Christ (v. 13). We will be glad with exceeding joy!

Peter tells us if we are reproached for Christ's sake we are blessed (v. 14). To be *"reproached"* is *oneidízō,* which means to "demote," to "chide," to "taunt," or to "revile." Jesus experienced such reviling as He hung upon the cross (Mark 15:32). In His Sermon on the Mount, Jesus said, "Blessed are you when they revile and persecute you, and say all kinds of evil against you falsely for My sake" (Matt. 5:11).

We should rejoice in such reproaching because it will affirm the fact that the Spirit of glory and of God rests on us (v. 11). The person who reproaches us is blaspheming, but Christ is being glorified through our lives. What a privilege is ours to suffer reproach for the name of Christ.

It is startling to us in our day to read in the Scriptures that "a murderer, a thief, or an evildoer" is to be confronted along with a "busybody in other people's matters" (v. 15). Although not many of us deserve the first three titles, many do deserve the last. Being a busybody does not befit the life of a Christian and does not bring glory to Christ.

When I was in college, I spent the summer working on a construction project with a group of rough and tough men. There was another Christian working on our crew who was ashamed to be identified as a believer. Instead, he joined the others in the life of overt sin and the constant flow of profanity. I found that I was teased a bit by my fellow workers for my personal faith in Christ, but I also had the opportunity of ministering to many of the men when they were hurting or in trouble. However, my Christian friend found himself suffering much more than I, not because of his Christian witness, but because of his sinful conduct. As Peter said, "It is better . . . to suffer for doing good than for doing evil" (3:17).

In fact, instead of being ashamed for suffering as a Christian, we should glorify God for the privilege (v. 16). Suffering for doing evil brings shame not only to the evildoer but to his or her family and loved ones. In contrast, suffering for Christ—for doing good—should bring glory to God, to the one who is suffering for Christ, and to the family of faith.

This glory should not only take place in the present tense, but also in the day of God's judgment (v. 17). For if His judgment begins first with us and the household of God, what will be the end of those who do not obey the Gospel of God? (v. 19).

In verse 18 Peter quotes from Proverbs 11:31, *"If the righteous one is scarcely saved, where will the ungodly and the sinner appear?"* (v. 18). That statement should bring us back to reality. Life is not lived merely in the present. We are accountable to God for all of our actions. There is a terrible consequence for sin, but great blessings for the believer and glory to God result when a Christian suffers for the name and cause of Christ.

I remember well a man who came to my office a number of years ago for counseling. He looked as if he had the weight of the world resting on his shoulders. He was stooped, his head was bowed, and his eyes were cast upon the floor. He was bearing a great deal of guilt for some trials and suffering he was experiencing. Some of his friends had convinced him that he must be living in sin or he would not be suffering so much.

He came to me so that I could assist him in identifying the sin which he had committed so that he could confess it to the Lord. As we visited and prayed together, I discovered that his friends were very wrong. He was suffering not for his sin, but because of his goodness and godliness. He was suffering as a Christian.

What a delight it was to share these verses from 1 Peter with him and to encourage him in being faithful in following Christ even if it meant some temporary suffering for the name of Christ. Peter reminded him that he should not be ashamed, but that he should glory in suffering for Christ.

I will never forget the change in the way that man looked when he left my office. His shoulders were erect, his head was high, and his face was shining with the glory of the Lord! Now he understood the reason for his suffering, and he was rejoicing and praising God for the privilege. He was not facing the judgment of God; he was facing the glory of God.

There is a marvelous solution for those of us who suffer according to the will of God. It is a profoundly simple solution—we should commit our souls to our Lord (v. 19).

He is the faithful Creator who made us in His image and who, through Christ, is in the process of making us become more and more like Him and less and less like the distortion which sin has created. He is to be trusted; He who calls us is faithful; He will do it (1 Thess. 5:24).

And, as we entrust ourselves to our faithful Creator, we should continue to do good. It is always the will of God, and it is always appropriate for the Christian to do good—even when we are suffering and hurting. That's what Paul and Silas did as they suffered in the Philippian jail; and that's what we should be doing day by day—to the glory of God.

NOTE

1. O. Hallesby, *Prayer* (Minneapolis: Augsburg Publishing House, 1931), p. 11.

CHAPTER FIVE

What Christian Leadership Is All About

1 Peter 5:1–14

God has given leadership gifts to those whom He has chosen to lead His Church. For example, in the fourth chapter of Ephesians we read that God has gifted some to be apostles, some prophets, some evangelists, and others pastors and teachers (Eph. 4:11).

But these gifts were not given as an end in themselves. They were given for the specific purpose of being used for the mutual and corporate benefit of the members of the Body of Christ—the Church. In short, God has given leadership gifts so that those leaders may serve the saints of God by equipping them for ministry—so that all of the members of the Body may be involved in active ministry—so that the Body of Christ might be built up—so that there may be a unity of the faith and of the knowledge of Jesus Christ—so that all of us may grow to become more and more like Jesus Christ, measured by nothing less than the full stature of Christ (Eph. 4:12–13).

That is one of the most important leadership models shared in all the Scriptures. In addition, Peter shares another vital leadership model in this final chapter of his first letter. It is a model all of us need to understand and then put into practice within our church and within our families. Christian leadership is a privilege given only by God. True Christian leaders are chosen by God—not by a mere human political system nor by the casting of lots. The Lord calls and the Lord anoints those who should give leadership to His Church.

PRIORITIES FOR CHRISTIAN LEADERSHIP

1 The elders who are among you I exhort, I who am a fellow elder and a witness of the sufferings of

Christ, and also a partaker of the glory that will be revealed:

2 Shepherd the flock of God which is among you, serving as overseers, not by constraint but willingly, not for monetary gain but eagerly;

3 nor as being lords over those entrusted to you, but being examples to the flock;

4 and when the Chief Shepherd appears, you will receive the crown of glory that does not fade away.

1 Peter 5:1–4

As we have noted earlier, Peter, the leader of the church of Jerusalem, was one of the most influential leaders of the first century church. He was the apostle who was a member of Christ's inner circle of three. He was the witness of the transfiguration of Christ. He was the human instrument upon whom Christ began to build His Church, as Peter stood on the Day of Pentecost and preached with the power of the Holy Spirit so that 3,000 persons were added to the church in one day. This same Peter now writes to the elders of the church and identifies himself not as their superior but as a fellow elder and a witness of the sufferings of Christ. That statement in itself is a powerful treatise on the role of godly leadership in the church.

This Peter, who had failed Christ so miserably when he attempted to serve Him in the flesh by falling asleep when Christ needed him the most (Matt. 26:40) and by denying Him at His hour of trial (Matt. 26:69–75), now teaches us how to give leadership, not in the flesh, but in the power and dynamic of the Holy Spirit. He shares with us four major priorities which we should follow in giving leadership to the church:

1. *"Shepherd the flock of God which is among you"* (v. 2). God has entrusted many of us with the marvelous privilege of shepherding His flock in the form of a local church. Notice that the emphasis is upon the fact that it is the flock of God. It is never "my" flock or "my" church. Christ is the Chief Shepherd (v. 4), and "I," Peter, am merely an undershepherd.

In order to be effective as an undershepherd, we need to be in close contact with the Chief Shepherd who is the Lord of the Church. We must live under His lordship and guide the members of the flock to follow Him as Lord. If we ever view the flock as "ours" or the ministry as "ours," we are in serious trouble, and so is the church.

The church at Corinth faced this difficulty. Some of the people decided to follow Paul as their shepherd while others chose to follow Apollos. Paul refuted this error and demanded that they follow neither Paul nor Apollos—but Christ. "Who then is Paul, and who is Apollos, but ministers through whom you believed, as the Lord gave to each one? I planted, Apollos watered, but God gave the increase. So then neither he who plants is anything, nor he who waters, but God who gives the increase" (1 Cor. 3:5–7).

Paul continues his teaching by asking his readers to put the human leadership of the church in proper perspective in the following manner: "Let a man so consider us, as servants of Christ and stewards of the mysteries of God" (1 Cor. 4:1). Indeed, that is a requirement of God if one is to be an effective undershepherd—to recognize that we are stewards of the flock of God which He has entrusted to our care. It is His flock, and we are His servants!

Within this same context, Peter instructs us to shepherd the flock of God. The Greek word for "shepherd" is poimainō, "to tend" or "to feed." It is the precise word that Jesus used when restoring Peter to fellowship with Him following Peter's denial. Jesus said to Peter, "Tend (poimainō) My sheep" (John 21:16). Without a doubt, that was the commissioning of Peter by Christ for his special ministry of tending or shepherding the flock of God.

Now Peter shares those same words of commissioning with us. To be the pastor of a church is more than merely a vocational choice. It is much more than merely fulfilling a job description prepared for us by a pastoral search committee. It is a holy calling and a sacred trust given to us by no one less than the Chief Shepherd of the flock of God! No one should be called to pastor a church who has not first been called and anointed by God.

As we consider that sacred and exciting task of shepherding, tending, and feeding the flock of God, the legitimate question becomes, How do I carry on that shepherding in the way in which God desires? In response to that kind of question, Peter continues his discourse on the four priorities of ministry by presenting three specific ways in which we should be involved in shepherding the flock of God:

2. *"Serving . . . not by constraint but willingly"* (v. 2). We should not serve by *"constraint,"* anagkastōs, which denotes serving by compulsion,

189

or because we have to. Unfortunately, there is that kind of mentality among many who serve in the church in the present day. The tendency is not to do it willingly or joyfully, but out of a sense of religious duty.

I have counseled with many pastors who are trapped in this syndrome. They feel that they are imprisoned by their calling to ministry. They would prefer to be somewhere else, they are not enjoying their ministry, or they are in a difficult situation from which they would like to escape. To them, ministry has become mere drudgery.

It need not be so! Peter reminds us that we should serve the Lord and tend His flock willingly. To serve *"willingly"* is *hekoúsios,* which means "voluntarily" or "willfully." That is the only way in which we can serve the Lord and serve His Church effectively. The Lord does not force us or coerce us to be involved in ministry. He calls us and invites us to ministry, but we have the freedom of saying "yes" or "no"!

To serve the Lord under constraint or because we feel compelled to do so against our will, is to not serve Him. If that is our motivation for ministry, it is much better that we not be involved in ministry; for not only do we suffer for that disobedience, but the flock of God which we are tending suffers with us.

3. *"Serving . . . not for dishonest gain but eagerly"* (v. 2). We should not serve for monetary or personal gain. The word here is *aischrokerdōs,* from a root word meaning "sordid gain" or "filthy lucre." It denotes a spirit of greediness.

Obviously, that should not be our motive for ministry. If we are involved in caring for the flock of God merely for our personal gain or for what personal gain we can derive from it, we are ministering for the wrong reason. The blessing of God cannot be upon us.

Within our society, most of us do not face the temptation for entering the ministry for purely monetary gain. Most persons involved vocationally in ministry could be earning more money in another profession and most lay persons involved in ministry make personal sacrifices in order to be involved. However, there are far more subtle kinds of personal gain which can be our reasons for ministry.

For example, one kind of personal gain which can be a temptation to those involved in ministry is that of personal recognition or personal power. In many churches, the pastor is the center of attention and has great power or authority which can be used for good or for evil.

All of us who are tending the flock of God need to maintain open and sensitive hearts to the Lord and to our brothers and sisters in Christ. We need to be on guard lest we slip into the trap of being involved in ministry for monetary or personal gain.

Instead, we should minister eagerly; not merely for what we can get out of it, but rather for what we can put into it. Investing in the lives of others is one of the highest callings and greatest privileges which God entrusts to any person. To serve *"eagerly"* is *próthumos,* which means to serve with a forward spirit—to serve with alacrity, readily, willingly.

Think of the difference in the effectiveness of our ministry if we are ministering with eagerness, initiative, and enthusiasm as opposed to doing it simply because we have to or because we are seeking personal gain or recognition. It is the difference between a boy carrying out the garbage because his mother made him do it as opposed to that same boy playing baseball because he wants to do it.

We have many pastors who act as if they are "carrying out the garbage" in their ministries. They need to be transformed into those who are eagerly "playing in the game" which God has prepared for them with excitement and enthusiasm, giving it everything they have—to the glory of God. We need to serve the flock of God not for monetary gain, but eagerly!

4. *"[Serve not] as being lords over those entrusted to you, but being examples to the flock"* (v. 3). God has not called us to be dictators to the flock of God, not even benevolent dictators. Unfortunately, that is the model being provided for us by many pastors and many local churches in the present day. To be sure, such a form of government may seem very efficient, but it can be very devastating.

Several years ago, I heard of a local church which had been founded and pastored by a sincere man who was such a dictator. The official board of the church was made up of himself, his wife, and his brother-in-law. Needless to say, when he departed, the church was in a state of absolute chaos. In an overreaction to the first pastor's style of leadership, the congregation called a young seminary graduate to be their pastor. For several years they gave themselves to dominating that young pastor and opposing most of his leadership.

After his departure, the church was served by an interim pastor. As he led the church through a wonderful time of healing and preparation for the pastor whom God was preparing to tend that flock, those observing his leadership learned many things about leadership style within the Body of Christ. One of the lessons became a deep conviction—it is never the leadership style of Jesus Christ for pastors to lord over the people of God. Rather, God has called us to serve His people, not to dominate them.

As Peter espouses this teaching, he is sharing from his own experience with Jesus. It was Jesus who had taught Peter and the disciples this important truth about Christian leadership, "You know that the rulers of the Gentiles lord it over them, and those who are great exercise authority over them. Yet it shall not be so among you; but whoever desires to become great among you, let him be your servant. And whoever desires to be first among you, let him be your slave— just as the Son of Man did not come to be served, but to serve, and to give His life a ransom for many" (Matt. 20:25–28).

Jesus practiced a "servant style" of leadership, and it is that "servant leadership style" which He has entrusted to us. An effective shepherd gives his life for his sheep, and an effective pastor gives his life for the flock of God.

Such a pastor does not merely tell his people where to go or what to do—he leads them; he is their example. In this passage, the word "example" is túpos, from the root meaning of a "die" or "stamp." Also, it means "model" or "pattern" or "print." That is one of the holy roles of a pastor—to be a model for his people. He is not a model of one who has reached perfection, but a model of one who has denied himself, is taking up his cross daily, and is following Jesus as the Lord of his life.

The pastor, like Paul, never attains full maturity in Christ, but he presses "on toward the goal for the prize of the upward call of God in Christ Jesus" (Phil. 3:12–14). He, with Paul, should say, "Imitate me, just as I also imitate Christ" (1 Cor. 11:1). Or, more specifically, "Follow my example as I follow Christ's" (NEB).

That is our four-step model: (1) to shepherd the flock of God which is among you (or entrusted to your care); (2) to serve not by constraint but willingly; (3) to serve not for monetary gain but eagerly; (4) to serve not by being lord over those entrusted to you, but by being examples to the flock.

As we are faithful to the Lord and to His flock, a marvelous promise is given to us: *"When the Chief Shepherd appears, you will receive the crown of glory that does not fade away"* (v. 4). In other words, we are accountable to the Chief Shepherd for the stewardship of how we care for His flock. He will reward those undershepherds who have been faithful in their ministry.

CLOTHING YOURSELVES WITH HUMILITY

5 Likewise you younger people, submit yourselves to your elders. Yes, all of you be submissive to one another, and be clothed with humility, for
"God resists the proud,
But gives grace to the humble."
6 Therefore humble yourselves under the mighty hand of God, that He may exalt you in due time,
7 casting all your care upon Him, for He cares for you.

1 Peter 5:5-7

As Peter has shared his counsel with the elders of the church, he now addresses the younger Christians specifically about a subject which most of us would prefer to ignore. It is the subject of submission.

1. *Be submissive* (v. 5). Peter has already written a great deal about the importance of submission in this letter: we should submit ourselves to every ordinance of man (2:13); servants should submit to their masters (2:18); wives should be subject to their husbands (3:1–5); and angels and authorities and powers are subject to Christ (3:22). (See commentary, p. 145.)

Submission is a vital part of authentic Christian lifestyle. We cannot truly follow Christ until we are willing to submit to Him as the Lord of our lives. Peter's initial counsel is to the younger people who are a part of the flock of God. They should submit themselves to their elders (v. 5). To *"submit"* is *hupotásso* which means "to be subject to" or "to submit yourself unto."

To be submissive is to obey. Obedience is vital to Christian lifestyle. One of the great problems of our society is the resistance to submission and obedience—even within the church. A major expression of sin is that of rebellion against authority. Christian young people need to learn to obey Christ, and they will be greatly blessed if they learn to be submissive to their Christian elders.

But young people should not only be submissive to their elders, all Christians should be submissive to one another (v. 5). All believers, even those with leadership responsibilities, should be submissive to one another. We use another word in our society which will help us understand the importance of submission to one another as members of the Body of Christ. It is the word "accountability."

Every one of us is ultimately accountable to Christ, the head of the Church. But we need also be careful to place ourselves in positions of being accountable to one another. For example, all of us who are pastors or leaders in the church should make certain that we are accountable to a group of God's people, whether this is a board of elders or deacons or the entire congregation.

This provides a necessary "check and balance" system for our ministry. People who love us and who love our Lord will "call us back" to truth if we should stray. They will encourage us when we are discouraged, and will love, support, and pray for us as we minister. No one should be involved in ministry without accountability to a group of other Christians. This will insure and assist us in our accountability to Jesus as Lord.

In the church of Christ, there should be no one lording over or dominating others. In love and honor, we should serve one another. We should be seeking first not to get but to give; not to be served but to serve.

2. *Be humble* (vv. 5–6). Submission and accountability are closely related to humility. Peter's instruction to us is that we should be clothed with humility. Within that context, someone has said, "Many would be scantily clad if clothed in their humility."

To be humble is to have the Spirit of Christ. "Let this mind be in you which was also in Christ Jesus, who, being in the form of God, did not consider it robbery to be equal with God, but made Himself of no reputation, taking the form of a servant, and coming in the likeness of men. And being found in appearance as a man, He humbled Himself and became obedient to the point of death, even the death of the cross" (Phil. 2:5–8).

Humility is essential for Christian lifestyle. Only when we are clothed with humility can we come to know Christ better and grow to become more like Him. As Thomas à Kempis wrote, "God walks with the humble; He reveals himself to the lowly; He gives understanding to the little ones; He discloses His meaning to pure minds, but hides His grace from the proud."

Peter quotes from Proverbs 3:34 when he writes, "God resists the proud, but gives grace to the humble." Therefore, he concludes, we should humble ourselves under the mighty hand of God (v. 6). In other words, we should see God as He really is, and we should see ourselves as we really are. God's hands are mighty. His weakness is mightier than our strength. His foolishness is greater than our wisdom.

He is the Creator, and we are the created. All things were made by Him and by Him all things exist. God determines the days of our lives. Whether we wish to be or not, we are in His hands—at His disposal. He alone is sovereign!

And so He has given us a choice. We can resist Him and ignore Him and even curse Him. We can go our own way and do our own thing. But that way leads to certain death—eternal death.

Or we can recognize Him for who He is. We can respond to His love and grace and forgiveness. We can humble ourselves under His mighty hand. And, if we do, His promise is that He will exalt us in due time (v. 6). And through Him we will have life eternal. The Scriptures declare, "Before honour is humility" (Prov. 15:33).

Because of the humility, submission, and obedience of Jesus Christ, "God also has highly exalted Him and given Him the name which is above every name, that at the name of Jesus every knee should bow . . ." (Phil. 2:9–10). And the Lord will also exalt His children who walk humbly with Him.

3. *Be dependent* (v. 7). As we humble ourselves under the mighty hand of God, we should become increasingly dependent upon Him. Peter says, "Casting all your care upon Him" (v. 7). "To cast" is *epirhíptō,* which means "to throw upon." That is exactly what we should do. Christ desires deeply to carry our cares. "He has borne our griefs and carried our sorrows" (Isa. 53:4). He has invited us, "Come to me, all you who labor and are heavy laden, and I will give you rest. Take My yoke upon you and learn from Me, for I am gentle and lowly in heart, and you will find rest for your souls. For My yoke is easy and My burden is light" (Matt. 11:28–30).

Peter's use of the word "all" is most interesting. He encourages us to cast all of our cares upon Him. For some reason, many of us contemporary Christians seem to be pseudo-sophisticated about such things. Many have worked out quite an elaborate scheme regarding what kind of problems they should bring to the Lord. As one woman said to me recently, "I don't bother God with my small problems. I only bring the big ones to Him."

God desires for us to be deeply dependent upon Him with all of our cares, sorrows, problems, needs, and questions. Nothing is too big for God nor is anything too small. Our Lord cares for a single sparrow and knows the very number of the hairs of our heads (Luke 12:6–7). And He cares about our small problems as well as the large. He desires for us to be dependent upon Him, to trust in Him with all of our hearts and to lean not unto our own understanding (Prov. 3:5).

We should cast all of our care upon Him because "He cares for you" (v. 7). Think of it. God cares for you. He loves you. He delights in caring for you! In this verse, the word for *"care"* is *mérimna*, meaning "to be anxious about" or "to be concerned." God is interested in you; He is concerned about your needs. He cares for you.

We can never know true liberty, we can never be truly free until we cast our cares upon the Lord. A mark of maturity in the life of the Christian is to become increasingly dependent upon Christ. The more we depend upon Him, the more mature and free we become in Christ.

A number of years ago, a successful businessman came to see me. Although he was a professing Christian, he never attended any church. However, he had founded a breakfast group of Christian businessmen and served as its president. He was a man who was always in control of every situation. He dominated his business, his breakfast group, and his family.

He came to see me secretly and out of sheer desperation. He was facing a major problem in his life and didn't know what to do. He couldn't bring it under control. His theology did not allow for such a thing. In his opinion, a Christian wasn't supposed to have problems.

As we shared together, I had the delight of introducing him to the wonderful message of this passage. I told him that he didn't have to carry the problem by himself; Christ wanted to carry it for him. He only needed to cast it upon the Lord.

I will never forget his response. He sat in complete silence for several moments as he contemplated the possibility of committing his problem to Christ. He was a strong, handsome, self-made man, and his will was not broken easily. Then his lower jaw began to tremble. Next tears began to form in his eyes. He tried to deny them, but they would not cooperate. Suddenly he broke into uncontrollable sobbing. The dam had broken!

That day was a turning point in his life. He gave his problem to

Christ—but he did much more than that. He heeded the counsel of God's Word as shared by Peter. He began to love in submission to Christ and to his brothers and sisters in Christ; he humbled himself before the Lord and cast his cares upon Him. What a remarkable difference took place in his life, and what a remarkable difference will take place in our lives as we cast our cares upon the Lord and begin to live with the confidence that He cares for us.

STANDING FIRM IN THE FAITH

8 Be sober, be vigilant; because your adversary the devil walks about like a roaring lion, seeking whom he may devour.
9 Resist him, steadfast in the faith, knowing that the same sufferings are experienced by your brotherhood in the world.
10 But may the God of all grace, who has called us to His eternal glory by Christ Jesus, after you have suffered a while, perfect, establish, strengthen, and settle you.
11 To Him be the glory and the dominion forever and ever. Amen.

1 Peter 5:8–11

As Peter comes to the close of his first letter, he shares some important counsel regarding how we should be standing firm in the faith. He begins with a warning.

"Be sober, be vigilant" (v. 8). "To be sober" is *nepho*, which means "to be watchful," "self-controlled," or "not under the influence of intoxicants." Peter used the same word to encourage us in verse 13 of the first chapter of this letter, and again when he encouraged us to be serious and watchful in our prayers because the end of all things is at hand (4:7). (See the discussion of the word *"sober"* on p. 123.)

We should be also *"vigilant"* (from *grēgoreō*), "to be watchful" or "awake." Jesus used this word with Peter in the Garden of Gethsemane when he said, "Watch and pray, lest you enter into temptation" (Matt. 26:41). Paul uses the same word in writing, "Watch, stand fast in the faith, be brave, be strong" (1 Cor. 16:13).

We should be on watch for our adversary, the devil, who walks around us like a roaring lion, waiting to devour us (v. 8). What a contrast from the previous verse in which we are told about Jesus who longs to protect us and take care of us! Here we read about the devil who desires to devour us. In fact, he is on the offensive, like a hungry lion stalking its prey.

Malcolm Collins, a missionary supported by our church as he ministers in Africa, recently gave the children's message in one of our morning services. What he shared was most interesting and helpful. He told the children (and scores of interested adults) what to do in case we ever met or encountered a hungry lion. The first thing to remember is that you should never try to flee. That would mean certain death. The lion can run much faster than we can. Next, you should try to look very brave and stare right into the lion's eyes. If you are successful, he will back down and run away. However, if that does not work, you should be prepared for the lion to attack you. Have your spear ready so that when he leaps upon you, he will land on the spear and be killed!

That is not only wonderful advice regarding how to meet a lion, it is also helpful advice on how to meet the devil. We should not try to flee from him. Instead, we should resist him by being steadfast in the faith (v. 9). To *"resist"* is *anthístēmi*, which means "to stand against" or "withstand." James gives us the same counsel. "Therefore submit to God. Resist the devil and he will flee from you. Draw near to God and He will draw near to you" (James 4:7–8).

We need to be alert and watchful so that we can resist the devil when he attacks us. Victory is promised to us as we submit to the Lord and draw close to Him. We should then resist the devil, and he will flee from us!

The two steps go hand in hand. You shouldn't attempt to do one without the other. First, you should draw near to the Lord and then you should resist the devil (see commentary, p. 82). Our only defense against the evil one is through the power of Christ. And, as we resist him, we should know that we are not the only ones who face the sufferings that come from the attacks of the devil. We should remember our brothers and sisters in Christ throughout the world who are suffering for the sake of Christ (v. 9).

As we resist the devil, we have seen that we should also submit ourselves to the Lord (v. 10). Peter reminds us again that the attacks of the devil and suffering for doing good are not wasted as we entrust ourselves to Christ Jesus. It is He who has called us to His eternal glory (v. 10). The God of all grace, who will allow us to suffer for a little while, will use that suffering to accomplish four important things in our lives.

1. He will perfect us. "To perfect" is *katartízō*, which means "to restore," "to mend," or "to complete thoroughly." That is exactly what God desires to do with our lives. He wants to restore what sin has taken from us, to mend what sin has broken, to complete us thoroughly so that we may grow to become more and more like Christ.

2. He will establish us. "To establish," *stērízō*, means "to turn resolutely in a certain direction," "steadfastly set," or "strengthen." Again, God will use the suffering in our lives to turn us resolutely to Him, to forsake sin, to be steadfast in Him, and to be strengthened by Him.

3. He will strengthen us. "To strengthen" is *sthenóō*, which means "to give vigor" or "to make firm." God desires to make us vigorous and strong for Him and to make us firm in our commitment to Him.

4. He will settle us. "To settle" (*themelióō*) means "to consolidate," or "to lay a foundation." Our Lord desires to use our brief times of suffering to consolidate all the fragments of our lives and to bring them under His control in order to lay a solid foundation in our lives—Jesus Christ Himself—and to settle us from all of our instability.

God uses our suffering for good! By it we are perfected, established, strengthened, and settled. By faith we submit ourselves increasingly to Jesus as the Lord of our lives. And as we do, we depend more and more upon Him and we give to Him the glory and the dominion forever and ever (v. 11). We recognize more clearly who He is and who we are—and that causes us to bow down and worship Him as Lord.

FINAL GREETINGS

12 By Silvanus, our faithful brother as I consider him, I have written to you briefly, exhorting and testifying that this is the true grace of God in which you stand.

13 She who is in Babylon, elect together with you, greets you; and so does Mark my son.

199

14 Greet one another with a kiss of love. Peace be
with you all who are in Christ Jesus. Amen.

1 Peter 5:12–14

Peter's words of closing are consistent with his spirit of pastoral concern and love which has been expressed through the letter. He refers to Silvanus (v. 12) who was either the secretary or courier for the letter, or both. Peter then summarizes the contents of the letter: "I have written to you briefly, exhorting and testifying that this is the true grace of God in which you stand" (v. 12).

He then brings greeting from the church in Babylon, which is probably Rome, as well as greeting from "Mark my son" (v. 13). This Mark is thought to be the John Mark of Acts 12:12, 15:37, the same person to whom Paul refers in several of his letters including his letter to the church at Colossae (Col. 4:10). It was also John Mark who wrote the second gospel—the Gospel of Mark.

His final words reflect two of the major themes of the Christian faith which are key words in the vocabulary of the Christian family— "love" and "peace." He encourages us to greet one another with a kiss of love (*agapē*). This was one of the beautiful customs of the early Christians who related to one another as members of the family of Christ. Paul shared this same instruction in several of his letters, including Romans 16:16 and 1 Corinthians 16:20.

"Peace" is a fitting word for the climax. The people of God who are suffering and dispersed and unsettled can enjoy God's peace, which is far more wonderful than our minds can comprehend and which no one can take from us! "Peace be with you all who are in Christ Jesus" (v. 14). Amen!

Introduction to 2 Peter

Several years ago, I was invited to speak at an evangelistic meeting sponsored by the Navigators in Denver, Colorado. As I shared a simple message on the adventure of knowing Christ, I closed my remarks by extending an invitation to anyone who would like to know more about knowing Christ personally as Savior and Lord.

Among those who responded was a master sergeant in the air force. He shared a story with me which I shall never forget. For years he had been assigned the task of training new recruits during their basic training. He was an alienated man who hated himself, God, and everyone who came into his life.

His favorite hobby was to destroy the religious faith of his young recruits. For example, whenever he recognized any trace of the Christian faith in the life of a recruit, he would attack that young man in every possible way in order to destroy his faith.

However, recently he encountered something new. As he was attacking the faith of some of his newest recruits, they responded to him in a most unusual way. They reached out to him with love. He did not know what to do. The more he hated and abused them, the more they loved him. They invited him to attend the Navigator meeting that evening, and he had come out of curiosity. As he listened to my explanation of the new life in Christ, the Holy Spirit convicted him of sin and the need of a Savior. He responded by coming to visit with me.

As he poured out his life story of sin, immorality, hate, and persecution of Christians and others, he asked me, "Could God ever forgive me?" How delighted I was to tell him about Saul, who was committed to persecuting Christians, who became the great Apostle Paul. That evening, the tough, bitter master sergeant opened his life to Jesus Christ and became a new spiritual baby. He was wonderfully converted, and just a few months later, during a Billy Graham Crusade, I had the joy of seeing him lead a young air force cadet to personal faith in Christ.

The epistle called 2 Peter is directed to Christians who are suffering the kind of persecution that the master sergeant brought to bear upon his recruits. Amid great persecution and trials under the Emperor Nero, there were false teachers who arose in the church who were attempting to lead the young Christians astray.

Peter begins with words of affirmation and encouragement and then presents a lengthy rebuttal against those false teachers, which includes part of chapter one, all of chapter two, and part of chapter three. He pleads with his readers to keep on following Jesus, to place their trust in God, and to resist the false teachers who would like to lead them astray.

He calls them back to the basics of the faith. He reminds us God is always on time and Jesus Christ is going to return at God's appointed time. The Lord keeps His promises. He does not desire for any to perish but that all should come to eternal life. And so, we should remain faithful, enjoying His peace, and resting in His righteousness.

The Author

The introductory statement of this letter, found in verse one of the first chapter is *"Simon Peter, a servant and apostle of Jesus Christ."* And yet the authorship of Peter has been challenged by many Biblical scholars both in the early church and in the present day of Biblical criticism. The reasons for this suspicion are many. For example, there is a difference in content and form between 1 and 2 Peter.

However, for our purposes, I propose we recognize the authorship of the Apostle Peter of this epistle based upon a number of strands of internal evidence, including his introductory statement (1:1), his reference to this as his second epistle (3:1) and to his being an apostle (1:1, 3:2), his apparent reference to being an eyewitness at the transfiguration of Christ (1:16–18), and his statement concerning his impending death as the fulfillment of the prophetic statement made by Jesus in John 21:18 (1:13, 14).

The Recipients

Those to whom this letter is addressed are not as clearly defined as are the recipients of 1 Peter and James. They are referred to as *"those who have obtained like precious faith with us by the righteousness of our God and Savior Jesus Christ"* (1:1).

Although we cannot identify the recipients by geographical location or nationality, we can discover some basic facts about them from the internal evidence of the letter. These were Christians who were grounded in the basics of the Christian faith. Peter is writing to stir them up and to remind them of the truth (1:12, 13).

They are also being besieged by false teachers who would lead them astray. Peter refutes the false teachers with a variety of warnings (chap. 2). Within this context, he gives strong encouragement to the Christians to remain faithful to God. They are to be diligent in making their call and election sure (1:10); then they will never stumble.

The Occasion

Because of the questions of authorship, scholars are not at all in agreement on the dating of this letter. Some believe it was written as late as A.D. 150. Personally, I subscribe to the view it was probably written by Peter from Rome in about A.D. 67 shortly before his death. The internal evidence which I have shared would tend to support this view.

Of some things we can be certain. Peter is writing to a suffering church which is facing the most difficult of all trials. In addition to the persecution by Nero, the Jewish leaders, and others who oppose the Christian faith, now the young church is being attacked from within.

Those who call themselves Christian teachers are attempting to lead the young Christians astray. Peter is writing to expose and to refute them as well as to encourage the Christians to return to the basics of the faith and not to depart from them.

Since we face some of those same challenges within our society, 2 Peter is an excellent book for contemporary Christians to study and master so we will not be led astray. The first and third chapters review the basic tenets of the Christian faith upon which we should build our lives.

Plan of Exposition

Our continued approach will be that of using the inductive approach of Bible study. As we have seen in these introductory remarks, the internal evidence of the epistle gives us clear indication of the author, the recipients, and the occasion for which it was written.

Within the content of this letter, we will discover basic similarities between this letter and the Epistle of Jude, including the punishment of fallen angels (2 Pet. 2:4; Jude 6), the angels' reluctance to bring a "reviling accusation" against Satan (2 Pet. 2:11 and Jude 9), and the reference to the coming of scoffers in the last days (2 Pet. 3:3, 4; Jude 17, 18).

NOTE

1. Michael Green, *The Second Epistle of Peter: An Introduction and Commentary*, The Tyndale New Testament Commentaries (Grand Rapids: William B. Eerdmans, 1979).

An Outline of 2 Peter

CHAPTER ONE

Keep on Following Jesus

2 Peter 1:1–21

Peter writes to the Christians of the early church who experienced so much suffering and persecution and who overcame so many trials. This is a letter of encouragement and affirmation. He encourages them and us to keep on keeping on! We must resist the evil one and his false teachers and keep on following Jesus.

Faithfulness is a high priority in Christian discipleship. In fact, faithfulness is one of the fruits of the Spirit shared in Galatians 5:22. In his message to the faithful church in Philadelphia, Jesus promises the one who is faithful and overcomes will be a pillar in the temple of God (Rev. 3:12).

GREETINGS

1 Simon Peter, a servant and an apostle of Jesus Christ,

To those who have obtained like precious faith with us by the righteousness of our God and Savior Jesus Christ:

2 Grace and peace be multiplied to you in the knowledge of God and of Jesus our Lord,

2 Peter 1:1–2

In his greeting, Peter exposes his humble spirit by referring to himself as a servant of Jesus Christ before he identifies himself as an apostle. This is more than literary style; it is the conviction of his life. In his first letter he taught the basic principles of servant leadership (1 Pet. 5:1-4) which he learned from Jesus, his Master (Matt. 20:25-28). As Peter's life was coming to a close, he had a clear understanding of who he was and who his Master was. He walked humbly with Jesus Christ as his Lord.

He addresses *"those who have obtained like precious faith with us by the righteousness of our God and Savior Jesus Christ"* (v. 2). Again, his spirit is like that which he communicated in his first letter as he identified himself as a fellow elder (1 Pet. 5:1). His spirit is not that of a dictator who is lording over his subjects.

To the contrary, he speaks with authentic humility as one who has followed Christ for many years. He left everything to follow Christ, was one of the inner circle of three disciples, failed Christ miserably by denying Him at a time of great need, was a witness to the resurrected Christ, experienced his own spiritual resurrection at Pentecost as he was baptized by the Holy Spirit, served as a leader in the early church as it spread throughout the world, and was now ministering to a suffering church as he himself was preparing for a martyr's death. Indeed, he walked humbly with God.

Within his greeting, Peter refers to the precious faith he "shares" (*isótimos*) with his readers. This is the common denominator that brings true believers together. As Peter shared in his first letter, this precious faith had been bought by the very blood of Jesus Christ, the Lamb of God (1 Pet. 1:19). This precious faith comes not through human righteousness but "by the righteousness of our God and Savior Jesus Christ" (1:1).

This is a marvelous truth. Most of us have enjoyed the experience of visiting a group of Christian believers in another community, state or even in another country. If they are true believers in Jesus Christ, and we both are walking in the fellowship of the Holy Spirit, we enjoy immediate fellowship—even when we do not understand the language of one another. This is the unity of the Spirit which is unique to the Christian family. We are all members of the Body of Christ with Jesus Christ being our Head.

GOD'S DIVINE POWER CAN BE OURS

3 as His divine power has given to us all things
that pertain to life and godliness, through the
knowledge of Him who has called us by glory and
virtue,

4 by which have been given to us exceedingly great
and precious promises, that by these you may be
partakers of the divine nature, having escaped the
corruption that is in the world through lust.

5 But also for this very reason, giving all diligence,
add to your faith virtue, to virtue knowledge,

6 to knowledge self-control, to self-control
perseverance, to perseverance godliness,

7 to godliness brotherly kindness, and to brotherly
kindness love.

8 For if these things are yours and abound, they
keep you from being either barren or unfruitful in
the knowledge of our Lord Jesus Christ.

9 For he who lacks these things is blind, cannot
see afar off, and has forgotten that he was purged from
his old sins.

2 Peter 1:3–9

As we have seen in Peter's first letter, he believes excellent defense
to be the best offense. Now as he begins his second letter, Peter
contends an excellent offense can be the best defense. He is concerned
these young Christians will be led astray by false teachers.

Rather than beginning his instruction by warning them against
the false teachers, he begins on the offensive by reminding them
and us of the basics of authentic Christianity. If we continue to live
by the divine power which God has given to us, and if we continue to grow in the grace and knowledge of Jesus Christ, we will
be victors. We will not fall into false teachings. And Peter gives us
the specific steps to follow if we are to be victorious through Jesus
Christ.

1. *Be aware that "His divine power has given to us all things"* (v. 3). The
statement made by Peter is not in the future tense. Peter contends
God has already given us His divine power and through that power
He has made everything we need available to us which pertains to
life and godliness.

Peter's teaching sounds like that of Paul when he declared "I can
do all things through Christ who strengthens me" (Phil. 4:13). Again,
he shared with the Colossian Christians, "For in Him [Jesus] dwells
all the fullness of the Godhead bodily; and you are complete in Him,
who is the head of all principality and power" (Col. 2:9, 10). In other
words, when you have Jesus Christ, you have everything you need!

The Lord has not given us a spirit of fear or weakness, but of "power and of love and of a sound mind" (2 Tim. 1:7). That is how we should live according to Peter. We must remember God has given us His divine power in order for us to follow, obey, and grow up into Him! Peter is calling upon us to live by that power which comes to us through the knowledge of Jesus who has "called us by glory and virtue" (1:3).

In other words, when we are born anew of the Spirit through faith in Jesus Christ, we receive the gift and power of the Holy Spirit just as Christ promised (Acts 1:8). We need to use that power to the glory of God. This is but one of the wonderful promises our Lord has given us.

2. *Appropriate the "great and precious promises" God has given to us* (v. 4). The promises of God are great and precious. The word "precious," *timios*, meaning valuable or costly, is a favorite word of Peter. He uses it extensively in both of his letters. For example, he uses it to describe our precious faith (1 Pet. 1:7) and the precious blood of Jesus Christ (1 Pet. 1:19). The promises of God are precious for at least two reasons:

First, they allow us to "be partakers of the divine nature" (v. 4). What a precious promise that is. Jesus first gave it to His disciples shortly before His crucifixion when He said, "It is to your advantage that I go away; for if I do not go away, the Helper will not come to you; but if I depart, I will send Him to you" (John 16:7).

That is exactly what happened to the disciples who gathered together on Pentecost. The Holy Spirit came upon them, and His divine nature replaced their own. And that marvelous promise is for us and our children (Acts 2:39).

And so, "if anyone is in Christ, he is a new creation; old things have passed away; behold, all things have become new" (2 Cor. 5:17). The implications of this promise are incredible for us. We have the potential to live by the very power of God. God's divine nature can replace ours as we follow Jesus as Lord and as we allow the Holy Spirit to possess us.

Second, the promises of God allow us to escape "the corruption that is in the world through lust" (v. 4). That is a major concern of Peter for the Christians to whom he is writing—including us. When we walk and live in the power of the Holy Spirit, we are walking in the opposite direction of our natural life. Paul stated that truth in Galatians 5:16, 17: "Walk in the Spirit, and you shall not fulfill the lust of the flesh. For the flesh lusts against the Spirit, and the Spirit against the flesh; and these are contrary to one another."

3. *Give all diligence to our faith* (v. 5). As Peter continues his practical advice concerning the basics of the Christian faith, he acknowledges the need for us to take the initiative to build our faith. He gives us seven steps we should follow in building our spiritual lives.

(1) Add virtue to faith (v. 5). As we have seen, the Christian life begins with faith and is carried on with "faith" (*pístis*). Without faith we cannot please God (Heb. 11:6). To our faith we should add *"virtue"* (*aretḗ*) which is sometimes translated as "goodness" or "moral excellence." Faith which is honoring to God is to have the character of goodness and moral excellence.

(2) Add knowledge to virtue (v. 5). Faith is not blind. It does not exist in a vacuum. If faith is to be active obedience to God, then we must have "knowledge" (*epígnōsis*) of God and of His will for us. This knowledge is in stark contrast to our former ignorance which led us to live former lusts (1 Pet. 1:14).

(3) Add self-control to knowledge (v. 6). To know is vitally important, but it is not enough. We are to do what we know we should do. In many of our lives, there is a great gulf between our knowledge and our conduct. It was to this problem James spoke when he wrote, "to him who knows to do good and does not do it, to him it is sin" (James 4:17). The Greek word for "self-control" is *egkráteia,* which is sometimes translated as temperance. It is one element of the fruit of the Spirit mentioned in Galatians 5:23. In the real sense of the term, it means more than self being in control. A more descriptive and accurate term would be "God-control." Only when we are under the control of the Holy Spirit can we be self-controlled.

(4) Add perseverance to self-control (v. 6). Both James and Peter write a great deal about the virtue of "perseverance" (*hupomonḗ*). This word means "enduring, continuance or patience" and comes from the root word *hupoménō* which can mean "to bear trials, to have fortitude, to abide or to endure." In our vernacular, we would say perseverance means "hanging in there." There are only seconds which separate those who fail from those who succeed in running most races. Too many people drop out of the race just before it is to be won. Those who persevere by "hanging in there" are those who win the prize.

(5) Add godliness to perseverance (v. 6). The Greek word for godliness, *eusébeia,* means "godly, pious, or devout." Godliness cannot be fabricated. We cannot merely pretend to be godly. The quality of godliness comes from God Himself. He must give that quality of life to us. We receive it as we are dead to self and alive to God

and as we allow the Spirit to live within us. The fruits of the Spirit are attributes of the character of God. The more we are possessed by God, the more we will act like Him and the more His character will be revealed in our lives.

(6) Add brotherly kindness to godliness (v. 7). "Brotherly kindness" or brotherly love is a special kind of love. The Greek word is familiar to us from our study of 1 Peter. It is *philadelphía*. Peter uses this word in instructing us regarding the importance of having unfeigned love of the brethren (1 Pet. 1:22); he teaches us to be kindly, affectionate to one another in brotherly love (Rom. 12:10). This is one of the amazing qualities of the Church of Jesus Christ. We are to love one another as brothers and sisters in Christ—and are members one to another (1 Cor. 12:27). We must live out our faith by having love for our brothers and sisters in Christ.

(7) Add love to brotherly kindness (v. 7). There is a wonderful quality of love between brothers and sisters. That is *philadelphía*. There is an even deeper quality of love which knows no limits and has no conditions. It is *agápē*—the very quality of the love of God. In fact, the most simple and profound definition of *agápē* in all of literature is simply this: "God is *agápē*" (1 John 4:8). *Agápē* is the highest expression of love and the ultimate mark of Christian lifestyle. By it we shall be recognized as the disciples or followers of Christ (John 13:35). *Agápē* is also a part of the fruit of the Spirit (Gal. 5:22). Peter believes in the priority of love. In his first letter he wrote, "And above all things have fervent love for one another, for 'love will cover a multitude of sins' " (Prov. 10:12; 1 Pet. 4:8).

In the foregoing steps, then, we have the progression of growing in our faith. Begin with a vital faith in Jesus Christ and then add virtue, knowledge, self-control, perseverance, godliness, brotherly kindness, and love. If we make these things ours and they abound, says Peter, two specific benefits will follow: (1) They will keep us from being barren (v. 8). None of us want to be *"barren"* (*argós*) in our Christian lives. To be barren is "to be useless or idle." The best defense against such a useless life is an active offense. If we are actively following Jesus Christ as Lord and are diligent in adding to our faith, we will never be barren in our Christian life.

(2) They will keep us from being "unfruitful in the knowledge of our Lord Jesus Christ" (v. 8). Jesus gave instruction to Peter and to all of us concerning the life of bearing fruit when He said, "Abide in Me, and I in you. As the branch cannot bear fruit of itself, unless

it abides in the vine, neither can you, unless you abide in Me" (John 15:4).

The secret of fruit-bearing is to abide in Christ and to allow Him to abide in us. Peter encourages us to follow Jesus aggressively by adding to our faith with all diligence; then we will never be unfruitful.

If these things are not ours, Peter says we will reap two negative results (v. 9). Again we follow the Biblical principle of reaping what we sow. The person who lacks these things faces two dilemmas:

(1) *He will be blind: he cannot see afar off* (v. 9). In other words, this is the kind of blindness which prevents us from seeing ahead. Such blindness is one of the expressions of the deceitfulness of sin. It blinds us and prevents us from seeing things as they really are. Sin leads us astray.

(2) *He "has forgotten that he was purged from his old sins"* (v. 9). How tragic it is to have our sins forgiven by our Lord and then to forget that forgiveness and live once again in our trespasses and sins.

You Need Never to Stumble

10 Therefore, brethren, be even more diligent to make your calling and election sure, for if you do these things you will never stumble;

11 for so an entrance will be supplied to you abundantly into the everlasting kingdom of our Lord and Savior Jesus Christ.

12 Therefore I will not be negligent to remind you always of these things, though you know them, and are established in the present truth.

13 Yes, I think it is right, as long as I am in this tent, to stir you up by reminding you,

14 knowing that shortly I must put off my tent, just as our Lord Jesus Christ has shown me.

15 Moreover I will endeavor that you always may be able to have a reminder of these things after my decease.

2 Peter 1:10–15

After making a strong presentation of the basics of the Christian faith, Peter now goes on to personal application. In fact, he presents more than application; he is deeply concerned about accountability.

He places himself in the position of reminding his readers of these truths, and of stirring them up to remain faithful. He is even concerned with providing them with a reminder after his death. As he shares these concerns, Peter makes three specific statements about application and accountability:

1. *"Make your calling and election sure"* (vv. 10, 11). Peter now appeals to us to be even more diligent to make our calling and election sure. The word "diligent" is *spoudē,* from the root word *speúdō,* meaning "to speed" or "to urge on." By diligence, Peter means we should move ahead with eagerness and earnestness.

The phrase *"make your calling and election sure"* is rather difficult for some Christians to understand since it doesn't seem to fit neatly into their theological system. We must understand the context in which Peter is sharing this teaching. He is deeply concerned for these believers as they face the onslaught of false teachers.

He wants them to be deeply anchored in the truth of God and in a personal relationship to Jesus Christ as Lord. He knows if they are grounded in the basics of the faith, and if they remain active in those basics, he will never need to fear their being led astray.

As we have seen, the basics to which he called them and calls us are all dependent upon a vital, present-tense relationship to Jesus Christ as Lord. The Christian life is not a list of propositions or a tight theological system; it is a vital relationship to a resurrected Lord. The commandments He gave us and the theological systems we devise as an understanding of those propositional truths exist only to help us live in a vital relationship with Christ day by day as we follow Him as Lord.

As these verses demonstrate, Peter is concerned that we be sure of that relationship in the present tense. We cannot merely clip coupons on the past, but we must follow Christ in the present! If we do this, and if we are faithful to those basics of the faith, we will enjoy two measurable results:

(1) We *"will never stumble"* (v. 10). That promise meets the basic concern Peter expresses about the false teachers, and his statement is consistent with our human experience. We do not stumble when we are giving attention to where we are stepping. We stumble when we become preoccupied with other things and do not pay attention to where we are going.

And so it is with our Christian walk. When we keep our eyes upon Jesus, following Him and practicing the basics of the faith diligently, we need not fear going astray or stumbling. We will not fall.

(2) *We will enter Christ's kingdom* (v. 11). Not only are we assured of not stumbling in the present tense, but we are assured an entrance will be supplied abundantly into the everlasting Kingdom of our Lord and Savior Jesus Christ in the future. As we follow Jesus and remain faithful to the basic principles of the faith, we are secure for the present and for eternity.

When I was in high school, I was involved in a number of sports, including track. I will never forget the first race I ran in competition—the 220-yard dash. I was so excited about the race I could not contain myself.

When the gun sounded, I was off like a shot. As I neared the finish line, I was several yards in front of my competitors. Then, a tragic thing happened: just a few yards from the finish line, I stumbled and fell. As a result, I did not win the race.

That is Peter's concern for us. We must not only begin the race, or complete most of it; we must finish the race in order to capture the prize! Peter assures us as we remain faithful to Christ and the basics of the faith, we will not stumble; we will finish the race and receive the prize of entering the everlasting Kingdom of our Lord and Savior Jesus Christ. Victory is ours through Jesus Christ!

2. *I will "remind you always of these things"* (vv. 12–14). Now Peter comes to the accountability factor. He speaks as a pastor with a father's heart. He loves his spiritual children, and he wants what is best for them. He desires deeply that they finish the race and receive the prize of life eternal.

And so he does not apologize for being committed to reminding them always of these things, even though he acknowledges that they already know these things and that they are established in the present truth (v. 12). In fact, he believes it is absolutely right for him to keep reminding them of these things just as long as he lives (v. 13). He sounds like a father or mother who deeply loves his or her child, and so without apology, keeps reminding the child of things that are important for his or her well-being.

I remember those kinds of statements coming from my parents: "Don't forget your coat!" "Watch out for cars when you cross the street!" "Never get into a car with a stranger!" And when I became a teenager, "Drive carefully!"

As a father, I find myself sharing the same kind of statements of concern with my children. I do it simply because I love them, and I want what is best for them. It is with this love and concern that Peter shares with his reminders.

Within this context, he pauses for a moment to acknowledge that he does not expect to live much longer. He shares that he must "put off [his] tent, just as our Lord Jesus Christ has shown [him]" (v. 14). He refers to the prophetic statement made by Christ concerning the death of Peter: " 'But when you are old, you will stretch out your hands, and another will gird you and carry you where you do not wish.' This He spoke, signifying by what death he [Peter] would glorify God" (John 21:18–19).

3. *"I will be careful to ensure that you always have a reminder"* (v. 15). Peter's love and concern for these spiritual children goes beyond his earthly life. As he acknowledges the imminence of his death, he states he will endeavor that they always may be able to have a reminder of these things after his decease.

What love Peter demonstrates! His concern for these spiritual children never ends. Although he does not reveal just how he would attempt to carry on that kind of accountability after his death, one probable vehicle is the letter he is now writing. His words of concern and calling to accountability have come down to us. And through Peter we hear our Lord calling us to be faithful, accountable, and to complete the race which we have begun.

GOD'S WORD IS TO BE TRUSTED

16 For we have not followed cunningly devised fables when we made known to you the power and coming of our Lord Jesus Christ, but were eyewitnesses of His majesty.

17 For He received from God the Father honor and glory when such a voice came to Him from the Excellent Glory: "This is My beloved Son, in whom I am well pleased."

18 And we heard this voice which came from heaven when we were with Him on the holy mountain.

19 We also have the prophetic word made more sure, which you do well to heed as a light that shines in a dark place, until the day dawns and the morning star rises in your hearts;

20 knowing this first, that no prophecy of Scripture
is of any private interpretation;
21 for prophecy never came by the will of man,
but holy men of God spoke as they were moved by
the Holy Spirit.

2 Peter 1:16–21

Peter now establishes his credentials and the trustworthiness of
the prophecies of the Word of God in contrast to the "cunningly
devised fables" being propagated by the false teachers whom he exposes and refutes in the second chapter of this letter. He makes three
specific contentions in establishing his credibility and the reliability
of the Word of God.

1. Peter begins by establishing his own relationship to Jesus Christ
as *"an eyewitness to Christ's majesty"* (vv. 16–18). He did not have to
contrive fables; he followed Jesus for the three years of His earthly
ministry. He has made known to his readers "the power and coming
of our Lord Jesus Christ" (v. 16).

This could have taken place in several ways. First, he may have
had the opportunity to preach the Gospel directly to those to whom
he is writing, or he may have shared this Good News with them
when he was sharing personal fellowship with them. Since he shares
with such deep pastoral concern, he may have been their pastor.
Or, he may be referring to his first letter in which he taught concerning
the coming of our Lord Jesus Christ. In any event, he has had the
opportunity to share with his readers the Good News of Jesus Christ.

He reminds them he was an eyewitness to the majesty of Jesus
Christ (v. 16). He then uses the personal experience of being a witness
to the transfiguration of Jesus Christ (vv. 17, 18). The Gospels of
Matthew, Mark, and Luke confirm that Peter was at the transfiguration of Christ along with James and John (Matt. 9:2, Mark 9:2, Luke
9:28).

Of all the stories and personal accounts Peter could have shared
from the life and ministry of Jesus, it is interesting that Peter should
share the account of the transfiguration of Jesus. He was deeply impressed with that spiritual experience.

The confirmation to Peter concerning who Christ really is came
when God spoke at the transfiguration, *" 'This is My beloved Son, in
whom I am well pleased' "* (v. 17). With conviction, Peter shares that
account with his readers to assure them of the credibility of Jesus

Christ as the Son of God when he was on the holy mountain (v. 18). And he now proclaims that message, "Jesus is the true Son of God!"

2. You will do well to heed the word of the prophets (v. 19). The prophets also spoke about this Jesus, and we would do well to listen to their prophecies and to believe them.

Peter uses this occasion to teach us about spiritual revelation. The prophets need to be heard not only with our intellect, but with spiritual perception. We need God to reveal truth to us through the prophets in the same way in which He revealed truth to them originally when He inspired and motivated them to write the words of prophecy (Peter speaks specifically about that process in the next two verses).

He uses the analogy of a light which shines in a dark place, until the day dawns and the morning star rises. God's Word comes to shine in our hearts when we are in darkness. But we cannot understand it until it breaks through into our hearts like the dawning of the day when the morning star arises just before the sun makes its appearance. That morning star must arise in our hearts and illuminate God's truth to us.

What a marvelous experience to have the light of God's truth shine into our hearts as the Holy Spirit reveals truth to us! Paul speaks about this experience when he writes that "the god of this age has blinded . . . [the minds of those] who do not believe, lest the light of the gospel of the glory of Christ, . . . should shine on them" (2 Cor. 4:4). Then he proceeds to speak about the miracle of spiritual revelation. "For it is the God who commanded light to shine out of darkness who has shone in our hearts to give the light of the knowledge of the glory of God in the face of Jesus Christ" (2 Cor. 4:6).

That is exactly what Peter is writing about. We can enjoy the marvelous experience of allowing the Holy Spirit to reveal truth to us through God's Word. In fact, the Bible will never become spiritually alive to us until that happens.

If you are ever bored with Bible study, or if you are unable to understand what God is saying through a passage, practice what Peter is encouraging us to do. Ask the Holy Spirit to reveal truth to you. Allow the light to shine into the darkness and expect the truth to emerge as the day dawns and the morning star arises.

3. Finally, we can rely on the Word of God because the prophecies of Scripture have come from God (vv. 20, 21). In the same way the Holy Spirit reveals truth to us from God's Word, so did the Holy

Spirit reveal the prophecies of Scripture to the prophets. To use the vocabulary of communications theory, the Holy Spirit was the "sender," and the Holy Spirit must reveal truth to the "receiver." Without a doubt, this is a spiritual dynamic!

Peter is explicit in his teaching: *"for prophecy never came by the will of man, but holy men of God spoke as they were moved by the Holy Spirit"* (v. 21). True prophecy comes not from men, but from God. The Holy Spirit was the source and sender of the communication; the holy men were merely the human vehicles through whom God chose to communicate truth.

In the same way, it is important that no prophecy or Scripture be of merely personal interpretation (v. 20). In other words, prophecies do not come from us, nor can they be adequately interpreted by us. Prophecies come from God and in order to properly interpret and understand them, we need the revelation of the same Holy Spirit who revealed the prophecies originally.

In matters of the Spirit, we must go back to the source—the Holy Spirit. False teaching flows from the minds of men and women; truth flows from the heart and mind of the living God.

When I was a seminary student, I knew of several classmates who came to believe the Bible was not any more inspired than the daily newspaper. These students denied the revelation of the Holy Spirit through the Word of God. To prove their point, one of the students preached a sermon using a story from a Chicago newspaper as his text.

His sermon fell flat. His source was merely human as opposed to the source of the Word of God and the prophecies proclaimed in the Word of God—God Himself in the Person of the Holy Spirit!

CHAPTER TWO

Keep on Resisting False Teachers

2 Peter 2:1–22

After establishing the basics of the Christian faith, the credibility of himself, and the prophecies of Scripture, Peter proceeds to refute the teachings of the false prophets with truth and directness. He begins by assailing the false teachings and then denounces the false teachers themselves. He assures them of their impending doom.

THE DESTRUCTIVENESS OF FALSE TEACHING

1 But there were also false prophets among the people, even as there will be false teachers among you, who will secretly bring in destructive heresies, even denying the Lord who bought them, and bring on themselves swift destruction.

2 And many will follow their destructive ways, because of whom the way of truth will be blasphemed.

3 And by covetousness they will exploit you with deceptive words, whose judgment for a long time has not been idle, and their destruction does not slumber.

4 For if God did not spare the angels who sinned, but cast them down to hell and delivered them into chains of darkness, to be reserved for judgment;

5 and did not spare the ancient world, but saved Noah, one of eight people, a preacher of righteousness, bringing in the flood on the world of the ungodly;

6 and turning the cities of Sodom and Gomorrah into ashes, condemned them to destruction, making them an example to those who afterward would live ungodly;

7 and delivered righteous Lot, who was oppressed with the filthy conduct of the wicked

8 (for that righteous man, dwelling among them, tormented his righteous soul from day to day by seeing and hearing their unlawful deeds),

9 the Lord knows how to deliver the godly out of temptations and to reserve the unjust under punishment for the day of judgment,

10 and especially those who walk according to the flesh in the lust of uncleanness and despise authority. They are presumptuous, self-willed; they are not afraid to speak evil of dignitaries,

11 whereas angels, who are greater in power and might, do not bring a reviling accusation against them before the Lord.

12 But these, like natural brute beasts made to be caught and destroyed, speak evil of the things that they do not understand, and will utterly perish in their own corruption,

13 and will receive the wages of unrighteousness, as those who count it pleasure to carouse in the daytime. They are spots and blemishes, carousing in their own deceptions while they feast with you,

14 having eyes full of adultery and that cannot cease from sin, beguiling unstable souls. They have a heart trained in covetous practices, and are accursed children.

15 They have forsaken the right way and gone astray, following the way of Balaam the son of Beor, who loved the wages of unrighteousness;

16 but he was rebuked for his iniquity: a dumb donkey speaking with a man's voice restrained the madness of the prophet.

17 These are wells without water, clouds carried by a tempest, to whom the gloom of darkness is reserved forever.

18 For when they speak great swelling words of emptiness, they allure through the lusts of the flesh, through licentiousness, those who have actually escaped from those who live in error.

19 While they promise them liberty, they themselves are slaves of corruption; for by whom a person is overcome, by him also he is brought into bondage.

2 Peter 2:1–19

An exposition of this passage is difficult because of its length. Peter does not divide his teaching into neat little packages or short paragraphs. Instead, his teaching flows freely as he presents an extensive exposé of the false teachers and their false teachings. In order to understand clearly the truth which Peter is presenting, let us divide the material into two major categories. Although Peter blends the material together, it is apparent he is presenting two major teachings: the first deals with how to identify or to recognize these false teachers; and, second, he speaks very directly about the doom which is faced by the false teachers. Let's explore these two areas.

The first could be titled, "How to recognize false teachers and their false teaching" (2:1–19). False teaching can come in many different expressions and by numerous approaches, and false teachers can be gifted and attractive people. How can we recognize them? Peter gives us 22 clues to help us in this vital venture of identification:

(1) They *"will secretly bring in destructive heresies"* (v. 1). Those who lead us astray usually sneak up on us. They approach us in the guise of light, in order to share heresies (Gk., *haíresis*) which are usually "doctrines containing some truth but which are cleverly blended with error." The various religious sects of our day are representive of clever heresies. The word *haíresis* can actually be translated as "sect." These heresies bring disunity to the Body of Christ.

(2) They *will even deny the Lord* (v. 1). No one knew any more about denying the Lord than Peter. How deeply concerned he was no one should follow in his footsteps! To deny is *arnéomai*, which means "to contradict, reject, or disavow." The next time a member of a religious sect calls on your home, ask him or her the direct question, "What do you think of Jesus?" If he is honest in his answer, his heresy will be clearly exposed.

(3) *"They will exploit you with deceptive words"* (v. 3). In the Authorized Version of the Bible, "exploit" is translated as "make merchandise of you." The Greek word is *emporeúomai*, which denotes the business of buying and selling. In fact, James uses the word within that context of buying and selling (James 4:13). False teachers exploit people. They use them as merchandise or objects.

(4) They *"walk according to the flesh in the lust of uncleanness"* (v. 10). In his first letter, Peter begs us to abstain from fleshly lusts which war against the soul (1 Pet. 2:11). And then he encourages us to live no longer in the flesh for the lusts of men, but for the will of God (1 Pet. 4:2). The lust of the flesh and the things of the Spirit are contrary

to one another (Gal. 5:16–18). False teachers do not walk in the Spirit; they live in the lusts of the flesh.

(5) *They "despise authority"* (v. 10). Jude writes of the same characteristic as he describes false teachers. He states they reject authority (Jude 8). A basic problem of sin is the resistance to submit to God or anyone else. God addresses this sin in the first commandment, "You shall have no other gods before Me" (Exod. 20:3, NIV). These false teachers despise the authority of God and refuse to live under the lordship of Jesus Christ. Instead, they prefer to establish themselves as the final authority.

(6) *"They are presumptuous"* (v. 10). Presumptuous (*tolmētēs*) means audacious, arrogant, rash or daring in a negative sense. Sin often leads to presumption. At best, sin is stupid!

(7) *They are "self-willed"* (v. 10). Self-willed (*authádēs*) means to be self-pleasing or strong in one's will. In other words, they always want their own way. They are concerned about doing their own thing as opposed to doing God's will. Their theme song is "I Did It My Way!"

(8) *They "speak evil of dignitaries"* (v. 10). They are so arrogant that they are not afraid to speak evil of dignitaries, angels, or those of high esteem. They feel that they are better than others. How much they need the counsel of Paul who challenges those with false feelings of superiority, "To everyone who is among you, not to think of himself more highly than he ought to think, but to think soberly, as God has dealt to each one a measure of faith" (Rom. 12:3).

(9) *They "speak evil of the things they do not understand"* (v. 12). False teachers are like brute beasts or irrational animals who abuse, sneer, and scoff at things they don't understand. Peter is obviously referring to the fact that since they are living in the flesh, they cannot understand the things of the spirit. Yet they mock and speak evil against those things.

(10) *"They are spots and blemishes"* (v. 13). They are "spots" (*spíloi*), unwanted ugly stains. And they are blemishes (*mōmos*), which can figuratively mean disgraceful persons. When we buy an object such as a piece of furniture or an article of clothing, we do not desire to purchase that which contains spots or blemishes. What a contrast this is to Paul's description of the church, "That He might present it to Himself a glorious church, not having spot or wrinkle or any such thing, but that it should be holy and without blemish" (Eph. 5:27).

(11) *They carouse "in their own deceptions"* (v. 13). Peter states these people count it pleasure to "riot" or "carouse" (*truphē*) in the daytime, and they carouse (*entruphaō*) in their own deceptions while they feast with you. Sin is deceptive and those who live in sin become entangled in their own "deceptions" (*apátē*). It is this kind of deception against which Jesus warned in His parable of the sower (Mark 4:19). The writer of Hebrews instructs us to "exhort one another daily . . . lest any of you be hardened through the deceitfulness of sin" (Heb. 3:13).

(12) *Their eyes are "full of adultery"* (v. 14). The seventh commandment is "You shall not commit adultery" (Exod. 20:14, NIV). Jesus said, "Whoever looks at a woman to lust for her has already committed adultery with her in his heart" (Matt. 5:28). The false teacher who is living in the flesh has his eyes full of adultery. He uses people for his own gratification.

(13) *Their eyes never cease from sinning* (v. 14). John warns us about the sin of loving the world. "For all that is in the world—the lust of the flesh, the lust of the eyes, and the pride of life—is not of the Father but is of the world" (1 John 2:16). The eyes can be used for lusting, and so Jesus warned, "If your right eye causes you to sin, pluck it out and cast it from you; for it is more profitable for you that one of your members perish, than for your whole body be cast into hell" (Matt. 5:29).

(14) *They beguile "unstable souls"* (v. 14). The Greek word for "beguile" is *deleázō*, which means to entice, allure, entrap, or delude. Sin does beguile and entice us. It promises us life, but it can deliver only momentary pleasure. Ultimately, it always leads to death. The wages or results of sin is always death (Rom. 6:23).

(15) *"They have a heart trained in covetous practices"* (v. 14). This literally means they have trained their hearts through continuous use to be greedy or to covet that which belongs to someone else. Again, this is the breaking of one of the Ten Commandments, "You shall not covet" (Exod. 20:17, NIV).

(16) *They "are accursed children"* (v. 14). These false teachers, who would lead others astray, are living under a curse from God. Because of the deception of sin, they are living under a curse and don't even know it. Literally, they are "children of curse."

(17) *"They have forsaken the right way and gone astray"* (v. 15). Isaiah declared, "All we like sheep have gone astray; we have turned, every one, to his own way" (Isa. 53:6). That is the problem of sin. We

leave the narrow way of righteousness for the broad way which leads to destruction (Matt. 7:13). To illustrate the sin of going astray, Peter recites the story of Balaam, who strayed away from God into sin and was verbally rebuked by a donkey which God had enabled to communicate (Num. 22). So are the stupid consequences of sin.

(18) *They "are wells without water"* (v. 17). A well without water or a spring that has gone dry can cause great frustration. They are of no purpose or use. They have lost their intended purpose or function. So it is of false teachers. They do not quench the spiritual thirst of their hearers.

(19) *They are "clouds carried by a tempest"* (v. 17). False teachers are like empty clouds which are being driven by a storm. They have nothing to offer, and they have no control of where they are going. Those who engage in false teaching have nothing to offer of any eternal worth, and they are driven by Satan himself. They are not under their own control, but his.

(20) *"They speak great swelling words of emptiness"* (v. 18). False teachers cannot bring us to truth. They can impress us only with their earthly wisdom and their knowledge, beautiful vocabulary, and their fluency. To use a contemporary expression, they are but bags of wind.

(21) *They allure those who have already escaped from the life of sin through the lusts of the flesh* (v. 18). Now we come to Peter's greatest concern. He has warned us loudly and clearly about being barren and unfruitful (2 Pet. 1:8). He has encouraged us to remain faithful to Christ and to the basics of the faith (2 Pet. 1:5–11). False teachers would attempt to allure (*deleázō*) with the lusts of the flesh rather than teaching us the truth of the Spirit.

(22) *They promise liberty but are themselves slaves of corruption* (v. 19). Sin always promises what it cannot deliver. It promises us liberty or freedom, but it gives us slavery. How pitiful it is to realize that the false teachers who promise liberty are slaves to sin and corruption themselves. Peter goes on to contend that a person is a slave of whomever or whatever overcomes or controls him. Spiritually, we are either dominated by sin or by the Holy Spirit. We are either slaves to sin, or we are willing slaves of Jesus Christ. Authentic freedom can only be ours when we are possessed by the Holy Spirit through faith in Christ.

The second truth on which Peter focuses in verses 1–17 is the certain doom of false prophets. As Peter teaches us how to recognize false teachers and their false teachings, he punctuates these verses with specific statements concerning the certain doom of these false teachers. Without a doubt, they are on their way to destruction!

(1) *They will "bring on themselves swift destruction"* (v. 1). The wages of sin is always death. Those who walk after the lust of the flesh are destined for destruction. We who are attempting to walk in the Spirit do not acknowledge that fact with happiness or satisfaction.

To the contrary, Paul shared with the Philippian believers, "I . . . tell you even weeping, that they are enemies of the cross of Christ: whose end is destruction" (Phil. 3:18, 19). It is only by God's grace we are not going to that end. By His grace, we deny ourselves, take up our cross daily, and follow Jesus (Luke 9:23).

This "destruction" (*apólia*) which they bring upon themselves is "swift" (*takinós*). It will not tarry, but will come rapidly.

(2) *"For a long time their judgment has not been idle, and their destruction does not slumber"* (v. 3). Again Peter shares a direct statement about their impending judgment and imminent destruction. His language is vivid and precise. God is not idle, sleeping, nor oblivious to their exploitation and deceptiveness (v. 3). He knows many will follow their destructive ways (v. 2). Judgment and destruction are on the way.

(3) *The false teachers are doomed* (vv. 4–11). Now Peter approaches the matter of the doom of the false teachers with specific Biblical evidence. He asks penetrating questions as he presents four specific examples:

The Angels (v. 4). If God didn't spare the angels who sinned, but threw them into hell and placed them in chains of darkness, in order to be reserved for judgment, don't you think He will bring the same kind of judgment upon false teachers who are leading others astray?

The Ancient World (v. 5). If God didn't spare the ancient world but allowed it to be destroyed by a flood (although He saved Noah and seven other righteous people), don't you think He will bring false teachers to destruction?

Sodom and Gomorrah (vv. 6–8). And if God condemned the cities of Sodom and Gomorrah to destruction and reduced them to ashes (delivering righteous Lot), don't you think He will bring that same kind of destruction to the false teachers who have led others astray with their false teaching?

Day of Judgment (v. 9). Peter answers those three questions as he comes to his summation statement: *"The Lord knows how to deliver the godly out of temptations and to reserve the unjust under punishment for the day of judgment."*

(4) They *"will utterly perish in their own corruption"* (v. 12). To utterly perish (*kataphtheirō*) means to spoil entirely or to completely destroy.

The word corruption (*phthorá*) also means perish or destroy. Peter could not use stronger language. He is talking about reaping what they have been sowing. They have been sowing destruction, and they are going to reap it utterly!

(5) They *"will receive the wages of unrighteousness"* (v. 13). Peter is emphasizing the same statement of destruction by using different vocabulary. But he means exactly the same thing. The wages of unrighteousness is eternal death (Rom. 6:23).

(6) They *will receive the gloom of darkness forever* (v. 17). This gloom of darkness is reserved for them. Within the Scripture, darkness is equated with the life of sin. Paul instructs us to "cast off the works of darkness" (Rom. 13:12), and asks the question, "What communion has light with darkness?" (2 Cor. 6:14).

In his parable on the talents, Jesus concluded by stating that the master "cast the unprofitable servant into the outer darkness. There will be weeping and gnashing of teeth" (Matt. 25:30). The implication is clear.

The false teachers are facing a gloom or mist of darkness which is being reserved for them. Swift destruction, doom, judgment, utter perishing, death, and a gloom of darkness await those who would be false teachers and lead others astray from the truth.

ENTANGLED AGAIN IN THE WORLD

20 For if, after they have escaped the pollutions of the world through the knowledge of the Lord and Savior Jesus Christ, they are again entangled in them and overcome, the latter end is worse for them than the beginning.

21 For it would have been better for them not to have known the way of righteousness, than after they have known it, to turn from the holy commandment delivered to them.

22 But it has happened to them according to the true proverb: *"The dog returns to his own vomit,"* and, "the sow that had washed, to her wallowing in the mire."

2 Peter 2:20–22

After speaking about the impending doom of the false prophets, Peter now addresses the fate of those who are led astray by those whom he describes as spots and blemishes. They will utterly perish in their own corruption. As he shares some graphic warnings with those young Christians to whom he is writing, Peter warns not only against the false teachers but also reminds us of the fact that we bear responsibility for ourselves. We are responsible and accountable for our own spiritual welfare, and if we allow ourselves to be led astray, we will pay a tremendous price for our sin.

Peter begins his warning by identifying those to whom he is directing his teaching. They are those who have escaped the pollutions of the world through the knowledge of the Lord and Savior Jesus Christ (v. 20); and they are *"the ones who have actually escaped from those who live in error"* (v. 18).

Peter is affirming the truth taught repeatedly in the Scriptures— the only way to escape sin and its accompanying pollutions of this world is through the knowledge of Jesus Christ as Savior and Lord. Here the word for knowledge is again *epignosis*. Peter uses that word three times in his first chapter. Each time he uses it to describe the privilege of knowing Jesus as Savior and Lord and to point out the value of the knowledge of God and Savior Jesus Christ (1 Pet. 1:2, 3, 8).

As we have seen, to walk in the Spirit whom we receive through faith in Christ is to walk the opposite direction from the lusts of the flesh. This is the only way to escape the pollution of the world and the ultimate death and destruction to which it always leads.

The statement in verse 20, *"If, after they have escaped the pollutions of the world through . . . Jesus Christ, they are again entangled in them and overcome,"* presents a difficult theological dilemma about which theologians have argued for centuries. There are those who contend once we have been born anew of the Spirit, we cannot become "unborn." There is also a point of view which says since God has created us free moral agents, we can choose to leave the faith just as freely as we came to choose the faith.

Peter does not address that issue directly. Instead, he exposes the deeper issue upon which both schools of theological thought would agree. It is simply this: a person who has once come to the knowledge of Jesus Christ as Savior and Lord and has escaped the pollution of the world is in serious trouble when he or she becomes again entangled in them and overcome by them. He declares they are worse off in their present condition than they ever were before coming to faith in Christ, *"the latter end is worse for them than the beginning"* (v. 20).

That is an extremely strong statement. It should stand as a strong refutation to those who think they can play games with God by dabbling in overt and premeditated sin while they claim to be living as Christians.

I counseled a man recently who openly admitted he was living in adultery. He claimed he couldn't help it; he was just too weak to resist. He was convinced God would ignore His overt sin because he was "trying hard in every other area of his life!"

Peter would say that man was deceiving himself and that he was in serious trouble. His condition is worse than if he had never come to the light. He is living in clear violation of the commandments of God. He is lusting after the flesh rather than walking in the Spirit. And he is in serious trouble.

"It would have been better for them not to have known the way of righteousness" (v. 21). This statement expands his teaching to make it so graphically clear none of us could fail to understand. It would be better for a person never to have known the way of righteousness, than after coming to that knowledge of Jesus Christ, to have turned his or her back on the holy commandments of the Lord Himself!

These two statements are difficult to refute or to "argue away." God does not offer us an eternal life insurance policy which allows us to "accept" Christ and then not follow Him; nor to be "born again" of the Spirit and then to lust after the flesh as our lifestyle; nor to "commit" our lives to Christ and then live for the devil. That is not Christianity; it is pure hypocrisy! And Peter will have no part of that kind of false teaching. It is an example of the vicious kind of false teaching which deceives us. Peter has already warned against that fallacious teaching which promises freedom but actually leads to the slavery of sin (v. 18).

To illustrate his teaching, Peter shares two vivid examples from Proverbs 26:11 to punctuate his contention. First, he states those who have turned from the knowledge of Christ are illustrated by the proverb "A dog returns to his own vomit" (v. 22). Second, such a person is like "a sow, having washed, [returned] to her wallowing in the mire" (v. 22).

Peter's twofold warning in this chapter can be summarized in two brief statements. First, beware of false teachers who are on their way to eternal destruction. Second, if you follow them, you are responsible for your own actions, and you will experience an end which is worse than if you had never come to the knowledge of God!

CHAPTER THREE

Keep on Trusting God

2 Peter 3:1–18

Peter's denunciation of false teachers and their false teaching has been vividly strong—they face certain doom. His vocabulary was confrontive and strong. In contrast, he now returns to speaking to the believers in gentle and endearing language. His message is one of love and encouragement.

He points them to God. Unlike the false teachers, God is the One who is always to be trusted. The day of the Lord is coming. God always keeps His promises. He is always on time!

REMEMBER THE BASICS

1 Beloved, I now write to you this second epistle (in both of which I stir up your pure minds by way of reminder),

2 that you may be mindful of the words which were spoken before by the holy prophets, and of the commandment of us the apostles of the Lord and Savior,

3 knowing this first: that scoffers will come in the last days, walking according to their own lusts,

4 and saying, "Where is the promise of His coming? For since the fathers fell asleep, all things continue as they were from the beginning of creation."

5 For this they willfully forget: that by the word of God the heavens were of old, and the earth standing out of water and in the water,

6 by which the world that then was, being flooded with water, perished.

7 But the heavens and the earth which now exist

are kept in store by the same word, reserved for fire
until the day of judgment and perdition of ungodly
men.

2 Peter 3:1–7

"Beloved" is a wonderful word of love and endearment. Peter has
a sincere love for the Christians who have suffered so much for their
faith in Jesus Christ. He wishes for them to walk with God and
not to be led astray. And so he writes to *"stir up"* their pure minds
as a way of reminder of what they already know and believe. In
fact, he states this has been the clear purpose of both of his letters
(v. 1).

The word translated *"stir up"* (*diegeirō*) means to arouse or awaken
fully. That was the need of the first century Christians, and it is a
primary need of Christians today. We need to be fully awakened
to the truth of God's Word and to the basics of the faith. Peter
suggests three specific areas of which we need to be reminded and
stirred up.

First, we need to remember the words of the holy prophets (v.
2). The holy prophets are far different from the false prophets about
whom Peter has been warning. These are the holy men to whom
Peter has referred in chapter one, verses 20 and 21. These holy prophets spoke as they were moved by the Holy Spirit. They wrote Scripture
which did not come by personal interpretation, nor by the will of
man, but by the Holy Spirit.

Peter encourages us to escape from the destructive heresies of the
false prophets (2:1) and to remember the words of the holy prophets.
In short, our trust should be in God and in His Word which He
has given us through Spirit-led prophets.

Second, we should remember the commandments of the apostles
(v. 2). When Peter was writing these words of instruction, the New
Testament canon had not been established. The words of the prophets
were among the canon of the Jewish Scriptures. They were certainly
to be heeded.

But from the beginning of the birth of the Church, the "apostles'
doctrines," or the commandments of the apostles of the Lord and
Savior (v. 2), were followed by the believers. Luke recorded this fact
when he wrote concerning the early Christians, "And they continued
steadfastly in the apostles' doctrine and fellowship, in the breaking
of bread, and in prayers" (Acts 2:42).

Last, Peter reminds us that God is in control (vv. 3–7). Remembering the words of the holy prophets and the commandments of the apostles of the Lord and Savior is essential and important because they take us back to God who is the source of the Word and commandments. Our trust should be in Him. He is in control of all things.

In this regard, the first thing to remember is that scoffers will come in the last days walking after their own lusts (vv. 3, 4). They are like the false teachers who walk according to the flesh in the lust of uncleanness (2:10).

These scoffers do not listen to the prophets, to the apostles, nor do they look to God. Instead, they merely look at outward circumstances and ask, "Where is the promise of His coming? For since the fathers fell asleep, all things continue as they were from the beginning of creation" (v. 4). The inference of Peter's teaching is clear. Don't listen to these scoffers. Don't follow in their ways. Look to God and trust Him. He has everything under control. God is the One who created the world, and He is still in charge!

Peter builds his argument upon God's creation (v. 5). He "stirs up" the minds of his readers to remember who God is. He is the creator of all things. By His word the heavens and the earth were created. The scoffers willfully forget this marvelous fact (v. 5).

In verse 6, Peter reminds his readers God did not merely create the world and then leave it. When the people of His creation disobeyed Him and chose to live in blatant sin, God brought the great flood upon the earth. He did not spare the ancient world, but saved Noah and seven others who were righteous while bringing the flood on the world of the ungodly (2:1; Gen. 6–8).

God is not only the Creator, but He has the power to bring judgment and even destroy that which He has created. It is a foolish thing to willingly forget or ignore who God is and who we are. By His word, He can create or destroy.

God has already declared through His holy prophets and apostles what lies ahead. Jesus prophesied of the end of the world when He said, "Therefore as the tares are gathered and burned in the fire, so it will be at the end of this age" (Matt. 13:40). The writer of Hebrews quoted from Psalm 102 in stating, "You, Lord, in the beginning laid the foundation of the earth, and the heavens are the work of Your hands; they will perish, but You remain" (Heb. 1:10–11).

John writes vividly about the destruction of the present heavens and earth in Revelation 20. He continues by writing, "And I saw a new heaven and a new earth, for the first heaven and the first earth had passed away. Also there was no more sea" (Rev. 21:1).

Peter confirms that teaching by stating that the heavens and earth which now exist are being reserved for fire until the day of judgment and perdition of ungodly men (v. 7). Those sobering words should remind us of the importance of trusting in the living God. We need to remember He is in control.

REMEMBER, GOD IS ALWAYS ON TIME

8 But, beloved, do not forget this one thing, that one day is with the Lord as a thousand years, and a thousand years as one day.
9 The Lord is not slack concerning His promise, as some count slackness, but is longsuffering toward us, not desiring that any should perish but that all should come to repentance.

2 Peter 3:8–9

God is not only in control; He is always on time. Scoffers would attempt to make us believe God has fallen asleep or He is inept or He does not keep His promises. Speaking once again with endearment to his readers as he calls them "beloved" (v. 8), Peter asks them not to forget that *"with the Lord one day is as a thousand years"* (v. 8). Peter practices what he has been preaching. He has encouraged his readers to heed the Word of God which has come from the prophets and the apostles. In verse 8 he does just that by referring to the teaching of Psalm 90:4, "For a thousand years in Your sight are like yesterday when it is past, and like a watch in the night."

Scoffers assert that since Jesus promised His second coming and has not yet come, He was either lying or is incapable of keeping His promise. Peter contends that Jesus is not limited by time as are humans. One day in the sight of God is like one thousand years, and one thousand years is as a day. The psalmist has declared it and Peter believed it.

Insisting that *"the Lord is not slack concerning His promise"* (v. 9), Peter gives a better reason for the fact Jesus has not returned. He remembers well the teaching of his Master on this subject, "It is not for you to know times or seasons which the Father has put in His own author-ity" (Acts 1:7). Jesus had also said, "But of that day and hour no one knows, no, not even the angels of heaven, but My Father only" (Matt. 24:36).

Thus, Peter concludes, the Lord is not "slack" concerning His prom-ise. He never stated the exact time in which He would return. It is in the Father's hands. Not even the angels know the time of His return.

The verb translated as "not slack" is *bradúnō,* which means to delay or tarry. God is never late. He is always on time. He is never delayed by outward circumstances or by others. He is always in control. His motive is always love. He so loved the world He gave His only begot-ten Son. And it's because of His love for the world that Jesus has not yet returned.

God's love is manifested in His longsuffering (*makrothuméō*) which denotes patience and forbearance. In his first letter, Peter referred to the longsuffering of God in the days of Noah before bringing judgment upon unrepentant people (1 Pet. 3:20).

"[He is] longsuffering toward us" because He does not desire for any to "perish but that all should come to repentance" (v. 9). Again, Peter bases his teaching upon the Word of God from the prophets and apostles. Ezekiel recorded the Word of the Lord, " 'Do I have any pleasure at all that the wicked should die?' says the Lord God, 'and not that he should turn from his ways and live?' " (Ezek. 18:23).

Paul contends God does not desire for any to perish, but wishes for all to be saved (1 Tim. 2:4). And Paul wrote to the church at Rome, "For God has committed them all to disobedience, that he might have mercy on all" (Rom. 11:32).

Thus, Peter concludes, the Lord has not returned for one simple reason—it is not yet the Father's time. And the reason it is not yet the Father's time is because of His longsuffering. He is not willing that any should perish, but that all should come to repentance.

THE KIND OF PEOPLE WE SHOULD BE

10 But the day of the Lord will come as a thief in
the night, in which the heavens will pass away with
a great noise, and the elements will melt with fervent

heat; both the earth and the works that are in it will be burned up.

11 Seeing then that all these things will be dissolved, what manner of persons ought you to be in holy conduct and godliness,

12 looking for and hastening the coming of the day of God, because of which the heavens, being on fire, will be dissolved, and the elements will melt with fervent heat?

13 Nevertheless we, according to His promise, look for new heavens and a new earth in which righteousness dwells.

2 Peter 3:10–13

As Peter has written directly regarding the false teachers, he now expresses himself very graphically and with great conviction concerning the coming of Christ's Kingdom. Indeed the Lord is going to keep His promise. It is not a matter of "if" He is coming, it is merely a matter of "when" He will return.

"The day of the Lord will come" (v. 10). The scoffers may doubt, and the world may totally ignore Him, but Jesus is coming again! Jesus said, "Therefore you also be ready, for the Son of Man is coming at an hour when you do not expect Him" (Matt. 24:44). Peter describes what will happen in that time.

Remember that Peter was present when the Lord shared His teaching regarding His second coming. Jesus had told Peter and the other disciples, "But know this, that if the master of the house had known what hour the thief would come, he would have watched and not allowed his house to be broken into" (Matt. 24:43). Thus, Peter reminds us the Lord will come like a thief in the night (v. 10).

"The heavens will pass away" (v. 10). The heavens (*ouranós*) are mentioned by Peter five times in this chapter. In verse 5, he refers to the creation of the heavens by God; in verse 7, he contends the heavens are kept in existence by the word of God; in verse 12, he speaks about the heavens being dissolved by fire when Christ returns; in verse 13, he speaks about the new heavens which will come after the destruction of the old; and in verse 10, we read that the heavens will pass away with a great noise.

The word translated as "a great noise" is *rhoizēdón*, which means "whizzingly" or "with a great crash." One is reminded of the prophetic warning given to the city of Ariel by the prophet Isaiah, "You will be punished by the Lord of hosts with thunder and earthquake and great noise, with storm and tempest and the flame of devouring fire" (Isa. 29:6).

Even though we live in the day of atomic power, space travel, and many scientific achievements, and even though we have witnessed the power and awesome destruction of nuclear weapons, it is difficult for us to comprehend just what it will be like for the heavens to be destroyed and to pass away. What a noise!

The earth "will be burned up" (v. 10). Not only will the earth be burned up, but everything upon the earth: "the works that are in it will be burned up." What an incredible and incomprehensible event. To burn with fire is *katakaiō* which means to consume utterly or to burn up utterly.

In short, there will be nothing remaining. The earth will be consumed and everything on it. And the heavens will be destroyed. What an awesome event. Until the development of the atom and hydrogen bombs it was difficult for mankind to imagine that such destruction could be possible.

Our generation has come to know that it is not only possible, but it is probable. Peter says it is not only probable, but it is absolutely certain. And it is part of God's master plan. Therefore, we should be prepared. In verses 11 and 12 Peter suggests four specific areas of our lifestyles to which we should pay heed if we believe the Word of God is to be believed and that all things are to be dissolved. He tells us what manner of persons we should be.

First, we are to live lives of holy conduct (v. 11). Peter speaks a great deal about holiness in both of his letters. His most specific teaching is found in 1 Peter 1:15, 16 (see commentary, p. 125), "But as He who has called you is holy, you also be holy in all your conduct, because it is written, 'Be holy, for I am holy.' "

In the Gospel of Matthew, Jesus shares the parable about the faithful and unfaithful servants. When the master returned from a trip, he found the good servant serving faithfully, who was rewarded. But the unfaithful servant was beating his fellow servants. He was to be cut in two and cast out with the hypocrites (Matt. 24:45–51). Like those servants, we should be ready for our Master to return.

Second, Peter tells us to live lives of godliness (v. 11). In order to live godly lives, we must live like Him! Of course, we cannot do that if we live in the flesh. Peter has already warned us against that kind of lifestyle (2:20 and 3:3).

We must be like the good servants in another parable of Jesus who did not bury the talents the Master had given them, but invested them wisely. Jesus concluded that parable by saying, "for to everyone who has, more will be given, and he will have abundance; but from him who does not have, even what he has will be taken away" (Matt. 25:29).

Verse 12 then tells us to look for His coming. Faithfulness is one of the great attributes of God, and He asks His children to follow Him with faithfulness. Peter's exhortation is clear: we should faithfully be looking for His coming with expectation.

Jesus illustrated this important truth by sharing the parable of the wise and foolish virgins. The foolish virgins were not faithful, and thus, not adequately prepared. But the wise virgins were looking for His coming and were adequately prepared. When the bridegroom came, they went in with him to the wedding, but the other virgins came after the door was shut.

The conclusion of Jesus is clear, "Watch therefore, for you know neither the day nor the hour in which the Son of Man is coming" (Matt. 25:13). He gave the same warning after speaking about Noah, the two women grinding at the mill, and the two men working in the field. "Watch, therefore, for you do not know what hour your Lord is coming" (Matt. 24:42).

And last, we should be hastening His coming (v. 12). Although Peter does not give us clear instructions regarding how we should hasten the coming of the Lord, the inference seems clear. If the reason the Lord has not yet come is that He is longsuffering and not willing that any should perish but that all should come to repentance (v. 9), then we should be involved in the spiritual harvest.

Jesus said, "I must work the works of Him who sent Me while it is day; the night is coming when no one can work" (John 9:4). That is also His instruction. He has given us His commission: "Go therefore and make disciples of all the nations" (Matt. 28:19).

We are not called to bask in the sunshine of God's Kingdom or to sleep as did the foolish virgins. We are called to labor in the Lord's vineyard. If we are to hasten the coming of the Lord, we should be those who live holy and godly lives, who are looking for His coming, and who are working faithfully to share His love and salvation with others.

The prophetic statements made by Peter concerning the passing away of the heavens and the destruction of the earth are not meant to be fatalistic. To the contrary, Peter is constantly calling us to the life of hope in Jesus Christ.

The old must pass away when the new comes (1 Cor. 13:10). And so Peter proceeds to a note of hope and triumph. There will be new heavens and a new earth when the Kingdom of our Lord comes, and we should be looking for them (v. 13). This, says Peter, is according to the promise of God. An example of that promise is found in Isaiah 65:17, "For behold, I create new heavens and a new earth; and the former shall not be remembered or come to mind."

As we have seen, the ultimate promise is given in Revelation 21:1, "And I saw a new heaven and a new earth, for the first heaven and the first earth had passed away." The promise is clear. The old is passing away by God's design, and the new is coming by God's plan.

The marvelous thing which Peter specifies about the new is the fact that righteousness dwells there. John writes that there will be no more curse and no more night (Rev. 22:3, 5); "And God will wipe away every tear from their eyes; there shall be no more death, nor sorrow, nor crying; and there shall be no more pain, for the former things have passed away" (Rev. 21:4).

No wonder we should look forward to His coming! His testimony to us is "And behold, I am coming quickly, and My reward is with Me, to give to each one according to his work" (Rev. 22:12).

How to Be Found by Him

14 Therefore, beloved, seeing that you look for such things, be diligent that you may be found by Him in peace, without spot, and blameless;

15 and account that the longsuffering of our Lord is salvation—as also our beloved brother Paul, according to the wisdom given to him, has written to you,

16 as also in all his epistles, speaking in them of these things, in which are some things hard to understand, which those who are untaught and unstable twist to their own destruction, as they do also the rest of the Scriptures.   *2 Peter 3:14–16*

Because the day of the Lord is imminent, and because we are those who are looking for the coming of Christ and His Kingdom, Peter states we should be diligent in being ready to be found by Him. The word *"diligent," spoudē* is the same word that Peter uses in chapter one when he urges his readers to be diligent to make their calling and election sure (2 Pet. 1:10; see commentary on p. 213).

As he comes to the close of his epistle, he makes the same appeal with a slightly different emphasis. It is certain we should make our calling and election sure, but it is within the context of being prepared for the coming of Christ. We should be diligent to be found in Him with the following attributes:

"In peace" (v. 14). Once again, Peter uses one of the key words which he addressed in his opening remarks. The word *"peace"* (*eirēnē*) means more than mere quietness. It has some of the sense of the Hebrew word *shalom* in that it implies prosperity or well-being.

That is Peter's concern for his readers—that we be at peace with the Lord, with others, and with ourselves. It is good to be resting in the Lord and in His faithful provision. Jesus shared that in the world we will have tribulation, but in Him we have peace (John 16:33).

"Without spot" (v. 14). In contrast to the false teachers who are spots and blemishes (2:13), Peter encourages us to be *"without spot"* (*áspilos*). This is the same word used by James when he instructs us to keep ourselves unspotted from the world (James 1:27). And it is the word which Peter uses in describing Jesus as the lamb without blemish and without spot (1 Pet. 1:19).

The teaching of Peter and of all the Scripture is clear: The Lord desires we would allow Him to make us pure and clean; that we would flee from the very appearance of evil; and that when Christ returns, He would find us without spot, cleansed by the very blood of Jesus Christ, the Lamb of God who has come to take away the sins of the world (1 John 1:7).

"Blameless" (v. 14). Blameless, what a startling word! To be blameless means we must be forgiven. There is only One in all of the universe who is capable of making us blameless. He is the One who is faithful and just to cleanse us from all sin (1 John 1:9). Indeed, it is Jesus Christ the Lord.

The human approach is to either ignore sin or to justify ourselves by rationalizing that we are as good or even better than others. However, God does not ignore or rationalize concerning sin. He takes sin so seriously that He sent His only begotten Son to rescue us from the eternal death which results from sin.

God deals truthfully with our sin. We can receive His righteous judgment or we can enjoy His forgiveness by repenting of our sin and turning to Christ for His forgiveness. God both forgives and forgets our sin. It is as though we had never sinned—we are blameless. "Though your sins are like scarlet, they shall be as white as snow; though they are red like crimson, they shall be as wool (Isa. 1:18).

Christ has given us the way to live in peace, to be without spot and blameless. If we are not found by Him to be enjoying such a marvelous lifestyle, we can only blame our own selfish wills.

My life is an illustration of the wonderful truth found in verses 15 and 16. How gracious, patient, and longsuffering our Lord has been with me. His love has been steadfast. His forgiveness has been generous and ever available. Without Him, I would be lost. Through Him has come my salvation.

Peter, Paul, and the other apostles experienced this great salvation. They not only taught it and believed in it—they enjoyed the benefits of the salvation of the Lord, and so can we. Peter states that this is the same salvation about which the Apostle Paul had written (vv. 15, 16).

To those who understand what Paul has written and have experienced the salvation of the Lord, it is wonderful news. But to those who continue to walk after the flesh and are untaught and unstable, they twist his teaching just as they do all of Scripture. The terrible result will be their own destruction.

What a contrast! To live in peace, without spot, blameless, and to enjoy the salvation which comes from the longsuffering of the Lord is the choice which Peter offers us as contrasted with the destruction which will come to those who twist the truth.

A FINAL WORD CONCERNING GROWING

17 You therefore, beloved, seeing you know these things beforehand, beware lest you also, being led away with the error of the wicked, fall from your own steadfastness;

18 but grow in the grace and knowledge of our Lord
and Savior Jesus Christ. To Him be the glory both
now and forever. Amen.

2 Peter 3:17–18

Peter is building to a climax. His aim is clear. His message has
not been hidden. He has warned against the false teachers and their
teaching which would lead others astray. Their end is also clear—it
will be certain destruction! But not only will they be destroyed, so
will the heavens and earth. The day of God's judgment is coming.

But so is the day of the Lord's salvation when Christ shall come
to reign as King of kings and Lord of lords! There will be a new
heaven and a new earth in which righteousness will dwell. The old
will pass away and the new will come.

Therefore, states Peter, you should be ready for the coming of
the Lord (3:14–16). And now he concludes, you should take the initiative in at least three measurable ways:

1. *Remember what you know* (v. 17). From the beginning of his letter
Peter has said he is writing to remind his readers of what they already
know (1:12). He has written both of his letters to "stir up" the pure
minds of his readers by way of reminder (3:1).

Now he translates those reminders into action. He asks us to live
as though we remember and believe those vitally important things
of which he has reminded us. Most of us do not need to know any
more until we begin to apply what we already know. Our knowledge
needs to be translated into lifestyle.

2. *Beware lest you fall from your steadfastness* (v. 17). Peter is writing
primarily to those who are steadfast (*stērigmós*) or stable in their Christian faith. Many of them had suffered greatly because of their faith
in Christ. They had withstood the attacks of Satan which had come
to them through persecution by Nero and others outside the Body
of Christ.

Now Peter is warning them and us against the attacks of Satan
which would come within the guise of those within the Church.
We need to be built solidly upon the rock, Jesus Christ (Matt. 7:24)
and to live constantly by the basics of the faith. We should remind
one another to "stir up" our brothers and sisters in Christ.

Then, we must be careful lest we be led away with the error of
the wicked and fall from our own steadfastness. There are those in
the Church who say we need not worry about falling. If that were

true, then Peter wrote his epistle in vain as did Paul when he said, "Therefore let him who thinks he stands take heed lest he fall" (1 Cor. 10:12).

The warnings of Scripture are numerous: Watch out! Be on guard! Beware! Resist the devil! Flee from evil! Consent not to sin! The list goes on and on.

But God tells us not only to beware of going astray, He has promised us a way to be secure in Him. He has promised to never leave us nor forsake us (Heb. 13:5). He is a friend who sticks closer than a brother (Prov. 18:24). And, as we have seen, the best defense is an active offense.

3. *"But grow in the grace and knowledge of . . . Jesus Christ"* (v. 18). When we are growing in Christ, we are resisting error. When we are following Him, we are going the opposite direction from error. When we pay heed to the Word of God and live the life of obedience to His Word, we need not worry about falling.

"Grow" (v. 18). In his first letter, Peter gave the answer to what we should do to grow when he wrote, "As newborn babes, desire the pure milk of the word, that you may grow thereby" (1 Peter 2:2). Peter is stirring up our memories concerning that basic and vital teaching.

The Bible has a great deal to say about growing up in Christ. For example, Paul writes about us growing up into a holy temple in the Lord (Eph. 2:21), and then teaches us how we should minister within the Body of Christ so we "may grow up in all things into Him who is the head—Christ" (Eph. 4:15).

"Grace" (v. 18). Peter encourages us to grow in grace. The word for grace is *cháris,* which means "unmerited" or "receiving without deserving." Grace flows from God. And the more we grow, the more we should become like Him and the more of His grace we should enjoy, and that grace should flow from our lives to others. Show me a person who is walking closely with God and growing spiritually as they draw spiritual nourishment from Him, and I'll show you a person who is not only experiencing the grace of God but who is sharing it with others.

We should be growing in the grace which comes from Jesus Christ, our Savior and Lord. This grace is at the center of Christian lifestyle and Christian community. Therefore, there is little wonder this grace was and is commonly used in the greetings and benedictions which Christians share with one another.

For example, Paul wrote to the Galatian believers, "The grace of our Lord Jesus Christ be with your spirit" (Gal. 6:18) and to the church at Ephesus, "Grace be with all those who love our Lord Jesus Christ in sincerity" (Eph. 6:24). May we be those who are growing in the grace of our Lord and Savior, Jesus Christ.

"Knowledge" (v. 18). We should not only be growing in grace, but also in knowledge. Not the kind of knowledge (*gnōsis*) which would make us puff up and be separated from others by the feeling of superiority (1 Cor. 8:1). But, instead, the kind of knowledge of Jesus Christ which brings unity to the Body and mutual growth to become more and more like Jesus Christ Himself (Eph. 4:12, 13).

This is not mere knowledge about Jesus; it is knowledge of Him. This is in stark contrast to those who are untaught, unstable, and who twist the truth to their own destruction (3:16). To know Jesus is to know the truth (John 14:6). To know Jesus is life everlasting (John 3:16).

"Jesus Christ" (v. 18). Without a doubt, Jesus Christ is the focus of Peter's epistles and his very life. Peter had grown wonderfully in the grace and knowledge of Jesus Christ, and he invites us to do the same.

Peter referred to Jesus the Savior; he had experienced the salvation of Jesus Christ in his own life. Also, Peter referred to Jesus as Lord; he had followed Jesus as Lord of his life. Then, Peter closed his letter by referring to Christ in the ultimate, "To Him be the glory both now and forever. Amen."

Introduction to Jude

Recently, I received a letter from a friend whom I had not seen for many years. To my surprise and delight, I heard from him at a very unexpected moment.

In his opening paragraph he stated simply that he was writing to me because I had been much in his mind and upon his heart during the preceding days. For some reason, the Lord had directed his conscious mind to me. His letter was in response to the guidance of the Holy Spirit.

The purpose of his writing was to affirm and encourage me in the ministry and to express his deep love for me. He assured me of his prayers, and he solicited my prayers for him and his family. I was greatly blessed by his letter. What a joy it is to love our brothers and sisters in Christ, to encourage and build them up in the faith, and to warn them against potential dangers. The Scripture refers to this wonderful ministry as edification.

That is the focus of the letter of Jude. Jude wrote to encourage and affirm those whom he loved in the truth. Within the context of edification, he also warned them very specifically against false teachers whose instruction would lead them astray. His warnings supplement those shared in 2 Peter 2. We have already noted the similarities between the epistles of Jude and 2 Peter (see commentary, p. 204).

Like Peter, Jude begins with words of love and affirmation which are followed by a strong warning concerning those who would cause divisions and who are sensual, not having the Spirit (v. 19). His warning is followed by a marvelous treatise on how to be a builder of spiritual lives. Then Jude concludes with a moving benedictory statement declaring the adequacy, wisdom, glory, and power of Jesus Christ.

The Author

"Jude, a servant of Jesus Christ, and brother of James," is the introduction which the author shares with his readers (v. 1). Both Mark and Matthew tell us in their Gospels that Jesus had brothers by the names of Judas (Jude) and James (Mark 6:3, Matt. 13:15). It is probable that since Jude is not mentioned within the Acts of the Apostles nor in any of the other books of the New Testament, he was not a leader in the early church. Therefore, it was quite natural to identify himself with one who was a leader in the church—his brother James.

As we have seen, there was only one James who was recognized as a leader in the early church (see p. 12). It was the same James who wrote the Epistle of James and who was the brother of Jesus.

Of much more importance, however, is his personal identification as a servant of Jesus Christ. Jude had come to follow Jesus as a willing servant. In fact, his humble and profoundly appropriate introduction of himself begins with his identification of being a servant of Jesus Christ. His priorities were correct. Nothing in all of our lives and relationships can be more important than following Jesus Christ as Savior and Lord and then willingly serving Him.

It appears that the author is indeed Jude, the brother of James and the half brother of Jesus. And, of even greater importance, this Jude is a servant of Jesus Christ.

The Recipients

"To those who are called, sanctified by God the Father, and preserved in Jesus Christ" (v. 1). These words of greeting give us little specific information concerning the recipients except that they were Christian brothers and sisters. In the third verse, Jude addressed them as though he knew them personally when he wrote, *"Beloved, while I was very diligent to write to you concerning our common salvation, I found it necessary to write to you exhorting you to contend earnestly for the faith which was once for all delivered to the saints."*

There are some Bible scholars who believe that this letter and 2 Peter were addressed to the same group of people. They base their conjecture upon the fact that the content of the two letters is so similar that Peter and Jude must have been writing to Christians facing similar needs and could therefore have been writing to the same people.

The Occasion

Most of the New Testament was written as "occasional theology." In other words, all of the epistles were written for very specific occasions. The authors were writing with love and concern to instruct those who were in need of instruction, to encourage those who were discouraged, or to correct those who were going astray.

In that sense, the occasion of Jude's letter was both encouragement and exhortation. He had planned to write a letter concerning their mutual salvation, but instead he wrote, *"I found it necessary to write to you exhorting you to contend earnestly for the faith which was once for all delivered to the saints"* (v. 3).

As we have ascertained, the specific audience to whom Jude is writing is not certain and thus the dating of this epistle is difficult to determine. However, many Biblical scholars believe Jude was written before 2 Peter since it is logical to conclude that Peter borrowed some of his material from Jude since his letter is longer.

A second option is that neither of them borrowed from each other, but that both were in Rome simultaneously and wrote their letters with encouragement and knowledge of each other, and that they both received some of their material from a common source or from a common experience! This seems the most likely to me.

In any event, it is probable that Jude was written either shortly before, slightly afterwards, or at approximately the same time as the writing of 2 Peter. Therefore, the approximate date was sometime between A.D. 67 and 70.

Plan of Exposition

As in the other books studied in this volume, we will continue to use the inductive approach, sincerely attempting to hear what the content and internal evidence has to say to us.

Because Jude is a very short letter and because much of the content is difficult for those in our culture to understand easily, this letter is often neglected. I have found relatively few Christians who have given serious study to this book or who have much knowledge of its teachings.

I trust that this exposition of Jude will "bring it alive" to all of those who read this volume. If that happens, we will find this letter to be of great assistance to us in our personal lives as we battle against the nominal expression of Christianity that is so prevalent in our society. And, by God's grace, we can be helped to become *builders* of the spiritual lives of our brothers and sisters and of the Kingdom of God rather than destroyers. "So let it be, Lord!"

An Outline of Jude

A Strong Warning against Nominal Christianity

Jude 1–25

Nominal Christianity has always been the enemy of the church. Jesus warned against the nominal kind of spiritual lifestyle when He quoted Isaiah in saying, "This people honors Me with their lips, but their heart is far from Me" (Mark 7:6, Isa. 29:13).

In 1981, I was privileged to participate in a consultation on world evangelization held in Thailand. Hundreds of Christian leaders gathered from around the world to prayerfully plan strategy to reach some twenty major categories of people's groups throughout the world who had not yet been reached with the Gospel of Jesus Christ.

Some of those unreached groups of people are more obvious than others. For example, there are millions of Chinese and millions of Moslems who have never been reached with the Gospel of our Lord Jesus Christ. But I was assigned to the category of "nominal Christians." And as many of us have discovered, nominal Christians are among the most difficult people to reach with the Gospel.

Jude understood that principle and was deeply concerned with encouraging believers to avoid the satanic trap of becoming merely nominal Christians. Like Peter, Jude believed that the best defense against nominalism and against false teaching was a strong, offensive, dynamic faith in Jesus Christ. We need to contend earnestly for our faith (v. 3).

THE PURPOSE OF THIS LETTER

1 Jude, a servant of Jesus Christ, and brother of James,

To those who are called, sanctified by God the Father, and preserved in Jesus Christ:

2 Mercy, peace, and love be multiplied to you.

3 Beloved, while I was very diligent to write to you concerning our common salvation, I found it necessary to write to you exhorting that you should earnestly contend for the faith which was once for all delivered to the saints.

Jude 1–3

Jude identified himself first as a servant of Jesus Christ and then as a brother of James (see commentary, p. 244). This greeting reflects his humble spirit and the authentic priority of his life. His highest calling and privilege was to be a servant of Jesus Christ. He was not embarrassed to be called a servant of Christ nor to be called the brother of James.

If Jude's brother was the same James who authored the epistle bearing his name and who was a leader in the early church, then Jude was not only the brother of James but the half brother of Jesus. Yet he did not glory in that fact. He was content to be called a servant of Jesus and a brother of James. His attitude was like that of Andrew who is consistently referred to in Scripture as the brother of Peter (John 1:40).

Jude greets *"those who are called, sanctified by God the Father, and preserved in Jesus Christ"* (v. 1). The word that Paul uses in writing to the church in Rome when he states that they are the called of Jesus Christ and called to be saints is *klētós*, "to be called" (Rom. 1:6, 7).

They are *sanctified (hagiázō)* by God—"set apart" (see commentary on 1 Pet. 3:15, p. 125)—and they are preserved in Jesus Christ. The Greek word translated as *"preserved"* is *tēréō*, which is often rendered as "kept" or "reserved." What a marvelous promise! Our Lord has called us, sanctified us, and has promised to keep us in His love and power.

After those wonderful words of affirmation, Jude extends the greeting, *"Mercy, peace, and love be multiplied to you."* This is a uniquely Christian greeting which was used in similar forms by many Christian writers including Paul as he wrote to the church at Corinth, "Grace to you and peace from God our Father and the Lord Jesus Christ" (1 Cor. 1:3).

Jude then moves on to the purpose of his letter. He admits that he had hoped to write them simply to encourage them *"concerning our common salvation"* (v. 3). However, he has heard about a need which they are facing, and so he *"found it necessary to write to you exhorting you to contend earnestly for the faith which was once for all delivered to the saints"* (v. 3).

Jude has two major concerns—that they do not drift and that they will not be led astray by false teachers. He prays that they will instead take the initiative and contend for the faith.

DON'T BE A DESTROYER

4 For certain men have crept in unnoticed, who long ago were marked out for this condemnation, ungodly men, who turn the grace of our God into licentiousness and deny the only Lord God and our Lord Jesus Christ.

5 But I want to remind you, though you once knew this, that the Lord, having saved the people out of the land of Egypt, afterward destroyed those who did not believe.

6 And the angels who did not keep their proper domain, but left their own habitation, He has reserved in everlasting chains under darkness for the judgment of the great day;

7 as Sodom and Gomorrah, and the cities around them in a similar manner to these, having given themselves over to sexual immorality and gone after strange flesh, are set forth as an example, suffering the vengeance of eternal fire.

8 Likewise also these dreamers defile the flesh, reject authority, and speak evil of dignitaries.

9 Yet Michael the archangel, in contending with the devil, when he disputed about the body of Moses, dared not bring against him a reviling accusation, but said, "The Lord rebuke you!"

10 But these speak evil of whatever they do not know; and whatever they know naturally, like brute beasts, in these things they corrupt themselves.

11 Woe to them! For they have gone in the way of Cain, run greedily in the error of Balaam for profit, and perished in the rebellion of Korah.

12 These are spots in your love feasts, while they feast with you without fear, tending only themselves; they are clouds without water, carried about by the winds; late autumn trees without fruit, twice dead, pulled up by the roots;

13 raging waves of the sea, foaming up their own shame; wandering stars for whom is reserved the blackness of darkness forever.

14 And Enoch, the seventh from Adam, prophesied about these men also, saying, "Behold, the Lord comes with ten thousands of His saints,

15 "to execute judgment on all, to convict all who are ungodly among them of all their ungodly deeds which they have committed in an ungodly way, and of all the harsh things which ungodly sinners have spoken against Him."

16 These are murmurers, complainers, walking according to their own lusts; and their mouth speaks great swelling words, flattering people to gain advantage.

17 But you, beloved, remember the words which were spoken before by the apostles of our Lord Jesus Christ:

18 how they told you that there would be mockers in the last time who would walk according to their own ungodly lusts.

19 These are the sensual ones, who cause divisions, not having the Spirit.

Jude 4–19

In this long and rather difficult discourse, Jude warns against nominal Christianity and against those false teachers who would divide the Body of Christ and who would seek to destroy the faith of believers rather than to build it. These destructive men have crept into the church unnoticed and have *"turn[ed] the grace of our God into licentiousness and deny the only Lord God"* (v. 4). As we have noted in our earlier commentary, there are some common denominators between this teaching of Jude and that of Peter in his second letter (see p. 204).

In studying this passage, it is helpful to divide all of this material into two categories. The first exposes the characteristics of these ungodly men and the distinctives of their false teaching. The second exposes the judgments which God is going to bring upon them and all who follow their evil ways.

1. *The characteristics of these ungodly men and the distinctives of their false teaching* (vv. 4, 8, 10, 12–13, 16–19). The Scripture teaches that we are known by what we say, what we do, and what we are. In other words, our conduct and speech reveal our character. Jude describes the character of these ungodly men at the same time he exposes their false teaching. He blends their character and false teaching all together as he exposes them for what they are. Let us follow his exposé by clarifying the twenty characteristics he reveals.

"Ungodly men" (v. 4). God is the source of truth (John 14:6), and those who would espouse non-truth cannot be of God. They are ungodly.

They *"turn the grace of our God into licentiousness"* (v. 4). The *"grace"* (*cháris*) of God is very expensive. It has been bought with the very blood of Jesus Christ. His grace has been bestowed upon us so that we will live the godly life of righteousness. But those who walk in sin would encourage us to misuse this grace as a means of license to live the life of immorality.

They *"deny the only Lord God and our Lord Jesus Christ"* (v. 4). The litmus test of authentic Christianity is the lordship of Jesus Christ. No one can belong truly to Him without acknowledging Jesus as Lord (Rom. 10:9, 10). In fact, no one can authentically acknowledge Him as Lord without the empowering of the Holy Spirit (I Cor. 12:3).

"These dreamers defile the flesh" (v. 8). How tragic. Sin always destroys and leads to ultimate death. Those who walk in the flesh rather than the Spirit are actually involved in defiling or polluting their own bodies. What a contrast to the Biblical teaching that our bodies are precious in the sight of God and are actually temples of the Holy Spirit (1 Cor. 6:19).

They *"reject authority"* (v. 8). One of the great sins of the latter part of the twentieth century has been the sin of rejecting God's authority. It is the breaking of the first commandment, "You shall have no other gods before me" (Exod. 20:3). Unfortunately, this philosophy has also slipped into the church. There are many who do not wish to live under the lordship of Christ, nor under the godly discipline of the church.

They *"speak evil of dignitaries"* (v. 8). Love and respect for godly leaders is given a high priority in the church. Paul teaches that we should esteem those who labor among us very highly in love (1 Thess. 5:13), and that the elders who rule well should be counted worthy of double honor (1 Tim. 5:17).

The writer of Hebrews instructs Christians to "obey those who have the rule over you, and be submissive, for they watch out for your souls" (Heb. 13:17). What a contrast is this teaching to that of the false teachers who would lead us astray. They slander even dignitaries and celestial beings. We should not be afraid of such false teachers as was Michael the archangel when he dared not bring a reviling accusation against the devil (v. 9). As James wrote, we should resist the devil and he will flee from us (James 4:7). (See commentary from 2 Pet. 2:10, pp. 222.)

"These speak evil of whatever they do not know" (v. 10). There is an old adage which states, "Listen very carefully when the speaker pounds the podium the most loudly; it is usually his weakest point!" In other words, it is a trait of the natural, sinful person to often speak most loudly and emphatically about that which he or she knows the least well or is the least sure. That, says Jude, is true of false teachers. And they not only speak with loudness, but also they speak with evil.

"Like brute beasts, . . . they corrupt themselves" (v. 10). These false teachers are like irrational or dumb animals. Without realizing it, they *"corrupt"* (*phtheírō*) or destroy themselves. This teaching is especially poignant when we recognize that one of the heresies which these false teachers were espousing was that of gnosticism, the earliest of heresies which contended, among other things, that its followers were particularly brilliant and elite in their spiritual understanding.

This is another one of those passages which parallels with the teaching of 2 Peter (see commentary from 2 Pet. 2:13, p. 226). The root word used here (v. 12) for *"spot"* is *spilás*, which literally means "a ledge or reef of rock in the sea." The warning is explicit. Just as a ship needs to avoid such a danger at sea, so should we seek to avoid the treachery of false teachers.

"Serving only themselves" (v. 12). The word translated as "serving" is *poimaínō* which means feeding or tending. It is the word used by Jesus in His dialogue with Peter when He said, "Feed my sheep" (John 21:16). These false teachers care only for themselves. They come to the love feasts not to share communion or fellowship but only to feed themselves.

"They are clouds without water" (v. 12). Again, Jude uses the same analogy as Peter (see p. 224). The inference is clear. Clouds without

rain are like wells without water—they are of little use. They are driven by the wind—out of control.

They are *"late autumn trees without fruit"* (v. 12). They are like trees in late autumn; they bear no fruit. They are quite unlike those who are abiding in Christ who bear much fruit (John 15:4, 5). And not only are they fruitless, but they are doubly dead since they have no spiritual roots through which they can draw up nourishment from Jesus Christ (Col. 2:6, 7).

They are *"raging waves of the sea"* (v. 13). These false teachers are compared to the raging or "wild" (*ágrios*) waves of the sea. These violent waves produce foam which is their own *"shame"* (*aiskúnē*) or "disgrace."

They are *"wandering stars"* (v. 13). These are like the stars that have gone astray or have moved out of their intended orbit. This statement reveals one of the great tragedies of the life of sin. It always takes us off course from enjoying the very best which God has prepared for us.

"These are murmurers, [and] complainers" (v. 16). Such false teachers are *"murmurers"* (*gongustēs*), and *"complainers"* (*mempsímoiros*). Those out of fellowship with the living God, who have strayed from their intended orbit, are *"complainers"* rather than praisers. The Children of Israel praised God when they enjoyed fellowship with Him, and they constantly murmured and complained when they strayed from Him and followed after their own lusts (Exod. 16:2).

They are *"walking according to their own lusts"* (vv. 16, 18). Twice Jude describes the false teachers as those who walk after their own lusts (*epithumía*). Peter begs his readers to abstain from fleshly lusts which war against the soul (1 Pet. 2:11). Unfortunately, these teachers do not warn against such conduct; they practice it in their own lives.

"They mouth great swelling words" (v. 16). Peter also refers to this characteristic of false teachers who speak with *"great swelling words"* (*hupéronkos*) in his second letter (2 Pet. 2:18). They are boasters, and they attempt to impress people not only with their bragging, but with the big words which they use.

They are *"flattering people to gain advantage"* (v. 16). The Proverbs reveal the truth concerning flattery. "He who rebukes a man will find more favor afterward than he who flatters with the tongue" (Prov. 28:23). "A man who flatters his neighbor spreads a net for his feet" (Prov. 29:5). At best, flattery is a form of lying since it is exaggerated or distorted truth. Evil people use it to deceive others for their own advantage.

"These are [the ones] who cause divisions" (v. 19). The Spirit of God brings unity to members of the Body of Christ. But those who walk according to their own ungodly lusts are the ones who cause divisions or separations within the Body. Wherever and whenever there is division in the Body, you can be certain that the lust of the flesh is being expressed rather than the unity of the Spirit.

They are *"sensual"* (v. 19). To be *"sensual"* (*psukikós*) is "to live in the natural as opposed to the supernatural." It is to walk after the flesh (vv. 16, 18) rather than after the Spirit. Paul teaches, "The natural man does not receive the things of the Spirit of God, for they are foolishness to him; nor can he know them, because they are spiritually discerned" (1 Cor. 2:14).

They are *"not having the spirit"* (v. 19). Now we come to the very summation statement of all that Jude has been teaching about the false teachers. Their basic problem is spiritual. They do not have the Holy Spirit. Jesus referred to the Holy Spirit as the "Spirit of truth, whom the world cannot receive, because it neither sees Him nor knows Him" (John 14:17). He also said, "When He, the Spirit of truth, has come, He will guide you into all truth" (John 16:13).

The Holy Spirit is the basic source of truth as well as the revealer of truth. Those who are acknowledging Jesus as Lord are controlled by the Holy Spirit. But those who walk after the flesh do not have the Spirit. Therefore, they cannot teach truth.

Most of us have seen vivid illustrations of this Biblical truth in the lives of other believers or even in our own lives. Several years ago, I counseled with a young pastor who was extremely discouraged. He was a brilliant young man who had an impeccable theological education. In addition, he was deeply committed to the ministry and had obvious aptitude for ministry.

As we visited and prayed together, I discovered that he had a basic problem. He was so deeply involved in ministering to people that he was neglecting his own walk with God. Without realizing it, he was ministering in his own strength rather than by the power and grace of the Holy Spirit. What an incredible change took place when he recognized his need, recommitted his life to the lordship of Jesus Christ, received anew the guidance of the Holy Spirit and again experienced His empowering. Instead of leaving the ministry, he began to thrive and his church grew in power as God poured His blessing upon the life and ministry of the young pastor.

Effective spiritual ministry always takes place through a human vehicle who is living under the lordship of Jesus Christ and who is ministering by the grace and power of the Holy Spirit. Those who do not have the Spirit are false teachers and should be called to accountability.

2. *The judgments which will surely come to these false teachers* (vv. 5–11, 13–15). After exposing the characteristics of these false teachers, Jude speaks very specifically about the judgments which will come upon those who walk according to their own ungodly lusts and who would seek to lead others astray.

The Lord "destroyed those who did not believe" (v. 5). Jude reminds his readers of how the Lord has dealt with unbelievers in the past. He uses the specific example of the Children of Israel after they had been delivered from Egypt during the Exodus led by Moses. The Lord destroyed those who did not believe (Numbers 14). In the same way, infers Jude, God will ultimately destroy those of the contemporary day who do not believe.

"He has reserved [disobedient angels] in everlasting chains under darkness for the judgment of the great day" (v. 6). Jude again parallels with the teaching of Peter concerning the judgment of disobedient angels (2 Pet. 2:4; see commentary, p. 225). The judgment of the great day seems to refer to that judgment described by the Apostle John, "And the devil, who deceived them, was cast into the lake of fire and brimstone where the beast and false prophet *are*. And they will be tormented day and night forever and ever" (Rev. 20:10).

They shall suffer "the vengeance of eternal fire" (v. 7). Jude now uses the historical example of Sodom and Gomorrah and surrounding cities which had given themselves to sexual immorality. Their destruction by fire is an example and warning to those who would seek after sexual immorality in the present day (Genesis 19).

"Woe to them!" (v. 11). Jude is declaring woe upon those who speak evil about things they don't understand, who think only in the natural realm, and who literally corrupt themselves (v. 10). He uses three Old Testament examples to reveal three specific sins of the false teachers. First, there is Cain who failed to please God because he murdered his brother (Gen. 4:1–15). Next, there is Balaam who not only sinned by his deceit and covetousness, but who also attempted to lead the Children of Israel astray (Numbers 22–24). Finally, there

was Korah who rebelled against the authority and leadership of Moses—an authority entrusted to Moses by God (Num. 16:1–36). God's judgment came upon Cain, Balaam, and Korah when they disobeyed, and His judgment will surely come upon all who disobey in the present day.

"For whom is reserved the blackness of darkness forever" (v. 13). As Jude refers to these false teachers as stars who have gone astray and have moved out of their intended orbit (see p. 254), he states that the blackness of darkness has been reserved for them forever. Throughout Scripture, we find sin and disobedience being portrayed as darkness, and righteousness and obedience as light. For example, John refers to Jesus as the true light who came to give light to every person. But the darkness did not comprehend it (John 1:1–13). Jesus called himself "the light of the world" (John 9:5), and He declared that people loved darkness rather than light because their deeds are evil (John 3:19–21).

"The Lord comes . . . to execute judgment on all . . . who are ungodly" (vv. 14, 15). In declaring this judgment Jude quotes from the apocryphal book Enoch. The full prophecy of Enoch is "Behold, the Lord comes with ten thousands of His saints, to execute judgment on all, to convict all who are ungodly among them of all their ungodly deeds which they have committed in an ungodly way, and of all the harsh things which ungodly sinners have spoken against Him" (Enoch 1:9).

Within the Jewish society of Jude's day, the book of Enoch was popular. Jude is not referring to it as Scripture, but rather as a common source with which his Jewish readers would be very familiar.

The message of Jude concerning the impending judgment of God upon the false teachers is loud and clear. The judgment of God will certainly fall upon them.

BE A BUILDER

20 But you, beloved, building yourselves up on your most holy faith, praying in the Holy Spirit,

21 keep yourselves in the love of God, looking for the mercy of our Lord Jesus Christ to eternal life.

22 And on some have compassion, making a distinction;

23 and save others with fear, pulling them out of the fire, hating even the garment defiled by the flesh.

24 Now to Him who is able to keep you from
   stumbling,
   And to present you faultless
   Before the presence of His glory with exceeding
   joy,
25 To God our Savior,
   Who alone is wise,
   Be glory and majesty,
   Dominion and power,
   Both now and forever.
   Amen.

Jude 20–25

When I was a college student, my home town of Pollock, South Dakota, was moved from a beautiful valley to a lovely hillside some one and a half miles away. The little town of 350 people had to be moved for the building of the large Oahe Dam on the Missouri River. The reservoir, which was to become Oahe Lake, would flow into the valley where the old town was situated and would form a smaller lake to be named Lake Poccasse.

I had the privilege of being involved in the construction of the new town. And, subsequently, I also was a participant in the destruction of the old town. The demolition of many of the old buildings I had come to cherish, including the gymnasium where I had played basketball, was a very emotional experience for me.

Through that experience, I learned a lesson that will be helpful to me as long as I live. It is simply this: one can destroy in just a few hours that which has taken years to construct. However, to be a builder is much more fulfilling than being a destroyer!

That is the message of Scripture. Our Lord has called us to be builders—not destroyers. Sin brings destruction, but spiritual life brings growth and building! After condemning the false teachers who would destroy and tear down, Jude instructs us to build ourselves up spiritually (v. 20). We are to be builders! And Jude shares six specific ways we may accomplish this:

1. By *"building [ourselves] up on [our] "most holy faith"* (v. 20). Faith is a vital essential to the life of spiritual growth. Hebrews declares that "without faith it is impossible to please [God]" (Heb. 11:6). And both Paul and the writer of Hebrews quote from Habakkuk 2:4 in

declaring that "the just shall live by faith" (Rom. 1:17; Gal. 3:11; Heb. 10:38).

This is a *"holy"* (*hágios*) faith which denotes that it is "separate, distinct or utterly different." This is a faith that comes from God and is toward God. Paul writes, "So then faith comes by hearing, and hearing by the word of God" (Rom. 10:17). This faith is lived out through active obedience (see p. 61).

2. *By "praying in the Holy Spirit"* (v. 20). Jude encourages us as builders to be those who would be praying in the Holy Spirit. To be sure, the battle against false teaching is not to be won by mere argument or intellect. "We do not wrestle against flesh and blood, but against principalities, against powers, against the rulers of the darkness of this age, against spiritual *hosts* of wickedness in the heavenly *places"* (Eph. 6:12).

God has given us spiritual weapons to be used not only in refuting error, but in growing and in building. One of God's greatest gifts to His children is the gift of prayer. Prayer is essential to spiritual vitality. Prayer is not something we do in the flesh; we are to pray guided by the Holy Spirit. Prayer is spiritual, and the Holy Spirit desires to empower us to pray; He wants to make intercession for us according to the will of God (Rom. 8:26, 27).

3. *By keeping ourselves "in the love of God"* (v. 21). If we are to be builders, we must also be lovers. And that love must flow from God Himself. Paul teaches us clearly about the relationship of love and building in his letter to the Ephesians, "But, speaking the truth in love, may grow up in all things into Him who is the head—Christ— from whom . . . causes growth of the body for the edifying of itself in love" (Eph. 4:15, 16). Paul also declared, "Knowledge puffs up, but love edifies [builds up]" (1 Cor. 8:1).

Jesus said, "Abide in my love" (John 15:9), and then proceeded to say, "If you keep My commandments, you will abide in My love" (John 15:10). That is the truth which Jude is teaching. Stay within the bounds of God's love. Don't stray away like a star out of orbit. Enjoy the love of God and share it freely with others.

4. *By "looking for the mercy of our Lord Jesus Christ"* (v. 21). The mercy of our Lord Jesus Christ is to be enjoyed day by day. As Jeremiah wrote, "Through the Lord's mercies we are not consumed. They [His mercies] are new every morning" (Lam. 3:22, 23).

But Jude reminds us of the ultimate of God's mercy—eternal life.

We are to wait or to look forward to that gift of His mercy. When our eyes are set on that goal, and as we enjoy the daily mercies of God, we are not as apt to be led astray by the false teachers (see p. 251).

5. *By having compassion* (v. 22). The mercy of God should not only be enjoyed by us, but we should joyfully share it with others. The word *"compassion"* is *eleéō* which is often translated as "mercy." It is closely related to the word *éleos* which is translated as "mercy" in the previous verse.

The word *eleéō* is used by Peter in his wonderful declaration, "[You] who once were not a people but are now the people of God" (1 Pet. 2:10, see commentary, p. 141). Those who walk with God through faith in Jesus Christ do receive His mercy. And we should share that mercy with those who have gone astray.

Jude states that we should do so "making a distinction." In other words, we should attempt to reach out with mercy and compassion to those who have gone astray. We should attempt to rescue them from the error of the false teachers. Our deepest concern should not be to condemn them but to restore them to the fellowship of Christ and His Church.

6. *By [saving] others with fear"* (v. 23). The act of mercy should reach so far as to attempt to actually snatch them from the fire of judgment. The ministry of rescuing those who have strayed from the faith is a vital one. In the closing words of his letter, James speaks about this important ministry (see p. 102).

This act of mercy of reaching out to snatch others from the fire should be done with "fear" (*phóbos*). Paul teaches the same truth in his letter to the Galatians, "You who *are* spiritual restore such a one in a spirit of gentleness, considering yourself lest you also be tempted" (Gal. 6:1).

And, as we have seen, it should be done with love and compassion for the sinner but with great hatred for the sin— *"hating even the garment defiled by the flesh"* (v. 23). We are to be like Jesus. He had a reputation for being a friend of sinners, but He hated sin. He came to be our Savior and to rescue us from sin.

The closing two verses of Jude's short letter are the best known and most quoted of the entire epistle. It is the final word on Christian living and on escaping the error of false teaching. The focus is squarely upon God! He is the One "who is able to keep you from stumbling," and He is the One who will "present you faultless before the presence of His glory with exceeding joy" (v. 24).

Our trust should be in Him. We should receive Him as Savior and follow Him as Lord day by day. Indeed, we should deny ourselves, take up our cross daily, and follow him (Luke 9:23). He is to be trusted with our very lives. We should follow Him by faith, by praying in the Holy Spirit, by keeping ourselves in the love of God, by receiving His mercy, and by having compassion on those who have gone astray, attempting to snatch them from the fire.

Jude closes with the highest tribute to God as a reminder to us of who God is and who we are. *"To God our Savior, who alone is wise, be glory and majesty, dominion and power, both now and forever. Amen."*

Bibliography

Barclay, William. *The Letters of John and Jude.* Philadelphia: Westminster Press, 1960.
————. *The Letters of James and Peter.* Philadelphia: Westminster Press, 1960.
Bromiley, G. W. *Historical Theology.* Grand Rapids: Eerdmans, 1978.
Buttrick, George. *The Interpreter's Bible,* vol. 12. Nashville: Abingdon, 1957.
The Cambridge Bible Commentary. Edited by P. R. Ackroyd, A. R. C. Leaney, J. W. Packer. Cambridge: University Press, 1967.
Green, Michael. *The Second Epistle of Peter and the Epistle of Jude.* Tyndale New Testament Commentary Series. Grand Rapids: Eerdmans, 1975.
Guthrie, Donald. *New Testament Introduction.* Downers Grove, IL: InterVarsity Press, 1973.
Harrison, Everett F. *The Wycliffe Bible Commentary.* Chicago: Moody Press, 1962.
Kelly, J. N. D. *A Commentary on the Epistles of Peter and Jude.* Grand Rapids: Baker Book House, 1981.
Leighton, Robert. *Commentary on First Peter.* Reprint, 1972. Grand Rapids: Kregel.
Mayor, Joseph B. *The Epistle of St. Jude and the Second Epistle of St. Peter.* Minneapolis: Klock and Klock Christian Publishers, 1978.
Stibbs, Alan M. *The First Epistle General of Peter.* Tyndale New Testament Commentary Series. Grand Rapids: Eerdmans, 1974.
Stott, John R. W. *Basic Introduction to the New Testament.* Grand Rapids: Eerdmans, 1979.
Tasker, R. V. G. *The General Epistle of James.* Tyndale New Testament Commentary Series. Grand Rapids: Eerdmans, 1975.
Thayer, Joseph Henry. *Thayer's Greek-English Lexicon of the New Testament.* New York: American Book Co.
Wesley, John. *The Journal of John Wesley.* Chicago: Moody Press. 1974.
————. *Sermons on Several Occasions.* New York: Carlton and Phillips, 1855.
Williams, R. R. *The Letters of John and James.* Cambridge: University Press, 1965.